HOW FEAR WORKS

CONTENTS

Introduction   1

1   Changing Stories of Fear   35

2   Waiting for the Time Bomb to Explode   71

3   Moral Confusion – the Main Driver of the Culture of Fear   107

4   The Perspective of Fear – How it Works   145

5   Creation of the Fearful Subject   177

6   The Quest for Safety in a Dangerous World   207

Conclusion: Towards a Less Fearful Future   237

Acknowledgements   261
Notes   262
Bibliography   287
Index   299

Introduction

Nothing in life is to be feared, it is only to be
understood. Now is the time to understand more, so
that we may fear less.

Marie Curie

When I published my book *Culture of Fear* in the summer of 1997, this
concept was almost unknown. Two decades later, talk of a 'culture
of fear' is everywhere: from political campaigns to discussions of
Islamist terrorism or avian flu. Yet there is still much confusion about
the causes and consequences of the culture of fear that grips our
society. This book aims to remedy that confusion. It sets the modern
obsession with fear in its historical context, and examines how the
way we fear now differs from the past. It analyses how our culture of
fear is founded on and reinforces a fatalistic view of our humanity.
And it seeks to point a possible way towards a less fearful future.

THE IDIOM OF FEAR

The term 'culture of fear' was a relatively new concept back in the
1990s, but one that gave voice to a pre-existing and pervasive
sensibility of anxiety and uncertainty. Even critics who did not accept
the arguments advanced in the *Culture of Fear* understood that fear
and culture had become closely entwined and that this development
had a significant impact on public life.

At the time, the alarmist and disoriented responses to a variety of concerns – the AIDS epidemic, missing children, Satanic Ritual Abuse, pollution, crime – indicated that society had become fixated on promoting a climate of fear and cultivating a disposition to panic. But there was much more to come. During the years that followed, society's attention became focused on dramatic catastrophic threats such as global terrorism, global warming, flu pandemics, and weapons of mass destruction. At the same time concern about high-profile threats was more than matched by a regime of constant anxiety about more banal and ordinary risks of everyday life. Diet, lifestyle and childrearing practices, along with dozens of other normal features of life, are now scrutinized for the risk they pose to people. Fear itself has become politicized to a point where debate is rarely about whether or not we should be fearful, but about who or what we should fear.

Compared to the late twentieth century, the language we use today has become far more inclined to embrace the rhetoric of fear. At times it appears as if the narrative of fear has acquired its very own inner momentum. Since the eighteenth century there have been numerous references to an 'Age of Anxiety'.[1] However, in recent decades references to this condition have proliferated to the point that they have acquired everyday usage. The emergence of catchphrases such as the 'politics of fear', 'fear of crime', 'fear factor' and 'fear of the future' indicates that *fear itself* has become a singularly significant point of reference in our public conversation.

When the expression 'Project Fear' emerged during the 2016 UK referendum on membership of the European Union, it indicated that the narrative of fear had acquired the status of common sense. The adoption of a similar rhetoric by Donald Trump and his rival Hillary Clinton during the course of the American Presidential Election a few months later confirmed that fear had indeed become a project. 'If this election cycle is a mirror, then it is reflecting a society choked with fear', was the assessment of a feature article in the *Rolling Stone* magazine.[2]

Of course, the question of whether society is indeed 'choked with fear' cannot be explained with sole reference to the language that is in currency. Nevertheless language serves as an important marker of people's attitudes and reflects the spirit of the times. More importantly, language works as a vital medium through which people voice meaning about their predicament. The growing usage of terms like the 'politics of fear' or 'culture of fear' indicates that a significant section of the articulate public has become concerned about the impact of fear on their lives. To gain insight into the meaning that society attaches to the term 'culture of fear', I explored the Nexis database of news sources to chart the evolution of the rhetoric that surrounds it and the development of its current meaning.

The first example of the use of the term 'culture of fear' that my search revealed was a *New York Times* article published on 17 March 1985.[3] The article referred to the action taken by a business executive who apparently 'brought discipline and planning' to his organization and who 'has worked to snuff out a culture of fear and despair fomented by past rulers'. The manner with which this early use of the term was deployed anticipated the subsequent tendency to associate it with an intangible climate of anxiety and fear. However, during the 1980s this term had only a limited currency and there were merely eight references to it in the sources available on Nexis. During this decade the term was used in reference to specific experiences such as the culture of an institution, and tended not to refer to a wider condition prevailing in society.

It was during the 1990s that the term 'culture of fear' gradually acquired the status of a distinct, stand-alone idiom that existed independently of any specific institution or experience. In May 1990, an Australian journalist described how a series of scary newspaper stories about crime have spawned 'a Culture of Fear'.[4] This usage of 'a Culture of Fear', pointing to the crystallization of a sensibility that transcended any specific experience, marked an important point of transition in the evolution of this concept. From this point onwards the term was increasingly used in association with cultural practices and patterns that impact on society as a whole.

During the 1990s references to the term 'culture of fear' rose from 8 to 533. By the middle of the decade, the term was sufficiently recognized to be used in headlines. The first example of a headline containing the term was in January 1996.[5] To a significant extent this increase in usage was stimulated by the appearance of two publications. My book *Culture of Fear*, published in 1997, and Barry Glassner's text with the same title, issued in 1999, led many commentators to adopt and use this term in their reportage. Frequently, culture and fear were communicated as intertwined concepts. That the term 'culture of fear' had acquired widespread usage was demonstrated during the first decade of the twenty-first century. In just one year, 2005, there were 576 references to the term in Nexis; a decade later, in 2015, the number of references had risen to 1,647, and by 2016, to 2,222.

Even taking into account the likelihood that Nexis has expanded the sources cited in its database, the steady expansion of allusions to the culture of fear suggests this idiom resonates with the public imagination and corresponds to an experience that it captures. Its usage is not confined to media communicators: this is one of relatively few sociological concepts that has entered colloquial language. One can often hear references to it in everyday conversations about the pressures, anxieties and concerns facing people in a variety of institutional settings. For example it is often used as a rhetorical weapon of condemnation to indict the behaviour of an individual or an institution. Adopting this posture, a critic of the UK government's school inspection body accused Ofsted of being 'responsible for a culture of fear in schools'.[6] The colloquial use of this term is widespread throughout the Anglo-American world, indicating that it speaks to a sensibility that transcends national boundaries. As shown by the title of Ben Shapiro's 2013 bestseller *Bullies: How the Left's Culture of Fear Silences Americans*, it has become routinely used as a term of condemnation.[7]

In everyday speech, the term culture of fear carries a diffuse connotation that can encompass a variety of feelings, from unease and discomfort towards unwanted remarks and pressure to an acute sense of insecurity, powerlessness, intimidation – as well as feeling threatened by crime or terror. The term culture of fear works as a rhetorical idiom rather than as a precise concept. Its meaning is often far from clear. It is used to describe people's emotional reactions and fears towards a wide variety of phenomena. Studies indicate that a rhetorical idiom can gain influence and widespread usage if it is able to draw on 'cluster images' that are integral to the public imagination.[8] The proliferation of images such as men wearing white protection suits and gas masks, or a picture of a missing child on the noticeboard of a supermarket, offer a visual landscape for imagining and then expressing fear.

What endows both the rhetoric and the reality of the culture of fear with force is that it gives a voice to moral uncertainties and the sensibility of powerlessness in contemporary society. The frequent usage, and over-usage, of this term indicates that it increasingly serves as a metaphor for interpreting life. At times it almost appears as if fear has become a caricature of itself. The casual manner with which people express their fear of this or that act or experience indicates that it has also become a rhetorical gesture designed to draw attention to a particular point or claim.

Recent decades have witnessed the emergence of competitive scaremongering, where different groups vie with one another about what we should and should not fear. So while one group of professionals advises parents to shield their children from the sun in order to protect them from skin cancer, another group points to the risk of children suffering from vitamin D deficiency because they have been shielded from the sun. Competitive scaremongering surrounds the debate on whether vaccinating children carries more risk than letting nature run its course.

People routinely accuse one another of promoting fear, playing the fear card, or allowing themselves to be manipulated by appeals to fear. Some critics of the culture of fear have become overwhelmed or at least disoriented by the targets of their censure. Barry Glassner claims that 'we are living in the most fear-mongering time in history'.[9] Perhaps he is right. But critics of the omnipresence of fear may have inadvertently introjected the very values they indict. Psychoanalytic theory states that introjection occurs when an individual adopts or incorporates the values and attitudes of others. It is a process through which people unconsciously assimilate external values: sometimes even those that they publicly criticize. In this case the introjection of the values associated with the culture of fear leads to unwitting scaremongering about the threat posed by fear-mongering.

Commentaries on the culture of fear often, and understandably, tend to overreact to this powerful phenomenon and convey the impression that the current levels of public fear are historically unprecedented. An article published in *Time*, titled 'Why Americans Are More Afraid Than They Used to Be', exemplifies the tendency to assume that public fear is at an all-time high.[10] Such accounts are rarely backed up by empirical evidence. They should be interpreted as testimony to the prevalence of a consciousness of fear rather than lived experience. With so much energy devoted to alarmist warnings about fear, it is not surprising that many people have drawn the conclusion that the power of this emotion is at a historical high.

To avoid being overwhelmed by the latest scare story it is essential to go beyond surface and investigate its inner dynamics. The chapters that follow explore what is distinct about our culture, in order to gain an understanding of the workings of twenty-first-century fear.

THE CULTURE OF FEAR THESIS

Debates on the culture of fear often fail to address the question of what is cultural about fearing. They therefore confuse the relationship between its impact and influence as a narrative with the lived experience of fearing. The narrative of fear attempts to offer a system of meaning; a background, context and set of assumptions that guide people in the way they go about making sense of, and responding to, threats.

The way people fear also depends on a variety of specific variables – such as their cultural, political and religious attitudes and affiliations, their socio-economic circumstances, their gender and age. But though the act of fearing is an individual accomplishment that is influenced by personal experience and influences, it is also mediated through the prevailing web of meaning. As the sociologist Norbert

Elias explained, 'the strength, kind and structures of the fears and anxieties that smoulder or flare in the individual never depend solely on his own "nature"' – they are 'always determined, finally by the history and the actual structure of his relations to other people'.[11] In other words, community values, attitudes and expectations provide a cultural context for the articulation of individual fears.

The argument developed in my 1997 study *Culture of Fear: Risk Taking and the Morality of Low Expectation* was not devoted to exploring people's individual fears; rather, it offered an analysis of the narrative that assisted the emergence of a fearful society. My follow-up essay, 'The Only Thing We Have to Fear is the "Culture of Fear" Itself', highlighted the role and influence of this narrative over people's attitude and behaviour.[12] The culture of fear thesis pointed to the growth and expansion of existential insecurity and risk aversion. It claimed that what fuelled the ascendancy of a narrative of fear was a radical redefinition and inflation of the meaning of harm, rather than an increase in the danger facing humanity.

My thesis also underlined the significance of a crucial development in the moral outlook of society – the transformation of safety into the fundamental value. (This issue is explored at length in Chapter 6.) These developments were paralleled by the dramatic demotion of the status of personhood. Since the late 1970s, pessimistic cultural attitudes towards the capacity of people to deal with adversity have become the norm. Everyday language reflects this shift through the regular use of terms such as 'vulnerable' or 'at risk' to describe people. The corollary of this emphasis on the emotional fragility and powerlessness of individuals is the constant inflation of the range of experiences defined as risky. The definition of harm and of its impact has also expanded to encompass experiences that in previous times were regarded as unexceptional and normal. Drinking water from a tap, or eating a large cheeseburger, are now targets of health alerts. In fact virtually anything that you eat has been associated with cancer! A study of 50 common ingredients, taken randomly from a cookbook, found that 40 of them were the subject of articles, reporting on their cancer risks.[13]

As the title of the book *Culture of Fear: Risk Taking and the Morality of Low Expectations* suggests, a focus on morality remains central to the thesis. It suggests that as a result of confusions about moral norms, Western culture has become less and less able to project a positive account of humanity and individuals' capacity to deal with risk and uncertainty. The frequent calls to avoid risks can also be interpreted as a reflection of a loss of faith in people. A mood of mistrust and misanthropy continues to influence public policy and debate. Since the publication of *Culture of Fear*, what I characterize as the 'morality of low expectation' has become even more entrenched. This development is particularly striking in universities where, in many instances, students are not expected to be able to deal with criticism, offence and pressure. Calls for safe spaces exemplify a demand to quarantine students from such things. The low expectation that higher education institutions have regarding students' capacity to cope is reproduced in other domains of daily life.

My arguments about the ascendancy of the culture of fear emphasized the proliferation of alarmist institutional reactions to an expanding range of human experiences. It pointed to the emergence of a sensibility that tended to portray threats to society as existential in nature and that used a language of catastrophe to describe risks that were susceptible to policy and technical solutions – e.g. the 'Millennium Bug', or the bird flu virus. The argument suggested that these developments fostered a disposition to fear the worst, overreact and panic.

Does the ascendancy of the culture of fear since the 1990s mean, as some have suggested, that society has become more scared than ever before? This question is impossible to answer with any degree of rigour or certainty. There are numerous surveys that attempt to measure people's fears over a period of time.[14] However, it is far from evident what scientific significance can be attributed to conclusions based on the construction of opinion statements offered on the spur of the moment. A methodology that relies on quantitative analysis is not an effective instrument for capturing what people mean when, for example, they say, 'I fear the future.'

It is simply not possible to measure differences in levels of fear over historical time. How we fear and what we say about it is subject to divergent influences, and historical and cultural variations. As an emotion, fearing is mediated through moral norms and social attitudes and expectations. In some circumstances, fearing is portrayed as an act of wisdom and responsibility. In other situations it is condemned as cowardly or irrational behaviour. Such important differences in cultural attitudes make it difficult, if not impossible, to reduce fearing to a common measurable property. Looking back in historical time, the only statement that we can make with certainty about the experience of fearing is that the way we express this emotion is subject to important variations.

While it is not possible to answer the question of whether we fear more than in the past, it is likely that Western societies devote an unprecedented degree of emotional and rhetorical resources to talking about fear. This point is also echoed by Peter Stearns, who has written important studies about the history of fear in America. Stearns contends that one important contrast between the nineteenth and the twenty-first centuries is that Americans are allowed, even encouraged, to express those fears more openly. He observed that there are 'either more fearful Americans than there once were, or ... their voices are louder or more sought after and publicly authorised'.[15] Anyone watching daytime television and various reality confessionals will concur that guests are continually exhorted to acknowledge their fears and are psychically rewarded for 'sharing' their pain.

Stearns usefully points to the changing context within which fear takes place. He observes that the public context for fearing has altered, and that consequently it has become more acceptable 'to talk about fears, and therefore (to some extent to acknowledge them to oneself')'.[16] To illustrate his argument he draws attention to the example of American military personnel preparing for action in the Second Gulf War, who readily and openly acknowledged to journalists that they were frightened.[17] The readiness with which members of the armed forces are ready to highlight their fear indicates that talking about feeling scared has become increasingly acceptable for a profession that used to boast it was fearless. Captain Scott O'Grady, the American pilot shot down during the war in Bosnia in 1995, personifies this trend. O'Grady managed to land safely and evade hostile Serbian troops on the ground. 'Can I have a tissue please?' he asked during a press conference honouring his recue. 'Everyone is saying "you're a hero", but all I was, was a scared little bunny rabbit trying to survive.'[18]

It is likely that pilots shot down during battle during the Second World War were no less scared than O'Grady. However, society at this point did not encourage soldiers to express their fears and anxieties in public. That does not necessarily mean that their experience of fear was the same as that of O'Gradys. Adversity is experienced through a system of meaning which is likely to communicate different ideas about how to engage with suffering, pain, risk and threats.

The proliferation of fear-talk encourages the normalization, even the banalization, of fearing. But whether or not this growing trend towards voicing fear proves that society has become more fearful than in the past is far from clear. Hopefully by the end of this book our exploration of the different dimensions of the current culture of fear will help to clarify this issue.

MEDIA AND CULTURE

In recent times I have given around eighty lectures on the culture of fear in different parts of the world. Whether the audience is in Singapore, Australia, USA, Holland or the UK, the one question that is inevitably raised is 'how important is the role of the media in making us fearful?' This concern is not surprising since most accounts of the culture of fear assign a central role to the media in promoting an alarmist message. The claim that the current climate of fear is the fault of the media is so often echoed that it has acquired the status of a self-evident truth.

Accounts of the public's fears are often represented as artificially manufactured by highly manipulative media moguls. 'Fox News Fear Factory' is the term used by one journalist to capture the image of a media industry devoted to the invention of scare stories.[19]

Commentators sometimes go so far as to hold the media guilty for turning its audience into fearful, even brainwashed, subjects. The filmmaker Jen Senko has made a film of her father, who she believes was indoctrinated to fear by the conservative media. 'All of these emotions, especially fear, whip people up into a state of alarm,' stated Senko, before asserting that it is 'like a disease infecting millions of people around the country'.[20]

The assumption that the media, and particularly, the social media is almost singlehandedly responsible for the culture of fear also often informs the work of academic commentators on the subject. Margee Kerr, a sociologist from the University of Pittsburgh, argues that the media and the 'immediacy with which we get the news' is 'why we are more fearful now than 200 years ago'. Kerr notes that constant exposure to news 'makes it feel more emotionally charged', and states: 'We start receiving notifications on our phone as soon as … disasters happen. So there's a false sense of involvement that we didn't have 150 years ago.'[21]

Paradoxically, commentators 150 years ago were no less certain than Kerr that the media was responsible for provoking a highly charged emotional reaction among the disturbed readers of mass-circulation newspapers, penny dreadfuls, and romantic novels. During the nineteenth century, panicky accounts about the destructive power of the media were themselves often the source of an early version of our culture of fear. For example, an anonymous author who wrote 'The Vice of Reading' in the London-based literary magazine *Temple Bar* in 1874 associated the act of reading with horrifying outcomes. Novel reading was held to be responsible for the corruption of morals. The anonymous author claimed that the compulsive reader resembled the alcoholic:

> The habit of novel reading, novel upon novel for reading's sake, is the principal cause of the general vice of reading; novel drinking is not so expensive, so outwardly repulsive, as dram drinking, nor can it be said that it brings the same ruin and disgrace upon families – but the individual is as surely enfeebled by it, taste corrupted, will unstrung, understanding saddened.[22]

According to this view, frequently repeated at the time, the media's corruption of helpless readers disposed the brainwashed individuals to adopt anti-social and immoral behaviour.

My research into the historical relationship between the media and its impact on people indicates that it has always been associated with alarmist fears.[23] Such claims emerged many centuries before the rise of the 24-hour news cycle and of the social media. The tendency throughout history to blame the media for people's irrational behaviour and allegedly unbalanced emotional state should make us wary of relying on this timeless argument to explain the novel and unique features of the twenty-first-century culture of fear.

Alarmist denunciations of media scaremongering often resemble the turbo-charged rhetoric of the practices that they criticize. In the very act of denouncing the media's rhetoric of fear, they unwittingly offer a substitute version, evoking an image of the media as an omnipotent, malevolent force responsible for creating an easily malleable public. According to one account, after 9/11 'the media, with its perverse fascination with violence and profit-driven espousal to round-the-clock, up-to-the-minute coverage' was responsible for inculcating the public 'with a sense of danger' and powerlessness. 'Still in shock from the realization that the US was vulnerable to such infiltration and aggression, American society began to transform itself into a culture of fear and docility,' Selena Harper and Professor Bruce Lusignan concluded.[24] This analysis, which offers a media-led and media-directed explanation for the transformation of America into a 'culture of fear docility', overlooks the fact that such a culture was in place before the tragedy of 9/11.

Simplistic media-blaming is often associated with an unflattering representation of the public as gullible and uncritical. From this perspective, people are portrayed as easily brainwashed into internalizing and acting on the latest media directive. Thus Harper and Lusignan contend that the media-constructed culture of fear led to 'the almost totally unchallenged consummation of the Bush Administration's agenda'.[25]

There is little doubt that the messages communicated by the media are often oriented towards capturing its audience's attention through appeals to people's sense of anxiety and fear. The alarmist repertoire of the media has been well documented.[26] The influence of the media and, lately, social media over the conduct of everyday life is evident. But how people think, behave and fear is not directly the outcome of their media consumption. People can reflect and talk to their neighbours and friends about the latest media-communicated scare story without being seriously affected by it and altering their behaviour. For example, studies of apocalyptic constructions of climate change communicated through the media indicate that such fear appeals are often ineffective.[27] Critics claim that constant exposure to exaggerated climate change messages may well turn people off.

What people fear is not necessarily the latest high-profile threat that they read about in headlines. In 2009, when I worked alongside European colleagues on a research project designed to find out which threats citizens of the European Union feared the most, it soon became evident that people's concerns were mainly directed at problems that had little to do with apocalyptic scare stories. The most important concerns raised by respondents in opinion surveys were traditional issues to do with the problem of economic insecurity, with rising prices and unemployment topping their list of concerns. Despite considerable media attention devoted to global terrorism, this issue proved to be the least of their worries. As we noted in our report, 'of all the high profile/dramatic threats discussed in the media, only "the fear of crime" featured as a major concern of the respondents'.[28]

So what is the relationship between the media and the culture of fear? In the current era, the mass media has become a uniquely powerful institution. David Altheide is right when he asserts that the mass media is 'our most important social institution'.[29] It exercises a formidable influence over public life and serves as the medium through which people become acquainted with a growing variety of problems and threats to their lives. The fears highlighted in contemporary society are far less based on direct experience than in previous times; and the media is the major source of information to people about matters with which they have no direct experience.[30] In this sense, the principal accomplishment of the media is to provide the public with a constantly evolving script about how it should experience and react to global threats.

As an institution, the media plays a significant role in the cultivation of the landscape of fear. As Stefanie Grupp points out, 'there has been a general shift from a fearsome life towards a life with fearsome media'.[31] But the media does not so much create fear as provide a medium through which it can be experienced second hand. The legal theorist Christopher Guzelian argues that this indirect aspect of fear is the most distinctive feature of contemporary fear culture. He contends that 'most fears in America's electronic age' are the results of 'risk information (whether correct or false) that is communicated to society', and concludes that it is 'risk communication, not personal experience, [that] causes most fear these days'.[32]

There is no robust evidence that media communication actually 'causes most fear these days'. Direct experience, personal circumstance, social context and emotional dispositions all play a crucial role in influencing how individuals fear. Studies indicate that age, gender, social class and education play a crucial role in how people react to threats such as crime or climate change. Social and cultural variables lead to a differentiated response to the threats depicted by the media. One study of the public's reaction to media warnings about 'extreme weather' indicated that people with lower incomes were far less concerned about this threat than their affluent and educated peers. Women were more troubled about this threat than men, and people who identified with the Republican Party were more likely to be sceptical of the media's warnings on this issue than their Democrat counterparts. The author of the study concluded 'that individuals experience extreme weather in the context of their social circumstances and thus perceive the impacts of extreme weather through the lens of cultural and social influences'.[33]

Often the public ignores or questions the risk information communicated through the media. Despite claims that the public passively internalized the media-promoted stories and explanations about 9/11, a significant proportion of Americans remained sceptical. In August 2006, a survey of 1,010 adults found that 36 per cent of the American public suspected that federal officials assisted the 9/11 attacks, or took no action to stop them, so that the US could justify going to war in the Middle East.[34] The refusal of a substantial body of opinion to accept the mainstream media's version of 9/11 indicated that their threat assessments and fear calculations were subject to other influences.

Despite its prominent role, the media is not an omnipotent force responsible for the construction of the culture of fear. Such a simplistic assessment of the relationship between the media and the public's fear actually distracts from understanding its vital role in the mediation of fear. Although at times the media appears to possess an autonomous capacity to select and frame the issues it wants to highlight to its public, it is necessary to note that this institution is itself underpinned by culture. Whatever the political or economic interests that dominate the agenda of a particular media organization, it cannot effectively communicate warnings and fear appeals that are manufactured out of thin air. The media is a constituent part of modern culture. It interacts with and influences cultural attitudes, but in the end its activities regarding the framing of fear are founded upon and guided by the prevailing *cultural script*.

The concept of the cultural script was developed by sociologists to explain how individuals, institutions and communities use cultural resources to make sense of their experience. A cultural script provides guidance and meaning to people as they engage with the troubles of everyday life. It transmits rules about feelings and also ideas about what those emotions mean. To a significant extent it scripts people's response to threats and provides a language and a system of meaning through which society engages with fear. A cultural script is informed by the taken-for-granted cultural facts that are reproduced by common-sense narratives and are founded on traditions, custom and values. It also expresses the prevailing spirit of the times, which is why a cultural script can reassure, while at other times it can unsettle the confidence of individuals.

The most significant contribution offered by the media in relation to influencing the way that society fears is to provide a cultural script with dramatic content and powerful symbols. In this way it plays an important role in constructing the background and ambient cultural sensibility that informs the dispositions of people towards the challenges, risks and threats that they encounter. From this perspective, the main outcome of the catastrophic apocalyptic rhetoric sometimes adopted by the media is to reinforce a pre-existing mood of pessimism and fatalism. In his important study, *Climate Change and Post-Political Communication Media, Emotion and Environmental Advocacy*, Phil Hammond points out that fear appeals on this issue are framed in a manner that invites people to feel despair and a sense of powerlessness.[35]

The most important contribution made by the media is not so much how it frames and communicates a specific threat, but its role in popularizing and normalizing a language and a system of symbols and meaning for interpreting society's experience. Take the example of the dramatic escalation of anxiety regarding the threat of paedophilia to children. As I argue elsewhere, the transformation of people's natural anxiety about the safety of children into a cultural obsession is closely associated with the moral disorientation and mistrust that prevails in Western societies.[36] The media did not cause these anxieties but has played an important role in creating the symbols and images that haunt our imagination. On this issue, at least, the media has helped to render our fears palpable, visual, dramatic and intensely personal.

The constant diet of stories about children being kidnapped, murdered, abused and bullied has created an environment where people's reaction to the mere photograph of a child is drawn towards worst-case scenarios. From this viewpoint, a playground is not perceived as an open space where children can run around, mess about and have fun, but as a hostile territory where youngsters face accidents, bullies and paedophiles. We imagine that children are constantly threatened by adult irresponsibility and moral turpitude. When viewers see an image of a child on a TV news item, they automatically anticipate a negative story.[37] So a majority of the people asked to give their interpretation of a photo of a man cuddling a child responded by stating that this was a picture of a paedophile instead of that of a loving father.

Back in 2011, I wrote about the cover page of *The Weekend Australian Magazine*, which showed a young girl sitting on the side of a boat, fishing with her dad. When I looked at it, I saw a lovely portrait of father and daughter at ease with each other as they gaze out to sea. But as a spate of letters to the magazine indicated, where I saw beauty they visualized horror. Instead of an innocent depiction of a child at one with nature, some detected warning signs of perilous danger and parental irresponsibility. One person was disturbed by the absence of a lifejacket and saw fear, uncertainty or discomfort showing on the girl's face. Another angry individual asked, 'Just how irresponsible can you get?' Apparently the sight of a child not wearing a helmet, goggles, lifejacket and other protective gadgets sent out a dangerous message to kids! It appears that even a picture shot in two feet of calm water can be perceived as confirmation of the pre-existing conviction that children are, by definition, at risk.[38]

The power of the media is also illustrated by its capacity to influence language usage and popularize the rhetoric of fear. Through the sheer repetition of terms such as superbugs, pandemics, extinction or toxic, a lexicon of doom helps endow threats with an existential quality. Since the 1980s, words that convey a sense of alarm have appeared with increasing frequency in the media. The Nexis database shows that most of the words that would be included in any scaremonger's dictionary are found far more regularly in newspapers today than, say, 20 years ago. This trend is no less evident in the language used by the so-called quality press as in 'sensationalist' tabloids.

Take the British daily newspaper, the *Guardian*. In 1988 the word *extinction* appeared 93 times in its editions. In 2007 mentions of this term had increased to 207. By 2016 there were 602 mentions.

Between the years 1988 and 2007, use of the word *pandemic* increased almost seven-fold from 11 to 73, and *epidemic* rose from 181 to 291. In 2016 there were 171 mentions of the term pandemic and 1,319 hits on epidemic. Usage of the term *risk* more than doubled – from 2,275 to 5,111 between the years 1998 and 2007. During the first quarter of 2016 alone, risk was used 7,463 times. A similar pattern is evident in other broadsheets such as *The Times*. The word *toxic* was used 248 times in 1988, 665 times in 2007, rising to 773 in 2016.

A sense of anxiety about the future is reflected through the popularization of new idioms and expressions. Take the term *tipping point*. It conveys a dark sense of foreboding about the world of the future, where one catastrophe will beget another. According to one newspaper account of natural disasters to come, 'a tipping point is a place of no return'. The paper helpfully provides a map of the world showing the 'risk of different tipping points being passed this century if global warming continues at 3–5° C'.[39] Back in 1988, neither the *Guardian* nor *The Times* had any reason to use this term. A decade later, in 1998, it was used once by the *Guardian* but not at all by *The Times*. In 2000 the former used it five times and the latter twice. It was in 2005 that the term tipping point acquired a more general usage, appearing 41 times in the *Guardian* and 48 times in *The Times*; by 2007, it appeared 199 times in *The Times* and 106 times in the *Guardian*. In 2016 this term was used 773 times in *The Times*.

What endows this media rhetoric with a particularly troublesome quality is that, although it exhorts urgent action, it tends to encourage a mood of 'paralysing dread'.[40] The *Oxford English Dictionary* defines dread as 'extreme fear; deep awe or reverence; apprehension or anxiety as to future events'.[41] Dread is an emotional orientation towards the future, which can be understood as an intense sense of anxiety towards as yet unknown or unclear threats. The term 'tipping point', which implies that soon it will be too late to save ourselves from the threats that lurk ahead in the future, serves as an exemplar of the kind of rhetoric that cultivates the sensibility of dread.

The media does not merely mobilize a pre-existing vocabulary of gloom – it also plays an important role in innovating or popularizing new terms inviting people to fear. Even an activity as banal as forecasting the weather has been transformed into a mini-drama, through adopting a rhetoric that inflates the threat posed by relatively normal conditions. Routine occurrences like storms, heavy snowfall or high temperature have been rebranded as extreme weather by the media. From the 1990s onwards the expression 'extreme weather' quickly gained widespread usage. In the 1990s headlines containing this term appeared in 69 instances on the Nexis database. It rose to 1,045 headlines in the following decade and appeared on 5,599 occasions between the beginning of 2001 and the end of 2006.

The term 'extreme weather' is a paradigmatic culture of fear expression. As an adjective, 'extreme' signifies a state that is far beyond normal. The conceptual linkage of weather with 'extreme' exemplifies the growing tendency to inflate the risks posed by natural phenomena, by highlighting the unexpected and unpredictable quality of this unnatural occurrence. It is not so much a scientific as a cultural metaphor that captures the anxieties of our time. In contemporary culture, extreme weather is often interpreted through a moralistic narrative that presents it as the inevitable outcome of irresponsible human behaviour.

My analysis of the relation between the media and culture emphasizes the element of interaction through which people's fears are expressed and crystallized. This analysis leads to the conclusion that the argument 'it's the fault of the media' is both simplistic and misplaced. Our analysis rejects the one-dimensional interpretations of the media, which indict this institution for being responsible for creating a climate of fear. There are of course instances when the media literally invents scare stories with which to entertain its audience.[42] However, the culture of fear is not reducible to the confusing consequences of hysterical tabloid headlines – on the contrary, the media itself is to a significant extent the bearer of pre-existing attitudes and values that inform society's ideas about emotions such as fear.

Since the turn of the twenty-first century, the term 'the media' has lost much of its meaning. In Western societies, and especially in the

Anglo-American world, the media has become increasingly divided and fragmented. Media consumption – especially online – is highly differentiated and segmented. The cultural and political divisions in society are reproduced and amplified by a fragmented media catering to different types of people. Consequently, there is no longer a unified media representation of threats.

News outlets also promote competing scare stories. The recent conflicts over Fake News mark an important escalation in scaremongering about the media. It also indicates that public opinion is bitterly polarized about how to view competing media fear appeals. This conflict, and the intense anxiety that surrounds it, suggests that the media has itself become the target of the kind of scare stories that it is usually accused of promoting. At times it seems that fear of the media creating fear surpasses traditional concerns about this institution's scaremongering. The current wave of anxiety about Fake News is symptomatic of the climate of suspicion that envelops journalism. These anxieties are particularly directed at other people's sources of news. From a sociological point of view, the fragmentation and segmentation of the media mirrors the wider climate of moral confusion and mistrust that permeates the culture of fear.

FEAR AND CULTURE
As indicated above, the scaremongering directed at the threat posed by the media shows how the influence of the culture of fear can capture the outlook of its critics. Indeed, one of the most disquieting features of the culture of fear is that its premises and practices are unconsciously accepted even by parties and individuals who are hostile to many of its manifestations. Unfortunately, criticisms directed at the culture of fear habitually target its consequences while unwittingly accepting its premise. This sentiment is most systematically articulated in the recurring criticism mounted against the culture of fear for misplacing the targets of fear: as indicated by the title of Barry Glassner's book, *The Culture of Fear: Why Americans Are Afraid of the Wrong Things*.

That people regularly worry about the 'wrong things' is not in doubt.

There are numerous studies that point out that people are often more worried about low-probability risks such as children being kidnapped rather than about more likely threats such as that posed by road traffic. It is well known that people's assessment of risks is distorted by the way that the media and wider culture portrays them – public anxiety about the potential risk to life posed by a nuclear power station, for example, bears very little relationship to the actual dangers associated with this form of energy. Numerous analysts have shown how our concern with safety from terrorism is disproportionate to the risks we face from this threat. John Mueller's book *Overblown* notes that since 2001 'fewer people have been killed in America by international terrorism than have drowned in toilets or have died from bee stings'.[43] One frequently cited example of the deleterious consequences of poor risk assessment is that an estimated 1,200 American people died because, in the aftermath of 9/11, they chose car travel over air travel.

Making wrong choices about what to fear can have tragic consequences. Children have died because their parents wrongly calculated that the side effects of vaccinating their children against a particular disease constituted a greater risk than that posed by the illness. However, the fact that people's assessment of the risks they confront is often misguided and confused has little to do with the twenty-first-century culture of fear. That people often fear phenomena posing little objective or material threat to their existence is arguably the *least distinctive feature of the fear culture of our times.*

Stories and legends from ancient times onwards point to examples where a poor assessment of risks led to tragic outcomes. Written 400 years before the birth of Christ, Thucydides' *History of the Peloponnesian War* offered a vivid account of the deathly consequences of Athenians 'fearing the wrong things' during the plague that afflicted their city-state. Fear and panic led many citizens to flee their homes and move into congested urban huts. Overcrowding helped spread the disease and, as Thucydides wrote, the 'mortality among them was dreadful'.[44] In the centuries to come, Europeans continued to be 'afraid of the wrong things'. In the course of battling with diseases, 'long-harbored fears about conspiracy and contamination came to focus on lepers and then on Jews (and eventually witches)', notes Philip Alcabes in his book *Dread: How Fear and Fantasy Have Fuelled Epidemics from the Black Death to Avian Flu.*[45]

Educating people about how to assess risk is obviously a worthwhile exercise. However, lecturing them about what they should and should not fear does little to improve matters. One problem with the 'people fearing the wrong things' argument is that it can inadvertently enhance the climate of fear. Criticism of 'fearing the wrong things' can seamlessly move on to an exhortation to 'fear the right things'. Competing views about what is the wrong or the right problem to fear fuel the process of competitive scaremongering. Such disputes serve to disorient public life and reinforce the mood of insecurity.

In any case, even the application of the most rigorous techniques of risk assessment cannot transform the emotion of fear and the forms of behaviour it encourages into an instrument of rationality. The relationship between the intensity of people's fears is rarely correlated to the gravity and likelihood of the risks they face. The rise of the so-called 'worried well' – people who do not need medical treatment but nevertheless are absolutely convinced that their condition requires it – exemplifies this point.[46] Research into the prevalence of the fear of crime or anxieties about health tends to show that in Western societies, it is usually the wealthiest, the most economically and socially secure individuals, who tend to be most concerned for their safety.

Numerous commentators have struggled to explain the coexistence of conditions of unprecedented prosperity and security with a pervasive climate of fear. As the Norwegian philosopher Lars Svendsen explains, 'a paradoxical trait of the culture of fear is that it emerges at a time when, by all accounts, we are living more securely than ever before in human history'.[47] Why Americans fear more when they have far less to fear than in other moments in the past is a question that puzzles numerous scholars.[48] One argument used to explain this 'paradox of a safe society' is that prosperity encourages people to become more risk and loss averse.[49]

There is no doubt some merit in the argument that prosperity is correlated with an aversion to risk and loss. However, it is unlikely that there is a direct causal connection between prosperity and an inclination to fear. Historically some of the most prosperous societies – Ancient Athens, Renaissance Italy, nineteenth-century Britain – were among those that were most oriented towards experimentation and the taking of risks. The argument developed in subsequent chapters is that it is not prosperity but prevailing cultural norms that have nurtured risk aversion and a dread of uncertainty.

Behaviours signalling fear are not always a direct reaction to physical threats. Aristotle pointed out that many of our most troubling fears are related to losing face and being disgraced or suffering slights to our reputation. How people responded to such slights or physical threat was informed by the prevailing rules of fear, which in turn were underwritten by moral rules guiding people to engage with their insecurities and fears. In a Greek city-state, as in the societies that followed, fearing was related to a cultural script about what ought to be feared and how people should deal with threats.

Today, as in ancient times, fear has an important historical, moral and cultural dimension. The emotion of fear also has a biological basis and has played a crucial role in the survival and the evolution of the human species. One of the founders of psychiatry, Sigmund Freud, seems to suggest that insofar as it is a signal to action, this emotion can have a 'purposeful aspect', such as fight or flight. Freud believed that what was 'purposeful' was not the fear but the action that emanated from it. He warned that if the fear becomes too strong, it 'defeats its own object' and paralyses 'every action, even flight'.[50] From this perspective, 'fearing the right things' can be a counterproductive reaction.

Though the emotion of fear has a biological foundation, it is also shaped by both 'individual experiences and social norms'.[51] In contrast to the way that animals respond to threats, humans also possess a disposition to fear that is culturally transmitted. This is a disposition that is based on the experience of the past and which, through the process of socialization and the values and attitudes promoted by a community, retains a certain degree of force as *living stories*. Fear is thus scripted. The sociologist Zygmunt Bauman describes this as a type of 'secondary fear' – which 'may be seen as a sediment of past experience of facing the menace point blank – a sediment that outlives the encounter and becomes an important factor in shaping human conduct even if there is no longer a direct threat to life and integrity'.[52] The troubles of the past, and the stories that are transmitted about them, continue to influence the human imagination.

Throughout history, philosophers, theologians, psychologists and sociologists have struggled to make sense of the workings of fear. As Freud wrote, 'it is certain that the problem of fear is the meeting point of many important questions, an enigma whose complete solution would cast a flood of light upon psychic life'.[53] Although there are numerous approaches towards the study of the problem, there appears to be a widespread consensus about the need to make a distinction between the condition of fear and that of anxiety. In his discussion of the 'General Theory of the Neuroses', Freud tentatively wrote: 'I think that anxiety is used in connection with a condition regardless of any objective, while fear is essentially directed toward an object.' Arguably, Freud's distinction is anticipated by the Danish philosopher, Søren Kierkegaard, who differentiated between two forms of angst: one being fear, which is a response to specific, focused, external threats, and the other being characterized as neurotic angst – a state when fear exists as a permanent neurotic condition.[54]

Freud was far from rigorous in maintaining the distinction between fear and anxiety. At times he used the term 'neurotic fear' to allude to conditions that are classically coupled with anxiety. He wrote of neurotic fear as linked to a condition of anxiety, which he described as 'a condition of free-floating fear as it were, which is ready to attach itself to any appropriate idea, to influence judgment, to give rise to expectations, in fact to seize any opportunity to make itself felt'. He also described this condition as 'expectant fear' or 'anxious expectation'.[55]

The most relevant of Freud's concepts for helping us grasp the workings of the culture of fear is the condition of *expectant fear*, which drives what I have described elsewhere as *worst-case thinking*.[56] This orientation towards expecting, and often acting, on the basis of the worst possible outcomes was already recognized in the fourth century BCE by Aristotle. He wrote in his *Rhetoric* that 'fear may be defined as a pain or disturbance due to a mental picture of some destructive or painful event in the future'.[57] The connection drawn by Aristotle between fear and visions of the future has important implications for understanding our current predicament. The proliferation of pessimistic accounts of the future highlights the general cultural condition of our times.

The frequency with which twenty-first-century fear is interlinked with expectations of threats that are not yet seen or known indicates that it is not always useful to distinguish between fear and anxiety. In practice, anxiety about the unknown reinforces the public's concern about specific threats and habituates it to fear. When society is habitually drawn towards worst possible outcomes it fosters a mood where fear can acquire the character of a habit, the acquisition of which endows fear with a banal and casual character. Svendsen refers to this form of fear as a 'low-intensity fear, a fear that surrounds us and forms a backdrop of our experiences and interpretations of the world'.[58] This relatively low-grade ambient fear provides the cultural setting within which individuals and communities deal with threats and manage uncertainty.

Cultural attitudes play a dominant role in defining the relationship between uncertainty and fear. Ideas about uncertainty are governed by the way society perceives the relationship between the present and the future. When, as today, the future is regarded as a dangerous territory, uncertainty is framed in a negative light. In such a setting, change itself is perceived as threatening. A potent undercurrent of apprehension towards change – whether technological, social or political – permeates the day-to-day affairs of the contemporary Western world. Uncertainty was at times regarded as an opportunity – that it now tends to be cast in a negative light is symptomatic of a mood of fatalism towards the challenges faced by society. This fatalistic attitude is summed up by the often-repeated catch-phrase –

'The question is "not if, but when?"' Warnings of catastrophic climate events, deadly flu epidemics or mass casualty terrorism usually conclude with this defeatist refrain, which implicitly and sometimes explicitly calls into question humanity's capacity to avert the destructive consequences of the threats it faces. In this way, the perils of the future acquire an immediate and intimate quality. They demand that we ring the alarm bells while implying that there is very little that can be done to avert the dangers that lie ahead.

In recent times, commentaries tend to suggest that it is the state of anxiety, rather than fear, which constitutes the main threat to collective and individual wellbeing. Often the terms are used as interchangeable. Svendsen argues that 'the dividing line between anxiety and fear is not, in practice, as clear as these conceptual distinctions maybe imply'.[59] Bauman's definition of 'fear' illustrates its conceptual intermeshing with anxiety:

> Fear is at its most fearsome when it is diffuse, scattered, unclear, unattached, unanchored, free floating, with no clear address or cause ... when the menace we should be afraid of can be glimpsed everywhere but is nowhere to be seen. 'Fear' is the name we give to our uncertainty, *to our* ignorance *of the threat* and of what is to be *done.*[60]

The condition described by this definition highlights an important feature of the working of the culture of fear. It is what I describe elsewhere as the *autonomization of fear* or the *objectification of fear.*[61] Unattached and free-floating anxieties that seem almost to be searching for a threat to dwell on appear as if they are driven by their own inner imperative. That is why the target of such apprehensions can so effortlessly shift in one day, from concern with one's physical appearance to unease about a child's safety to a sense of disquiet about mass immigration and crime.

The autonomization of fear as an emotion or phobia that exists in isolation from any specific threat can sometimes express itself as the *fear of fear*. This term is said to have first been used by the sixteenth-century French essayist Michel de Montaigne, who stated that 'the thing I fear most is fear'.[62] Though this sentiment has a long history, only in more recent times has it come to be seen as a risk that needs to be taken seriously. Consequently, a fear that is detached from any external referent is sometimes treated as a problem that requires the intervention of risk managers.[63] The act of fearing is in some cases perceived to be as much of a problem as the threat faced by society.

Classically, societies associated fear with a clearly formulated threat – the fear of death or the fear of hunger – and the threat was defined as the object of such fears (death or hunger). Today we frequently represent the act of fearing as a threat itself. A striking illustration of this development is the way that society engages with the fear of crime. Today, it is conceptualized as a serious problem that is, to some extent, distinct from the problem of crime. As one criminologist observed, 'fear of crime has come to be regarded as a problem in and of itself, quite distinct from actual crime and victimization, and distinctive policies have been developed that aim to reduce fear levels, rather than reduce crime'.[64] Indeed, some social scientists claim that the fear of crime is 'now recognised as a more widespread problem than crime itself'.[65] In many instances, the police appear to be spending as much time dealing with the *fear of crime* as with the detection and prevention of criminal activities.

In the popular media, everyday conversations and commentaries on the culture of fear tend to be depicted as the outcome of conscious manipulation, media propaganda, or the activities of profit-seeking businesses and professional scaremongers. As should be evident from the arguments outlined so far, such subjective explanations cannot account for the ascendancy of the culture of fear. The autonomization of fear, its free-floating and apparently arbitrary trajectory, indicates that at least some of the trends that are integral to the culture of fear have acquired their own inner dynamic. As we explain in Chapter 4, this development has lent fear the character of a perspective from which the different aspects of life are assessed.

Any serious analysis of the culture of fear needs to take the first word of this term seriously. Culture is not an optional add-on. It provides the script through which fear is nourished, cultivated and in the end experienced by communities and individuals. Of course there are many individuals and groups – fear entrepreneurs – who seek to promote fear and benefit from the anxieties that people possess. But though they contribute to the expansion of a climate of fear, their success depends on being able to draw on cultural resources that exist independent of their activities.

FEAR AND MORALITY

The flipside of the culture of fear is a tendency to inflate the nature and range of threats faced by society. The propensity to imagine that humanity is confronted with an existential crisis is even evident among analysts struggling to explain the contemporary climate of fear. Unlike accounts that emphasize the role of media manipulation and organized fear promotion, academic studies of 'Risk Society' tend to provide structural explanations for the emergence of contemporary fear culture. The main argument advanced by such structural explanations is that the rapid pace of change promoted by constant scientific and technological innovation and globalization has created a variety of potent risks whose consequences are impossible to know or calculate. According to this thesis, some of these risks – climate change, superbugs, global terrorism – pose a threat to both humanity and the planet it inhabits.

The claim that we live in a world that is far more dangerous than before is frequently motivated by arguments that echo the tone of fundamentalist eschatological warnings about the end of time. 'Time is running out' is a favourite refrain of a genre of fear analysis that often comes across as overwhelmed by the topic under investigation. Writing in this vein, Bauman offers the 'prophecy' that unless the threats faced by humanity are 'bridled and tamed', catastrophe becomes 'inescapable'. He warns that 'what threatens the planet now is not just another round of self-inflicted damage ... and not another of the long string of catastrophes ... but a catastrophe to end all catastrophes, a catastrophe that would leave no human being behind to record it'.[66]

Unlike most other alarmist narratives of catastrophes to come, Bauman succeeds in tempering his account by reminding his readers of the moral component of fearing. In others words, fearing is also a moral accomplishment and not simply a response to objective threat. He rightly notes that 'all moral tales act through sowing fear'.[67] Since the beginning of time, human fears have been formulated through the grammar of morality. What we fear and how we fear are guided by the norms and values of the prevailing moral code. Even some of our most primeval fears, such as the fear of death, are mediated through moral norms. Fears about human survival often draw on religious stories and themes. Historically, depictions of disasters possessed a profound religious significance. They were often perceived as 'Acts of God' – a form of divine retribution for human transgression.

Bauman points out that fear and evil are closely linked with one another. They are the moral equivalent of 'Siamese twins'; what we fear is evil and what is evil we fear.[68] Many of the fear appeals that circulate in the contemporary world originate in particular circumstances and are responses to perceived specific problems. However, in order to turn these problems into threats they deploy an ideology of evil that is well known in society. Historically, the concept of evil helped to explain why bad things happened; it provided an answer to society's need to understand the cause of misfortune, and guidance as to who should bear the blame. Traditionally in Western societies, sin was portrayed as the main catalyst for evil behaviour.

In modern secular times matters are more complicated because we eschew explicit references to good and evil. Western societies feel uncomfortable with the language of morality and therefore often lack a coherent narrative through which they can give meaning to fear. In such circumstances, we struggle to find the right words. This sentiment was expressed by the German sociologist Ulrich Beck, who lamented that 'we unleash unforeseeable, uncontrollable, indeed *incommunicable* consequences that threaten life on earth'.[69] The word 'incommunicable' draws attention to the absence of a language with which to give meaning to the threat facing humanity.

Even in the contemporary secular world, fear, evil and moral concerns intersect with one another. The example of the controversy surrounding the Millennium Bug illustrates how fears about a technical problem can so readily assume a moral dimension. During the year leading up to the new millennium, there were ominous hints about the dreadful hazards that lay ahead. Experts warned that on midnight, 31 December 1999, there would be catastrophic problems with computer programmes, which would behave as if it was 1900 instead of 2000. Apprehension concerning a potential technical glitch with what was initially known as the Y2K bug swiftly turned into a powerful scare about the breakdown of computer systems around the globe.

What was fascinating about the predictions of gloom concerning the devastating consequences of the Millennium Bug were the quasi-religious and end-of-time themes that were communicated by their authors. Religious preachers prophesied a future in which widespread computer failures would unleash a cataclysmic struggle between good and evil. For example Morris Cerullo, a Pentecostal healing revivalist, predicted a catastrophe of biblical proportions:

> This panic that will sweep the nation will translate into a global depression. Shutdowns of banks will paralyze the world's financial markets. Global economies will crash ... the Bible predicts an end day when the world will see a global economic crash in one hour! Riots will break out in cities ... at the tick of midnight, 2000, America could be less than thirty minutes away from nuclear devastation.[70]

Numerous fear entrepreneurs jumped on the apocalyptic bandwagon and invented the most fantastic and frightening scenarios. One book, *Time Bomb 2000*, predicted that Y2K would lead to global chaos. Grant Jeffrey's *The Millennium Meltdown: The Year 2000 Computer Crisis* prophesied a computer meltdown that would set the stage for the rise of a conspiratorial world government of the Antichrist.

The interweaving of eschatological anxieties with the search for technical solutions should be interpreted as an attempt to find a language with which to highlight a sense of foreboding about the future. The absence of language with which to communicate insecurity about the future, to which Beck alluded, invites people to search for meaning. That at least some commentators found refuge in the ideals and rhetoric of the biblical Apocalypse raised interesting questions about fear and evil in the current era.

Communities throughout history have protected themselves from the threats they faced through the stories and guidance provided by their moral codes. Whether or not people felt well or insecure was influenced by their relationship with the prevailing sense of meaning. The sociologist C. Wright Mills viewed the relationship between a system of meaning and people's perception of feeling threatened in the following manner: 'when people cherish some set of values and do not feel any threat to them, they experience *well-being*', but 'when they cherish values but *do* feel them to be threatened, they experience a crisis'. 'And if all their values seem involved they feel the total threat of panic,' adds Mills. Mills also projected a scenario that captures an important dimension of the construction of social anxiety today. 'Suppose, finally they are unaware of any cherished values, but still are very much aware of a threat,' he stated, before concluding, '*that is the experience of uneasiness, of anxiety, which, if it is total enough, becomes a deadly unspecified malaise*' (my emphasis).[71]

The consequences of being unaware of any cherished values are extremely significant for an understanding of the way that fear works today. At times, belief in the immortality of the soul helped people come to terms with their fear of death. Ancient Greek schools of thought – Epicureans, Sceptics and Stoics – developed a philosophy that rejected the fear of death as irrational. They provided a system of values that helped people to come to terms with their fear of death. Some societies were better than others at providing a web of meaning through which people made sense of the world and developed a capacity to make sense of the threats they faced. In societies with a strong moral code, fearing was related to a cultural script about what ought to be feared and how people should deal with threats. For example in Ancient Greece, the virtue of courage played an important role in the public management and performance of fear.

Contemporary society struggles to give concepts of right and wrong a self-conscious moral content. As the subsequent chapters argue, both the rhetoric and the reality of the culture of fear give voice to the moral uncertainties and sensibility of powerlessness that prevail in contemporary society. In today's fragile moral climate we lack a virtue that can serve as an antidote to fear. Consequently we rely on non-moral resources – psychology, therapy, expertise – to guide our responses to the threat we face. Moral confusion both sustains and reproduces the culture of fear.

To understand how fear works and what is unique about its contemporary manifestation, *How Fear Works* will focus on how it is scripted and acted out. In our references to the concept of a cultural script we have pointed to its role in providing people with guidance about how to interpret and respond to uncertainty and threats. Our cultural script provides the norms, rhetoric and taken-for-granted assumptions that inform the way we fear. It also provides a story concerning what it means to be a person. The ideas it communicates on this score inform us about how we are expected to behave in distressful situations. A cultural script also has a lot to say about how to feel in difficult circumstances and it helps guide the emotional experience of individuals. It transmits rules about feelings and also ideas about what those feelings mean. Individuals interpret and internalize these rules according to their circumstances and temperament but express them through culturally sanctioned idioms.

All cultures have their unique scripts about fear and its meaning. Since fear is so much immersed in cultural assumptions about the meaning of life, it is subject to historical variations. Indeed, one of the most useful approaches to the study of contemporary fear is to compare how it works to other historical moments. This approach helps facilitate the development of our understanding of the unique features and distinct attributes of our culture of fear. Attending to the study of the historical variations of fear is essential for answering the question of 'what's different about the way we fear compared to the past?' It also helps us to imagine a world where fear ceases to possess a commanding influence over our lives.

How Fear Works principally draws on the experience of the Anglo-American world. However, the influence of the culture of fear has become truly global. As I write these words, I am in Lima, Peru. During the past ten days I have been incessantly reminded to stay clear of places designated as 'unsafe', and informed about what restaurants and which taxi companies are 'safe'. My introduction to Lima's narrative of fear is informed by the expectation that *gringo* tourists welcome guidance on the subject. But when I talk to – mainly middle class – Peruvians it becomes evident they too have internalized aspects of the Anglo-American outlook on fear. Conversations in places as different as Singapore, Budapest, Amsterdam or Milan have convinced me that, to a greater or lesser degree, the culture of fear has acquired widespread global influence.

I have come to the conclusion that society has unwittingly become estranged from the values – such as courage, judgement, reasoning, responsibility – that are necessary for the management of fear. The culture of fear is not a product of nature; in many respects its strength derives from the way that young people are socialized. *How Fear Works* argues that, more than any other historical development, it was the adoption of new methods of socializing young people that served as a catalyst for the ascendancy of the culture of fear. Young people are socialized to feel fragile and overawed by uncertainty. This book is written in the hope that they will find a way of transcending the disempowering effect of the current regime of socialization.

1

Changing Stories of Fear

The contemporary meaning of fear stands in sharp contrast to the way it was perceived in previous historical epochs. Until the twentieth century fear was often regarded as an emotional state that meshed with moral concerns. According to the different cultural norms that were dominant until the end of the nineteenth century, fearing was regarded as a medium for cultivating moral values. Distinctions were often drawn between good and bad fears, and communities provided people with moral and practical guidance on this subject. Religious and moral codes praised the positive attributes of fear – so long as it was the right kind of fear.

Today, when fear itself is often abhorred and dreaded, it tends to be medicalized as a disease to be avoided. The purpose of this chapter is to explore the changing conventions and rules that governed fear in the past. It focuses on one period in particular: the interwar years of 1918–39, when many of the features of the twenty-first-century culture of fear began to take shape.

FEAR RULES

The previous chapter highlighted the case of Scott O'Grady, an American pilot who publicly talked about how scared he was after being forced to land in enemy territory. His reaction was very different to those of two former British sailors – Bill Wake and Bill Ness – to the horrors they faced after landing in France on D-Day. They recalled that 'everybody was beyond scared' and added that 'we were frightened, of course', but 'we had to have a brave face'.[1] In both cases the soldiers were frightened, but the old British veterans knew they were expected not to show it. They had to put on a 'brave face'. According to the rules of fear that prevailed during the Second World War, military personnel were expected to demonstrate stoicism in public, regardless of their inner state of emotional upheaval.

Since biblical times, authorities have taken a great interest in managing the fears of their soldiers before and during battle. The Second Book of Chronicles exhorts the Jews to 'be strong and courageous'. It states: 'do not fear or be dismayed' by the powerful army of the king of Assyria, because 'the one with us is greater than the one with him'.[2] The claim that their God was greater than those of others was offered to steady the nerves of soldiers facing an army with superior numbers. During the First World War, every Prussian infantryman had the words *Gott Mit Uns* – God is with us – stamped on their belt buckle. The phrase suggested that God was on their side, they had little to fear.[3]

How soldiers responded to their anxieties, and particularly to the fear of death, has been an issue of concern to military and civil authorities throughout the centuries. Communities provided their soldiers with a very clear story about how they were expected to respond to the dangers of the battlefield. Their religions and moral code frequently sought to disparage the fear of death in war. They acclaimed heroism and the willingness to make sacrifices for the sake of a higher cause.

Societies have different accounts and stories about the fear of dying. The American sociologist Arlie Hochschild, in her fascinating study of the sociology of emotions, characterizes these informal expectations of what constitutes an appropriate emotional response to situations as *feeling rules*.[4] Feeling rules instruct us concerning how and what we ought to fear, which in turn has a bearing on how we act. Through community conventions and custom, these rules influence people's response to threats and uncertainty.

One of the first explicit attempts to prescribe feeling rules about fear can be found in the writings of the ancient Greek philosopher, Plato. In *The Republic*, Plato directly addresses the question of how people should fear death. An important objective of this book – written around 380 BCE – was to provide its readers with guidance about socializing citizens to fear the right threats. Speaking through the voice of Socrates, Plato outlined a strategy for immunizing his Republic's soldiers from the fear of death. To realize the goal of making soldiers courageous, Socrates advocated the careful vetting of written communication and of orally transmitted poems and legends. Socrates wanted to ensure that anecdotes and examples of people fearing death were deleted from stories communicated to children. Not even Homer's magnificent poetry escaped this censorious project. In particular, Socrates was perturbed about Homer's description of the horrors of the afterlife in the underworld of Hades because he was worried that such passages would cause warriors to fear dying in battle.[5]

Socrates argued that in order to promote the values of courage, valour and sacrifice, and to ensure that soldiers feared defeat in battle more than death, the Republic had to adopt intelligent policies of manipulation that today would be considered as a form of social engineering. Socrates insisted that the content of stories transmitted to the guardians of the Republic should promote the project of cultivating desirable attitudes towards the fear of death. From this perspective, Greek heroes were to be depicted as courageous warriors who preferred to perish in battle than to be enslaved.

In Book III of *The Republic*, Socrates asked Glaucon, his interlocutor, about how to ensure that children – the guardians of the future – are 'to be courageous'. He continued: 'Shouldn't they be told stories that will make them least afraid of death? Or do you think that anyone will ever become courageous if he's possessed by this fear?'[6]

After Glaucon replied, 'No, I certainly don't', Socrates went on to enquire: 'And can someone be unafraid of death, preferring it to defeat in battle or slavery, if he believes in a Hades full of terrors?'[7] The main conclusion to emerge from this dialogue was the importance of providing cultural support for a positive representation of the underworld. It followed that the prohibition of any negative representation of the afterlife was mandatory in order to diminish soldiers' fear of death and to promote military courage. To ensure that Hades was depicted in a positive light, Socrates argued for deleting all negative references to it in poems and stories, stating that 'the most frightening names' used to describe the underworld 'must be struck out'. Socrates even held that the act of public mourning and lamentation of the dead should be curbed in the interest of promoting courage, stating: 'We'd be right, then, to delete the lamentations of famous men, leaving them to women (and not even to good women, either) and to cowardly men, so that those we say we are training to guard our city will disdain to act like that.'[8]

Plato's psychological template for regulating the fear of death went beyond censorship. He also proposed policies that would weaken soldiers' attachment to their families and friends as well as to material possessions. Similar to today's culture of martyrdom that surrounds the mystique of the twenty-first-century radical jihadist suicide bomber, Plato offered fallen warriors the status of immortal heroes.[9]

In centuries to follow, successive societies have attempted to control the corrosive effects of the fear of death on their military personnel. The feeling rules they developed drew on a moral code that celebrated the values of sacrifice, patriotism, loyalty and honour. Through the ages it was recognized that, since feeling fear in battle could not be eradicated, it needed to be neutralized by directing this emotion towards a higher end. Authorities frequently perceived people's fear of God as an antidote to the fear of death. In his fascinating account of early twentieth-century Russian military psychiatry and its engagement with fear, Jan Plamper noted that in the first half of the nineteenth century, the authorities still looked to religion and morality to contain the problem of fear. He cited a publication, *The Experience of the Military-Medical Police, or: Rules for the Healthcare of the Russian Soldiers of the Land Forces* (1834), that referred explicitly to fear only once. Fear was mentioned in the context of discussing the 'advantages of the Russians, Ukrainians, and Cossacks over other ethnic groups' in the Tsarist Empire. Its preference for these three groups was justified on the grounds that their people tended to be 'brought up in fear of God'. Plamper observed that in this publication, 'the categories in which fear could be discussed or almost discussed were still in the realm of morality and religion rather than medicine and psychology, and the strong ethnic component in the description of soldiers deduced national character from climate and religion rather than genes or individual personality types'.[10]

Throughout most of the nineteenth century, the military sought to train soldiers to regard fear of death as disgraceful cowardice. Yet by the early twentieth century, acknowledgement of the disorienting influence of the fear of death among soldiers had become widespread within the military establishment. Plamper cites the role of the Russo-Japanese Wars, the Balkan War of 1912, and the First World War in boosting the importance of military psychiatry. These wars saw a spectacular rise in the number of reported cases of 'hysteria and nervous exhaustion and fear', and consequently it emerged as a key issue for military psychiatry.[11] By the end of the First World War, the traditional feeling rules governing soldiers' fear of death in battle had unravelled. Plamper wrote that a 'century earlier there was hardly any military psychology, but there was also hardly any mentioning of soldierly fear in first-person sources'. But by 1918 fear had become not only of central concern to the psychological science of the military but also 'both a symptom and a product of this era'.[12]

Conventional explanations for the emergence of fear as a mental health issue that requires psychological intervention focus on the changing character of warfare. The new technologies of destruction were represented as more awesome and destructive than the threat posed by the bayonets of rifles. Wars lasting many years, and which relied on the mobilization of large numbers of civilians to fight in the trenches, were said to have had a corrosive impact on the morale of soldiers.[13] However, though the devastating consequences of modern warfare contributed and continue to contribute to a heightened sense of fear, this alone does not provide a satisfactory explanation for the emergence of a radical shift in attitude towards the public articulation of fear in the early twentieth century.

The immediate aftermath of the First World War brought a reorientation towards the rules of fear, not only within the military, but throughout the whole of society. The interwar era saw a significant expansion of the influence of psychology, and it is at this point in time that the subject of fear and anxiety came to be seen as a problem in its own right. Stearn has observed that fear culture changed in America in the 1920s, and a similar shift is apparent in many parts of Europe.[14] Though the influence of the narrative of fear as an independent variable or as a cultural force was relatively modest compared to in the late twentieth and early twenty-first centuries, it had already become disconnected from the way it was framed in more traditional settings.

The reframing of the rules of fear was not simply a response to the catastrophic experience of the First World War. The war served as a catalyst that brought to the surface pre-existing doubts about the relevance of traditional values and moral codes. The 'mass slaughter of self-sacrificing elites' called into question the values that had previously served to contain the fear of death.[15] The difficulty that society had in replacing its old moral code was principally responsible for uncoupling fear from its traditional moorings.

The transformation of feeling rules towards death did not occur overnight. Authorities throughout the world attempted to uphold traditional military values and, indeed, continue to do so today. However, the military establishment recognizes that it can no longer rely on the influence of the traditional warrior ethos and has opted to influence feelings about the fear of death through psychological techniques. That is why the American army provides advice on what it calls the 'emotional cycle of extended deployment' to soldiers and their families, along with guidance about dealing with 'fears about fidelity or marital integrity' and fears about 'separation anxiety'.[16]

One of the consequences of the shift away from traditional values is that death has become disassociated from any positive moral connotations, and is viewed merely as an incomprehensible, and unacceptable, personal tragedy. Within the military these cultural attitudes are reflected through the adoption of practices and tactics designed to avoid casualties to their own forces. This ethos of casualty aversion is most strikingly shown by the reluctance of the military establishment to 'put boots on the ground' and avoid extended combat operations. The doctrine, called Revolution in Military Affairs (RMA), can be seen as an attempt to avoid having to commit troops to a protracted and bloody encounter. According to one study, many 'statesmen and generals believe, with absolute and unquestioning conviction, that the United States can no longer use force successfully unless American military casualties are virtually nil'.[17] The main merit of the frequent use of unmanned drone-strikes for the Obama and the Trump administrations is that it avoids casualties among American military personnel.

Paradoxically, the loss aversion of Western military forces has provided their opponents with an incentive to exploit this fear. *The Report of the National Commission on Terrorism* (2000) took the view that 'if the terrorists' goal is to challenge significantly Americans' sense of safety and confidence', even a relatively small chemical or biological attack 'could be successful'. The impact that the threat of terrorist action can have on the imagination of the Western public empowers these apparently 'fearless' people. Indeed, it is the very fearlessness of the suicide bomber, who regards death as the road to a glorious martyrdom, which serves to amplify the apprehension of its targets. The suicide bomber, who apparently fears God far more than death itself, exemplifies at least some of the virtues praised in Plato's *Republic*.

A sense of historical amnesia deprives Western culture from recalling that not so long ago many of its youth stood ready to die in battle. Writing in the early stages of the First World War, the renowned German sociologist Max Weber declared that a community of solidarity created on the battlefield provided meaning and motivation comparable to the experience of religious brotherhood. He stated that a 'war does something to a warrior which, in its concrete meaning, is unique', because 'it makes him experience a consecrated meaning of death which is characteristic only of death in war'. Unlike normal death, which in a modern secular world has no special meaning, in war and '*only* in war, the individual can *believe* that he knows he is dying "for" something'.[18]

Weber's sacralization of an individual's sacrifice of life was not simply wishful propaganda. His claim regarding 'the very extraordinary quality of brotherliness of war, and of death in war', still had meaning for many soldiers – from all sides – who had volunteered to fight in this war, and was still present during the Second World War. Its gradual exhaustion only became visible during and in the aftermath of America's war in Vietnam.

FEAR OF DEATH

Throughout history it seemed to many thinkers that it is the fear of death that serves as the foundational frame for the public articulation of fear in general. Moreover, anxiety about death, which is also a very private fear, is said to lurk in the unconscious and is bound up with a basic concern with existential security. This view continues to influence contemporary reflections on this subject. Bauman claimed that the 'fear of death' is the 'most primal fear – prototype for all fears'.[19] Ernest Becker's influential 1973 book, *The Denial of Death*, argued that anxiety about death constitutes humanity's deepest fear; it is so deep-seated that it spawns many of the specific fears and individual phobias that prevail in society.[20]

The psychological and cultural significance of the fear of death was recognized by the Greek philosophers, many of whom interpreted this phenomenon as linked to apprehensions about the future. Some – for example, the Epicureans, Sceptics and Stoics – were also prepared to confront this fear, and sought to counter its effects by arguing that it was a pointless expenditure of emotion. Epicurus (341–270 BCE) advanced the thesis that once death was correctly understood there was little point in fearing it. He portrayed the fear of death as a projection of a threat into the future: it was the prospect of pain rather than of a specific hurt that underpinned this fear. He wrote that since the object of this fear 'caused no annoyance' in the present, it was therefore 'groundless', adding:

> Death, therefore, the most awful of evils, is nothing to us, seeing that, when we are, death is not come, and, when death is come, we are not. It is nothing, then, either to the living or to the dead, for with the living it is not and the dead exist no longer.[21]

Epicurus believed that the fear of death could be overcome if people understood that death does not harm the living. Nor does death hurt the dead, since they no longer exist.

Among the Ancients, it was the Roman poet Lucretius (99–c.55 BCE) who offered the most eloquent and powerful critique of the fear of death. His philosophical poem *De rerum natura – On the Nature of Things* – offers one of the earliest attempts to reflect seriously on 'a ubiquitous fear forming a basic element of the human psyche'.[22] Like Epicurus, Lucretius emphasized the irrational dimension of fearing death. His version of the argument relies on unpicking people's anxiety about ceasing to exist. He claimed that since people do not feel a sense of dread about their non-existence in the past – before they were born – it made little sense to be apprehensive about the state of non-existence in the future. This point was elaborated by the Roman philosopher Seneca (4 BCE–AD 65) in his discussion 'On Taking One's Life':

> Would you not think him an utter fool who wept because he was not alive a thousand years ago? And is he not just as much a fool who weeps because he will not be alive a thousand years from now? It is all the same; you will not be and you were not. Neither of these periods of time belongs to you.[23]

Seneca, like Lucretius, sought to counter people's fear of death by underlining the point that the dead will not be around to worry about their non-existence.

One of the limitations of the Epicurean philosophical critique of death was a narrow focus on people's anxiety about their own demise. Although at times Lucretius appears to look for the causes of fear beyond people's anxiety towards their own death, his analysis tended to avoid the question of what the possible wider concerns articulated through the fear of death might be. Contrary to the views of Lucretius and Seneca in the centuries that followed, 'non-existence' rather than physical death became increasingly perceived as the main focus of fears. 'Fear of being forgotten after death is one of man's most deep-rooted anxieties,' argues one study, titled *Death: A History of Man's Obsessions and Fears.*[24]

In his exploration of death, Lucretius identified 'a certain hidden force' that crushes human affairs. One study of Lucretius notes that this hidden force 'belongs to the uncontrollable violence of nature, storms, earthquakes, tidal waves, and other disruptive phenomena of nature', and that it 'operates in human life too' influencing 'ideas of love and death'.[25] The 'hidden force', which today is sometimes referred to as anxiety, is not of course simply a reaction to the prospect of death, and understanding its workings continued to preoccupy thinkers throughout the centuries.

Echoes of some of Lucretius's insights are to be found in the work of Sigmund Freud. Writing in 1915, six months after the outbreak of the First World War, Freud argued that the fear of death was simply a sublimated expression for some other, deeper anxiety. Freud took the view that 'we cannot' really 'imagine our own death' since 'whenever we try to do so we find that we survive as spectators'. He posited the idea that in 'the unconscious every one of us is convinced of his immortality'. Freud did not underestimate the impact of the fear of death over human life, but he argued that this sentiment was the outcome of unconscious anxieties that people find difficult to acknowledge. 'The fear of death, which controls us more frequently than we are aware, is comparatively secondary and is usually the outcome of the consciousness of guilt,' he contended.[26]

A perceptible shift from philosophy to psychiatry is evident in the contrasting interpretations of the fear of death offered by the Greeks and by Freud. Freud's account of acts of heroism in the face of death is based on his theory of the unconscious and the impulses it generates. 'The idea of death finds absolutely no acceptance in our impulses,' he wrote, before speculating that 'this is perhaps the real secret of heroism'.[27] Freud suggests that unconscious impulses and instincts are responsible for manifestations of what he described as 'impulsive heroism'. He recognized there was also a rational basis for heroism, which depended on 'the decision that one's own life cannot be worth as much as certain common ideals'.[28] But on balance he portrays heroes as individuals who act on impulse and who irrationally 'cannot believe in their own death'.[29]

Unlike Freud, Aristotle believed that heroism in the face of death had a rational and, significantly, a moral foundation. He believed that the antidote to the fear of death was the virtue of courage. As one commentary on this subject explained, for Aristotle what endows human acts with courage is a person's belief that they are acting for a noble end. Consequently such people will 'endure what is fearful for a human being even when they realize that they will not succeed'.[30] Aristotle's philosophy of fear emphasized the significance of cultivating the virtue of courage in order to mitigate the effects of the fear of death. In the course of his discussion of this subject, Aristotle asserted that from a moral point of view, the problem was not the act of fearing but that of *fearing the wrong way*. In his *Nicomachean Ethics*, he wrote of people fearing the 'wrong things, or in the wrong way, or at the wrong time', and distinguished between noble and base fears. He claimed that there is nothing wrong with fearing many of the things that threaten us; however, to realize noble objectives it is necessary to show courage in the face of fear. Aristotle stated that a courageous person does not fear death if a noble cause is at stake, particularly in battle.[31]

Sections of the *Nicomachean Ethics* can be interpreted as offering a guide as to how to fear in a virtuous manner. Like Plato before him, Aristotle sought to neutralize people's fear of death by providing a philosophical affirmation for the virtue of courage. However, in Greece and in most societies, it was the resources of religion rather than philosophy that were mobilized to confront the fear of death. The account that religion provided about life, the afterlife and the meaning of death played a central role in mitigating some of the disorienting feelings attached to the fear of death.

FEAR OF GOD

According to Peter Harrison, the 'oldest known "theory of religion" is the "fear theory"'.[32] From the Greeks onwards, studies of religion – especially those of a critical orientation – have often maintained that it emerged as a response to primitive society's demand for an institution that could manage its fear. 'The ancient saying that the first maker of the Gods was fear receives voluminous corroboration from every age of religious history,' wrote William James, the American psychologist and philosopher.[33] The proposition that divinities are a sublimated expression of a fundamental fear of the unknown is frequently allied to the thesis that the fear of God is a prerequisite for the maintenance of the moral order. It is frequently asserted that a belief in God assists human beings to manage and come to terms with their fears.

The Greek atomist philosopher Democritus (c.460 BCE–?) is often credited with the original authorship of the fear theory of religion. Democritus held the view that when 'men became frightened when the sky thundered', they imagined 'gods to be the causes of such phenomenon'.[34] He believed that it was human fear and superstition that led people to attribute responsibility and causation for uncommon and extraordinary natural phenomena to an act of God. At the end of the fourth century BCE, Theophrastus (371–287 BCE), a student of Aristotle, elaborated on the fear theory of religion through his analysis of the word *deisidaimon*. This word encompassed the meaning associated with superstition and the fear of God. Theophrastus posited the fearfulness of humans as the mental state leading to what we would now characterize as religion.[35] Lucretius famously stated that 'fear was the first thing on Earth to make gods'.[36] From this perspective, the fear of divine punishment existed in a mutually reinforcing relationship with a paralysing fear of death. These arguments about the fear theory of religion appeared to be empirically validated by the way communities responded to 'unnatural' natural occurrences. Often unease and apprehension towards the eruption of disturbing natural occurrences was heightened by expectations of divine punishment.

Take the example of the Middle Ages. Throughout this period, unusual natural events were regularly interpreted as ominous signs of divine displeasure. As one study shows, 'solar eclipses and comets were seen as catastrophes, because they were interpreted as signs of divine anger against human sins, as were earthquakes and volcanic eruptions'.[37] Such a dramatic interpretation of acts of nature continued to shape people's imagination well into modern times.

In early modern times, Shakespeare succeeded in gaining great dramatic effect through the symbolic use of strange and unnatural climatic episodes. In *Julius Caesar*, the audience discovers that a terrible storm is raging during the night before the Ides of March. A petrified Casca, with his sword drawn, recounts to Cicero all the bizarre and unusual events that he has witnessed. He claims to have seen heaven 'dropping fire', a man whose hand is ablaze but not burning, a lion on the prowl in the Capitol, and an owl hooting in the marketplace. A few scenes later in Caesar's house, Calpurnia interprets the storm as a portent of an evil omen and begs her husband Caesar not to go to the Capitol.

It was not so much the intensity of human suffering as the powerful signals sent by a major act of physical disruption that shaped the medieval perception of a catastrophe. Thunderstorms and unusual climatic occurrences were considered unnatural during the sixteenth century; it was widely believed that 'the hailstorm could be a sign from God, the work of the Devil or a result of witchcraft'.[38] The belief that supernatural forces were responsible for most forms of human tragedy was widely entrenched in the mind-set of the pre-modern and pre-scientific era.

Critics of superstitious belief also attempted to expose what they saw as the fallacy of fearing God. Epicurus did not question the existence of gods, but asserted that since gods have nothing to do with the human world, there is no reason to fear them. He took the view that gods did not interfere with the lives of human beings since they were happy living in their own world. Epicurus also put forward the proposition that it was pointless to fear the gods' punishment of people in the afterlife, since there was no life after death.[39]

The sceptical views towards divine punishment advocated by Lucretius and Epicurus were very much ahead of the times. Plato's insistence that atheists should be jailed and punished for denying the 'foundations of the law' was a far more representative view of this subject.[40] Even thinkers who became sceptical about the power of divine punishment tended to accept the view that the fear of God was essential for the perpetuation of the moral order. Philosophers like Cicero understood that the wise do not need to be superstitious and fear divine power to behave virtuously, but nevertheless believed that ordinary people needed to fear the gods.

In the Renaissance era it was recognized that 'an elite of philosophers or statesmen' had a right to 'private unbelief', but this view coincided with the consensus that people who did not fear God could not be trusted. According to a study on the 'Fear of God in Early Modern Political Theory', the sixteenth century saw the emergence of a theory 'which made fear of God and the hangman' the foundation of social order. The influence of this theory was so strong that 'thereafter for a hundred years it went virtually unchallenged'.[41] Calvin's proposition, that it was the fear of God that turned a sinner into a citizen, echoed the sentiment that prevailed among Europe's elites in the post-Reformation era.[42] That the fear of God underpins authority and sustains the moral order retains significant influence even today.

It was during the eighteenth century that the sceptical Greek fear theory of religion gained renewed intellectual credibility. In his powerful and bold essay, *New Science* (1725), the Italian political philosopher Giambattista Vico (1688–1744) put forward the argument that all human civilization has as its origins in fear. Vico argued that fear of natural elements and forces were personified in gods by early human beings. Terror and fear created gods, and the same impulse led to the development of religion, culture and civilization.[43] Vico's ideas were developed at a time that saw the appearance of the beginning of a trend towards uncoupling moral life from the fear of divine retribution. The English moral philosopher Lord Shaftesbury (1671–1713) attempted to develop a moral theory that 'in no way depended upon fear of divine punishment, a moral theory which would bind atheists as well as believers'.[44]

During the eighteenth century, it was the Scottish philosopher David Hume (1711–76) who provided the most systematic and sophisticated exploration of the relationship between religion, superstition and the fear of God. His philosophy of fear was motivated by his objective of countering superstitious beliefs and passions. He argued that the mutually reinforcing influence of superstition and fear had a destructive and distorting impact on the conduct of human affairs, writing that the human 'horror of death' was bad enough, 'but when the menaces of superstition are joined to this natural timidity' it 'deprives men of all power over their lives'. For Hume, superstitious religion was an 'inhuman tyrant'.[45]

In his essay *The Natural History of Religion* (1757), Hume built on the Greek critique of the fear of God. He observed that 'the primary religion of mankind arises chiefly from an anxious fear of future events'. Hume wrote that when such anxiety is fixed on 'invisible and unknown powers', fear can literally acquire a dynamic of its own:

> Every image of vengeance, severity, cruelty, and malice must occur, and must augment the ghastliness and horror which oppresses the amazed religionist. A panic having once seized the mind, the active fancy still farther multiplies the objects of terror; while that profound darkness, or, what is worse, that glimmering light, with which we are environed, represents the spectres of divinity under the most dreadful appearances imaginable. And no idea of perverse wickedness can be framed which those terrified devotees do not readily, without scruple, apply to their deity.[46]

Hume acknowledged that religious ideals are inspired not only by fear, but also by hope. However, when fear and superstition reinforce one another, religion becomes corrupted and disorients and confuses the believer.

In modern times, Vico's thesis has been developed and elaborated by secular and rationalist contributors on the subject. In his March 1929 lecture 'Why I am Not a Christian', the British liberal philosopher Bertrand Russell stated that fear, specifically the fear of the unknown, was the foundation of religion. He argued that 'fear is the parent of cruelty', and 'it is no wonder if cruelty and religion has gone hand-in-hand'.[47] By this point in time, the practice of cultivating a fear of God had become a frequent target of liberal, secular and leftist criticism.

Three years after Russell's lecture, the highly acclaimed scientist Albert Einstein ventured his opinion on the subject of what he described as the 'religion of fear'. Following on from Vico and others, he wrote that 'with primitive man it is above all fear that evokes religious notions – fear of hunger, wild beasts, sickness, death'. According to his theory, this fear 'though not created' was 'stabilized by the formation of a special priestly caste which sets itself up as a mediator between the people and the beings they fear'. Einstein believed that as communities became civilized, the religion of fear would give way to what he called a 'moral religion', one where it is not fear but love that defines people's relation to God.[48]

Einstein's attempt to draw a contrast between a religion of fear and one that was moral was integral to a wider project that aimed to decouple religion from its tradition of exhorting the pious to fear God. The implication of Einstein's argument – that the dogma of fearing God was not moral – was quite misplaced. The traditional religious construction of the fear of God was motivated by the impulse of moralizing fear. That is why a religion that draws on the fear of God is no less moral than one that focuses on love. In the eyes of the faithful, fear constituted a profoundly moral experience. Advocates of the fear of God perceive their project as inherently a moral one, and can appeal to the authority of tradition. In the Judeo-Christian context, fear, specifically the fear of God, is praised for helping people to discover and embrace moral virtues. At the same time, religion is avowed on the grounds that it helps people come to terms with their fearing by endowing this emotional experience with moral meaning.

According to the Judeo-Christian tradition, it is through the fear of God that the righteous can gain access to moral knowledge. That is why the fear of God is a central feature of Jewish and Christian theology. The earliest term for religion in biblical Hebrew and other Semitic languages is 'fear of God',[49] and the usage of the term 'fear of God' as a synonym for religion continued until relatively recently. Penelope Nelson, the author of an article written in 1980 on this subject, recalled how her great-great-grandfather went to the Caribbean in the late 1830s 'to spread the fear of God'. The journal of this Presbyterian missionary records that the 'negroes were to be taught from the Bible fear of God and the duty of man to God'.[50] Fear was considered essential in order to acquire the moral insights necessary for a good life.

Both the Old and the New Testaments treat the fear of God as the prerequisite for the acquisition of moral virtue. The Bible offers a veritable cultural script providing guidance on what, and what not, to fear. Time and again Moses encouraged the Jews to forsake their fear of their enemies and to fear God instead. Moses exhorted his people, 'Thou shalt fear the Lord thy God',[51] and continued: 'do not be afraid of the nations there, for the LORD your God will fight for you'.[52] Elsewhere, he advised the Jews to 'Fear not, stand firm, and see the salvation of the Lord, which he will work for you today.' 'For the Egyptians whom you see today,' he promised, 'you shall never see again.'[53]

Throughout the Old Testament, the fear of God is endowed with positive attributes and is depicted as a moral duty. The Book of Job informs us that 'the fear of the Lord' is 'wisdom'.[54] The representation of the fear of God as the source of wisdom is constantly reiterated in the book of Proverbs. To take a few examples:

The fear of the Lord is the beginning of knowledge. (1:7)

Because they hated knowledge and did not choose the fear of the Lord. (1:29)

The fear of the Lord is the beginning of wisdom. (9:10)

The fear of the Lord is instruction in wisdom. (15:33)

According to the Bible, the wisdom gained through the fear of God is moral knowledge. The emphasis that religion placed on the act of fearing was based on the conviction that it was an indispensable cultural practice for the maintenance and the reproduction of the moral order. As Robin points out, 'whether religious or secular, pre-modern thinkers argued that fear had to be deliberately cultivated and sustained by a moral understanding of who men and women are and how they should conduct themselves as ethical beings'.[55] Theologians did not perceive the cultivation of fear as a negative or destructive activity, but as integral to moral conduct. Many Christian theologians went so far as to assert that fear has its source in love. Thomas Aquinas systematically advanced this argument in *Summa Theologica*, stating that 'all fear arises from love; save no one fears save what is contrary to something he loves'.[56]

Present-day adherents of a Thomist view of fear believe that the Christian approach towards the cultivation of fear provided an indispensable prerequisite for the conduct of a good life. In an interesting essay titled 'Thomas Aquinas and the Culture of Fear', Scott Bader-Saye revisits the question of fear as a moral issue. He takes the view that 'excessive' fear fosters a climate of suspicion and mistrust and that therefore it can have negative consequences, such as undermining 'Christian virtues such as hospitality, peacemaking, and generosity'.[57] However, he claims that set in the context of a coherent moral universe, fear can become freed from its corrosive and destructive dimensions. He notes that in the past, when religion had a greater influence over Western society, 'fear was understood in the context of an ordered world and a provident God from which certain assumptions about politics, morality, and identity flowed'.[58]

According to a Thomist argument, once fear is ripped out from its religious context it acquires a disorienting and destructive dimension. Bader-Saye states that with the declining influence of religion and the guidance it communicates, fear became dispossessed of its moral attributes: 'in modernity, as we lost our sense of a common story, political fear came loose from this moral and political nexus and took the forms of generalized anxiety and naked terror'.[59] From this perspective, the disorienting influence of the culture of fear in the twenty-first century can be attributed to the separation of fear from a moral grammar of meaning.

In the modern era, religious advocates of the virtue of fearing God were overwhelmed by the tide of secularism that decried it as dangerous superstition. Critics of the project of securing the moral order through directing people to fear God sought to counter and discredit what they perceived as harmful superstition. Some went so far as to claim that science and reason could strike a blow against fear itself. Bertrand Russell told his audience that 'science can help us, to get over this craven fear in which mankind has lived for so many generations'. He held out an optimistic view of the future, one where a 'fearless outlook' would prevail. Russell's vision of the future was one where it was no longer necessary to 'invent allies in the sky' and humanity could rely on its intelligence and efforts to 'make this world a fit place to live in'.[60]

The steady decline in the cultural influence of religion in Western society during the decades that followed Russell's lecture appeared to confirm his prognosis that the fear of God would weaken its hold on the public imagination. But he was to be disappointed in his hope that a 'fearless outlook' would prevail. The weakening hold of religion and the loss of cultural valuation for the fear of God did not mean that society had become more fearless. All that happened was that the manner in which people feared altered, as did its focus and character. Deprived of religious legitimation, fear lost much of its moral bearing. The most dramatic indicator of this trend was that the fear of God was increasingly displaced by an unfocused, and therefore confusing and often meaningless, force: the fear of fear itself.

FEAR OF FEAR

Contrary to the expectations of many secular and liberal commentators, the loss of cultural valuation for the fear of God did not lead to the ascendancy of a 'fearless outlook'. Fear, which was previously mediated through a system of meaning provided by religion, lost many of its moral connotations. Consequently, a fear that became detached from the institutions that controlled and morally guided it often appeared to be both menacing and unpredictable. In this new secular cultural landscape, fear was often experienced as an entirely negative and destructive force.

In terms of historical time, the disassociation of fear from the grammar of morality occurred relatively swiftly. As late as the final decades of the nineteenth century, the sentiment of fear was often associated with an expression of 'respect' and 'reverence' or 'veneration'. From this standpoint, the act of 'fearing the Lord' still conveyed connotations that were culturally valued and affirmed. However, there were signs that even within Christianity, fear had become a subject of unease and controversy. The Danish philosopher and theologian Søren Kierkegaard struggled with this problem and seemed to believe that fear and pride stood in the way of the love of God. By the late nineteenth century, more and more Christians felt estranged from the depiction of a fearful God. A significant constituency of Christian thinkers sought to depict their religion as one of love rather than of fear.

It was not simply the fear of God that lost some of its theological appeal – the fear of Hell also began to fade as a central theme in the Christian catechesis. Until this point the promotion of the need for the righteous to fear Hell was seen as indispensable for the conduct of moral behaviour. Consigning the sinful to Hell served as a powerful threat that no pious Christian could overlook, and this awful threat haunted the imagination of a sinner. The following excerpt, from a nineteenth-century sermon delivered by Walter Elliott to American Catholics, reminded the would-be sinner: 'Ah! But when the sinner hears of a fire which is never going to be quenched, of a gnawing worm which shall never die, it strikes terror to his soul, you will see his face turn pale, you will see the tears start unbidden to his eyes.'[61] Sermons echoing a similar theme continued for many decades to come. Geoffrey Rowell pointed out in his fascinating study, *Hell and the Victorians*, that the fear of Hell played a major role in promoting moral conduct from infancy to a person's final days.[62] Yet by the end of the nineteenth century, serious questions began to be raised about the existence of Hell and the desirability of fearing it.

As a study on *Death in the Victorian Family* explained, by the end of the nineteenth century the perception of the 'bad death had changed, with the decline in both Evangelical fervour and the fear of hell'.[63] Secular and scientific-minded commentators became less and less inhibited about confining their rejection of the idea of a Hell to private conversations. In March 1878, the editors of the *Popular Science Monthly* argued in an article titled 'Concerning the Belief in Hell' that belief in Hades had become an obsolete sentiment. They denounced the idea of Hell because of its association with 'fierce intolerance' and 'cruel civil codes and vindictive punishment'. They claimed that the fear of Hell 'had a use as a means of the harsh discipline of men when they were moved only by the lowest motives', but that such a sentiment was inconsistent with the 'advance of human nature'.[64] At the time, these comments provoked a backlash. Many committed Christians found it difficult to give up their belief in a fearful God and a terrible Hell. 'We have often heard it expressed that individuals should love God without the fear of hell,' wrote the Afro-American theologian Bishop John B. Small, in a dismissive tone, in 1898, adding that, 'we have our doubts of the candour of the lovers of God who have no fear of hell'.[65] For many Christians, the dismissal of the fear of Hell constituted a serious blow against their faith.

The turn of the twentieth-century debate about the status of Hell and belief in an afterlife indicated that attitudes towards the rules of fear were in a state of flux. As the historian Joanna Bourke explained in her study *Fear: A Cultural History*, 'by the turn of the century' even 'devout believers professed competing religious views on the nature of hell'.[66] Though many educated Christians became less and less persuaded about the reality of Hell, in popular culture the fear of Satan retained much of its force. The fear of God, fear of Hell and damnation, and fear of the Apocalypse provided zealous religious leaders and scaremongers with plenty of material with which to strike terror in the hearts of common folk. James Joyce's novel *A Portrait of the Artist as a Young Man*, published in 1916, offered a vivid illustration of the anxieties that could still be provoked by the fear of Hell. At one point, the novel's main character, young Stephen Dedalus, 'listens to a priest describe what life is like for those unlucky souls who go to hell'. According to the priest: 'the blood seethes and boils in the veins, the brains are boiling in the skull, the heart and breast glowing and bursting, the bowels a red-hot mass of burning pulp, the tender eyes flaming like molten balls'. The novel's readers would have understood the emotional upheaval and profound sense of guilt felt by Stephen. Throughout the First World War, visions of the Apocalypse coexisted with eschatological fears.[67] Despite the growing influence of secular thought and scepticism towards the narrative of the Bible, the fear of Hell continued to haunt the popular imagination.

Yet Hell was fast losing plausibility in an increasingly secular world. And though such scepticism was most pronounced among the educated, it gradually gained authority over society as a whole. Church leaders, too, had come under the influence of this wave of scepticism, and some even dismissed the fear of Hell as an ancient legend.[68] Even those church leaders who remained wedded to the old doctrines were conscious of the backlash against the traditional account of religious fear. A point of transition in cultural attitudes towards fear had been reached, and those who still embraced the traditional narrative of fearing God were forced on the defensive.

Articles published by the New York-based *Methodist Review* during the years following the First World War communicated a sense of ambivalence and uncertainty towards the role of fear in religion. The commentator E. F. Little asked, 'shall we be a priest restrained by fear or a prophet led by faith', before going on to criticize those who 'fear change'.[69] A commentary on the use of fear in religion, titled 'Are there Evil Spirits?' questioned the need to fear the 'Devil and his Angels'. 'I am thoroughly in sympathy with anything that free us from an exaggerated fear of them', concluded the author of this contribution.[70] These tentative attempts to move Methodism towards a less fearful version of Christianity serve as testimony to a mood of transition towards the conceptualization of how the fear of God ought to be interpreted.

Not every contributor to the *Methodist Review* was reconciled to embracing the changing attitudes regarding preaching the fear of God. 'Shall the Severity of God Be Preached' was the title of an essay in the *Methodist Review* in January 1919 written by Andrew Gillies Rochester. It cited from an article, previously published in 1917, that outlined the issue facing Methodist preachers:

> Methodists fifty years ago persistently preached the terrors of the Judgment and an eternal hell. Probably all our preachers still retain their belief in the dreadful consequences of unrepented sin continuing beyond the grave. They would not expunge the doctrine from our standards of faith. But most of them have laid it away in the attic of their intellect, an antiquated memory of the olden times to be brought out occasionally for exhibition. Very few of our pulpits are blackened with the smoke or scented with the brimstone of a fiery hell.[71]

That the 'pulpits of the Methodist Episcopal Church are now silent on those solemn themes' was presented by Rochester as in part a reaction to past practices, when Christianity 'went mad over heaven and hell'. Yet he was unable to reconcile himself to sanitizing his faith from any mention of Hell, and could not quite grasp the cultural influences that led the pulpits to go silent on the subject.

Rochester clearly understood that the theological principles that he upheld faced a formidable challenge from psychology and from the emergence of novel cultural attitudes towards fear. His response to what he described as psychology's 'stock argument' against preaching the 'Severity of God' was one of resentment. This 'stock argument', which asserted that 'the appeal to fear is psychologically wrong and spiritually injurious', was one that his colleagues found difficult to answer. He took exception to the influence of a psychological outlook on matters that had hitherto pertained to the sphere of morality.

Nevertheless, he also sensed that it was simply not possible to return to the practices of the past. Consequently he called for a compromise; a balanced approach to preaching, which 'drives home' both 'the severity and the goodness of God, the wages of sin as well as the gift of God, the horrors of hell and the glories of heaven'.[72]

The manner in which the *Methodist Review* reflected Christianity's relationship to fear showed sensitivity and awareness of the remarkable revision of attitudes towards fear within wider society. Rochester tried to counter and neutralize the influence of these new attitudes. Others adapted to the temper of the times and embraced psychology as their new theology. In October 1919 a Protestant Pastor, Dr William Rosecrance Prince, informed his audience at the New School of Christian or Applied Psychology in Los Angeles that the 'devil was an ancient fetish of fear', and that there was 'neither hell or devil'. His denunciation of old superstition served as a prelude to an enthusiastic celebration of the promise of psychology. 'With the perfection of psychology mankind will reach the perfection predicted for the millennium,' prophesied Dr Prince.[73]

By the late 1930s, advocates of the traditional doctrine of Hell were clearly on the defensive. In 1938 Father Winfrid Herbst, a Catholic priest, outlined the problem in the following terms:

> Fear of death and purgatory and hell does not seem to disturb people overmuch, to judge from the fact that so many are not even enough afraid of these terrible things to refrain from committing grievous sin. An increase of a salutary fear of God were, indeed, much to be desired.[74]

There was no significant increase in the 'salutary fear of God' during the decades to follow. On the contrary: though it retained some influence among many evangelical churches, the significance of fear as medium for the attainment of moral knowledge became increasingly marginalized throughout wider society. Attempts made to accommodate to the new rules of fear meant that with the passing of time, mainstream Christianity became more and more prepared to replace the traditional theological conception of fear with a psychological one.

Changing attitudes towards fearing God and Hell were integral to a wider cultural shift that engulfed the Western world in the twentieth century. Secular scepticism and the growing authority of scientific thought drastically undermined the authority of the classical religious construction of fear. With the loss of its traditional moral underpinning, the meaning of fear altered its character. Until this point, the positive moral attributes of fear tended to outweigh its negative side effects. Now it stood de-moralized and exposed as an emotion that psychologists characterized as negative. In effect, the cultural script of fear was seriously revised and reframed in the new language of psychology.

The traditional idealization of fear that evolved over centuries met its demise in the interwar era. In historical terms its demise was remarkably rapid. That is why today, when ideas about fear are framed almost entirely through its destructive qualities, it is often difficult to comprehend that not so long ago this emotion was perceived as a positive moral value in itself.

The attitude expressed by John of Salisbury (c.1115–80), arguably the most sophisticated political theorist of the twelfth century, towards *fear itself* serves as a direct contrast to sentiments in the twenty-first century. For this medieval philosopher, fear itself was divinely inspired. In the course of distinguishing between a tyrant and a prince, John of Salisbury stated that 'beyond doubt the greatest part of the divine virtue is revealed to belong to the prince, in so far as at his nod men bow their heads and generally offer their necks to the axe in sacrifice, and by divine impulse everyone fears him who is fear itself'.[75] In this account, it is through 'divine command' that the Prince enjoys the gift of divine virtue and is able to personify fear itself.

Since the interwar era, fear has lost much of its divine connotation and is much more likely to be seen as a harbinger of a disease than of a virtue. This important twist in the construction of fear was most strikingly captured by the growing trend towards the diseasing of this emotion – psychologists and psychiatrists turned the fear of Hell from a virtue into a disease. 'A Case of Obsession: Fear of Hell', a title of an article published in January 1934 in *The Psychoanalytic Review*, summed up this attitude. According to the psychoanalyst René Allendry, the patient's obsession with the fear of Hell was the outcome of her dysfunctional weaning.[76] By this point, even some religious leaders adopted a therapeutic language in their deliberations on fear. In his essay 'The Defeat of Fear', the Reverend Archibald Parsons favourably cited the Chief Medical Officer of one of England's large asylums, who claimed that the 'three prime causes of mental unbalances are alcoholism, venereal disease and fear' and 'the most prolific of the three is fear'.[77]

In the cultural script that surfaced in the interwar era, fear became more or less stripped of its redeeming qualities. Accordingly, fear appeared as not merely a response to a threat – *it had become a threat itself*. When in the course of his 1933 inaugural speech as President of the United States, Franklin D. Roosevelt stated that 'the only thing we have to fear is ... fear itself', it was evident to him and his advisers that this formulation of the problem would resonate with the public imagination. Roosevelt described the fear of fear itself as a 'nameless, unreasoning, unjustified terror which paralyzes needed efforts to convert retreat into advance'. Through highlighting the destructive character of this form of fear, Roosevelt drew attention to a condition that the poet W. H. Auden would in the next decade describe as 'The Age of Anxiety'. And since the 1940s, constant references to an Age of Anxiety indicate that the 'fear of fear itself' has become a constituent part of the human predicament.

During the 1930s, constructions of the threat of 'fear itself' identified the human condition as one that was constantly unsettled by these sentiments. Commentators wrote at length about the expansive influence of anxiety – 'millions of men are obsessed with uncontrollable fear,' warned Reverend Dr Henry Tweedy of the Yale Divinity School in July 1931. Urging his audience to control fear, Tweedy concluded that 'greater faith in God' was 'the only solution' for confronting this problem.[78]

The cultural transformation of fear itself into the object of fear drew on the legitimacy of psychology and psychoanalysis. The condition of neurosis – a psychological disorder in which there is disabling or distressing anxiety – became a widely discussed topic in the 1920s and 30s. Fear was typically dismissed as an irrational reaction to life and was regularly diagnosed as a symptom of an underlying malady. One medical specialist writing an advice column in a London-based magazine posed the question, 'How many people spoil their lives by going in perpetual dread of ill-health?'[79] Pointing to the problem of a 'fear that kills', he warned his readers that 'fear is one of the deadliest of diseases'. In this medical model of fear, there was no room for even a hint that this emotion could have any positive moral qualities.

According to a study of interwar Britain, 'much of the public discussion of neurotic behaviour was subsumed under the banner of "fear"'.[80] The diagnosis of neurotic behaviour conveyed the implication that fear was characteristically a negative emotion that had disturbing consequences for the health of the individual and society alike. Neurosis was not simply an individual affliction but the condition of the era. At this time, the conditions that, in a more advanced form, would in the 1990s be characterized as the culture of fear were often conveyed through the use of the idiom of *psychology of fear*. Our perusal of English-language publications during the interwar era suggests that this phrase referred to a general mood that prevailed in society. The term 'psychology of fear' encompassed a wide range of dispositions towards fearing and also towards panicking. In some instances, behaviours that were regarded as irrational were described as the outcome of the power of the psychology of fear over the actions of the individuals concerned. For example, in 1935, a group of American workers protesting against the import of cheap lace from France were described as being 'possessed' by the 'psychology of fear'.[81] This usage of the term hinted at the irrational behaviour of people who appeared to be gripped by a force they could neither understand nor control.

The term psychology of fear was also used to describe a disturbing condition of anxiety that permeated public life. It served as a diagnosis of the social climate rather than of individual behaviour. In the 1930s there were clearly a lot of unsettling developments working towards the flourishing of the psychology of fear. The diagram below, based on a search for the phrase the 'psychology of fear' in Google Ngram Viewer, shows a dramatic spike in its usage during the 1930s by publications stored on its database:

The phrase psychology of fear was used to characterize the *zeitgeist*. It was also often deployed to account for the behaviour of people in precarious economic conditions. Alternatively, this idiom served as a way of describing a mood of unease, anxiety and, in some cases, panic. Often, references to its absence were treated as a hopeful sign regarding future prospects. An article in the *New York Times* on the rising stock market concluded that 'recovery ... [was] ... welcomed as indicating the disappearance of the "Psychology of Fear".'[82] One headline in the *Chicago Daily Tribune* wrote of 'An Optimistic City with no Fear Psychology'. An article in the *New York Times* pointing to the rise in real estate activity indicated that the 'vanishing of fear psychology is a Helpful Sign'.[83]

One commentator in *The Times* (of London) focused on government plans designed to abolish the psychology of fear in the United States.[84] The psychology of fear was also used as an idiom of condemnation. *The Times* reported in November 1934 that Labour Party politicians were worried about attempts to create a 'psychology of fear'.[85] As always, the media faced criticisms: in 1937 President Roosevelt accused American newspapers of 'fostering a psychology of fear'.[86]

The phrase 'psychology of fear' encapsulated the new feeling rules that were penetrating into the public discourse of the 1930s. It conveyed a negative psychological and medical view of fear, signalling the view that fear was a fearsome force that could not be reasoned with through logical and intellectual means. Fear was a psychological problem that required therapeutic solutions. Psychoanalysts at the time argued that the instinct of fear led to a nervous breakdown. In some cases, old themes about the dreadful power of the fear of death were recycled in the narrative of psychology. A paper given by the British psychoanalyst Mary Chadwick to the Psycho-Analytical Congress in Innsbruck in 1927 described the fear of death as akin to a fear of a giant 'over whom we have no control'. She stated that this is 'invisible, intangible, and therefore of a quality so UNKNOWN as to be terrifying in itself'.[87]

At this historical juncture, fear was often imagined as a stand-alone, autonomous force, which possessed the power to wreak havoc on society. The act of fearing fear became seen as a particularly virulent form of threat to the self. Fear was more than a negative emotion – it was also interpreted as a powerful force that exerted an irrational and disruptive influence on public life. A 1933 essay on the 'worship of fear' lashed out at the British Establishment's failure to respond effectively to Hitler, describing its response as 'just a blind cowardly fear which is not ashamed to cry that nothing is worse than death and war'.[88] Throughout the 1930s, popular publications attempted to offer advice about how to manage the fear of fear. Responding to the question of 'what can be done to fight the fear of fear?', one columnist advised;

> If we are poisoning our lives – fearing something quite unexplainable and something that may never happen – we must either conquer the negative emotions and face the future without fear, or live in perpetual danger of placing ourselves as prey to unreasoned hauntings of the unknown.[89]

Fear hovered in the background and, unlike in previous times, it ceased to have any redeeming features. The fear 'poisoning' people's lives worked as an invisible force lurking in the background.

In public life the attention of people tended to be focused on the specific high-profile fears of the interwar era such as the fear of war, fear of communism, fear of fascism, fear of unemployment and fear of economic depression. By the end of the 1930s, the public's insecurities tended to be directed at the deterioration of the international situation. But alongside all the specific concerns facing society, *fear itself* had become a problem in its own right. In all but name, the fear of God had been replaced by the fear of life.

THE DE-MORALIZATION OF FEAR

In his study *American Fear*, Peter Stearns draws attention to the radical transformation of the landscape of fear in the twentieth century. Stearns argues that at least in outline, a new fear culture began to emerge in the early twentieth century and that its 'contrast with an earlier nineteenth century take on fear is quite dramatic'.[90] To substantiate his argument, Stearns points to the new worries and concerns about fear and its emotional damage, 'which began to affect mainstream values in the 1920s'. Consequently 'a more confident approach to fear that had been forged in the nineteenth century' gave way to pessimistic accounts about the capacity of people to deal with this emotion.[91] Our study of the trends working towards the de-moralization of fear resonates with the thesis advanced by Stearns.

The world has undergone a profound transformation since the 1920s, and the manner in which fear worked at that time has undergone important modifications. However, many of the distinctive features of the twenty-first-century culture of fear can be usefully understood as the crystallized forms of the trends that gained momentum in the interwar era. The shift from the moral to a psychological interpretation of fear also altered cultural norms regarding how individuals were expected to deal with their fears. Previous rules of feeling, which provided people with religious or philosophical guidelines about how and what to fear, helped endow the experience with meaning. The new psychologically informed rules of fear that emerged in the interwar era treated this emotion as a threat to people's wellbeing. The imperative of quarantining people from this toxic emotion was soon to become a matter of public health. But as is often the case with novel attitudes and standards, it would take some time before psychology's pathologization of fear was internalized by popular culture and the language of everyday life. In their day-to-day affairs, people were still expected to manage their fears, and the display of courage in the face of fear was not yet displaced as a cultural ideal.

The growing influence of a psychologically informed ethos indicated that the values that had hitherto influenced feeling rules were giving way to ones that were explicitly medical and non-moral. The ascendancy of the authority of psychology in the interwar period was to a significant extent assisted by what was often described as a moral crisis facing Western society. Historical accounts of this era often rightly focus on the rapid escalation of political crisis, the spread of radical ideologies, the inexorable drive towards a new world war, and the disastrous consequences of the economic breakdown of global markets. People living through these momentous events were entitled to feel insecure and to fear the future. However, new attitudes towards fear were not simply a response to the frightening political and economic developments facing the world.

At the time, commentators often interpreted the powerful sensibility of fear that prevailed as a reaction to the global catastrophe inflicted on humanity during the First World War. The state of fear was portrayed as the legacy of this conflict in numerous commentaries during the 1920s and 30s. One essay titled 'Fear of Living', in *Nash's Pall Mall Magazine*, directly contrasted the mood of confidence that prevailed before the Great War with the state of fear in the 1930s. It continued:

> In the last decade, the fear which was born in the war – fear of not having a good time, of not getting the most out of life, fear of ending unnaturally and too soon and that worst of all fears, of not being able to end when everything of which the world consisted has already ended – has grown to strange and diverse maturity.[92]

In her outline of a list of existential fears, the author Rosita Forbes attributed the 'new condition of anxiety to a loss of belief in both the church and the state'. Beliefs in values, which acted as a 'form of insurance' and underwrote a sense of existential security, had lost much of their force, she stated.

During the 1930s, the crisis of belief tended to be understood as a problem that mainly afflicted the sphere of religion. But the kind of ambivalent attitude displayed towards the preaching of the fear of God by religious leaders that we noted earlier was also replicated in the domain of secular thought. Most of the central ideals of the Enlightenment – progress, universalism, the promise of science and rationality, democracy – were severely tested during this period. Cultural pessimism and anxiety about the future were widespread and many commentators were themselves overwhelmed by a 'crisis of confidence' that afflicted society. The mood of demoralization was eloquently summed up in 1922 by the French poet Paul Valéry: 'we think of what has disappeared, we are almost destroyed by what has been destroyed; we do not know what will be born, and we fear the future, not without reason. We hope vaguely, we dread precisely; our fears are infinitely more precise than our hopes.'[93] Valéry's musing on 'what has disappeared' referred to the loss of a web of meaning through which society made sense of the future.

In his study of the crisis afflicting French society, the intellectual historian Henry Stuart Hughes described the 1930s as one of 'almost unparalleled squalor'. He claimed that the 'unsavoury features of this period' can be categorized under the 'heading of moral decay'.[94] The awareness that society was experiencing a moral crisis was voiced by public figures on both sides of the Atlantic. This crisis, which was most strikingly experienced as a loss of belief in previously held values, freed fear from its moral context. To a significant degree, this moral crisis assisted the emergence of a narrative that depicted fear as an autonomous self-propelled psychological problem.

As we noted previously, psychology played an important role in the *de-moralization* of fear, diagnosing it as a medical problem and tending to label it as negative and harmful. The prominent position achieved by psychology in the public deliberation of fear was not merely the outcome of its scientific advance and achievements. The first three decades of the twentieth century saw a constant rise in the demand for answers to the kind of questions of existence that had hitherto been the provenance of religion and secular morality. For significant sections of the educated public, psychology appeared to provide answers that were modern and that therefore seemed more relevant than the outdated ones from the past. Psychology was the main beneficiary of the new demand for answers about how to react to threats and deal with fear.

Psychology not only provided intellectual and cultural resources to the de-moralization of fear; it also assisted the construction of a narrative that depicted fear as an uncontrollable, autonomous and paralysing force. Roosevelt's description of 'fear itself' self-consciously endorsed this narrative when it referred to it as 'unreasoning and unjustified terror that paralysed people'. Although rarely commented upon, Roosevelt's use of the terms *unjustified* and *unreasoning* is worthy of serious reflection.

Roosevelt's designation of fear as unjustified and unreasoning was one that was often used – especially by liberal commentators – at the time to account for what they saw as the irrational mood of the public. The word 'unreasoning' referred to emotional behaviours that were irrational or at the very least disconnected from reasoning. 'Unjustified' condemned this fear as pointless and, since it had no justification, it was akin to a mild form of a panic. Yet this unjustified expenditure of emotional energy had the terrible power to paralyse people and society. In this account what renders fear awesome is not the threat it confronts, but that it itself is a terrible threat.

What was remarkable about Roosevelt's speech is that, despite the pessimistic climate that dominated the mood of the time, he projected an optimistic vision. When he stated that the 'only thing we have to fear is ...' he was actually signalling his conviction that the target of this fear – 'nameless, unreasoning, unjustified terror' – was there to be overcome.[95] The manner in which Roosevelt projected his confident approach to fear was by focusing attention on the economic problems facing America. His account avoided the wider anxieties about existence that underpinned the mood of the times when he stated that we face 'common difficulties', which 'concern, thank God, only material things'. Roosevelt understood that it was easier to find a solution to economic problems than to people's existential insecurities.

Apprehension towards economic insecurity in the 1930s was a very real phenomenon, but there was much more to the cultural construction of 'fear itself' than merely concern about 'material things'. Not even Roosevelt's self-assured performance could counter the effects of the gradual demise of a cultural script that projected a degree of confidence about humanity's capacity to deal with its fear. 'Fear itself' may 'seem to be most absurd and irrational', noted one commentator, but 'once it is closely scrutinized by the aid of modern methods of psychological analysis, it is found to be of real and profound significance'.[96] This irrational but very real power was more and more visualized as a threat over which the mind had little control. Yet although people were advised that fear was akin to a disease that they should do their best to avoid, they were also informed that it was a natural part of their lives. More importantly, the narrative of an omnipresent 'psychology of fear' pointed to a condition that transcended the individual and afflicted society as a whole.

It would take many decades before the de-moralization of fear would develop into the phenomenon that we now know as the culture of fear. The 1920s and 30s were a period of transition in the evolution of the cultural rules of fear. Traditional ideals of valour, courage and fearlessness still enjoyed a degree of cultural valuation. Criticism of slavish attitudes towards fear, the worship of 'safety first' and the 'absence of courage' was still often heard.[97] People were still exhorted to overcome their fears. When an advice columnist insisted that an adult in charge of a young child 'should never show fear in his presence', she could be relatively confident that her words would be seen as sensible by her readers.[98] Yet something important had changed.

Back in the 1920s Bertrand Russell hoped that science could help humanity overcome the 'craven fear' with which it had lived for centuries. Looking back over the experience of the past century it is evident that the gradual demise of the fear of God has not liberated humanity from its dread of the future. What has changed is *how* we fear, and it is to this question that we now turn.

Waiting for the Time Bomb to Explode

The hope that Bertrand Russell invested in the capacity of science to conquer 'craven fear' was based on the assumption that reason and knowledge could provide humanity with the resources to both understand and manage the unknown. Russell was right to assume that science would help render more of the unknown knowable: and yet, 'craven fear' has not been conquered. What has altered is the way that twenty-first-century society perceives the unknown and deals with uncertainty. Since the way we fear is inextricably bound up with our capacity to engage with the uncertainties of life, it is necessary to turn our attention to the question of how we manage the unknown.

In principle, uncertainty can give rise not only to fear but also to hope. In the twenty-first century, the flame of hope still flickers on but it is increasingly overshadowed by a dark mood of intangible anxiety. This chapter is devoted to an exploration of how twenty-first-century society perceives and responds to uncertainty. It argues that a pessimistic *teleology of doom* pervades the public deliberations on this subject.

A TICKING TIME BOMB

Outwardly, one of the most noticeable features of the way we fear in the present day is the tendency grossly to inflate the threats we face and transform relatively normal risks into a potential catastrophe. An apparently innocent activity, such as having a barbecue, can be turned into an instrument of environmental and physical destruction. Take the following joining up of planetary risks with more mundane health threats: back in 2006, Professor Paul Hunter of the University of East Anglia discovered that, due to warmer weather conditions, people in the UK were likely to eat outside and have more barbecues. He feared that, as a consequence, they would suffer from more food bugs and salmonella infections. On top of that, higher temperatures could lead to a few cases of malaria, and heavy rains to more cases of diarrhoea-inducing cryptosporidium.[1] The use of charcoal in barbecues has also been indicted for its allegedly significant carbon footprint,[2] and it has been suggested that barbecued meat may be linked to cancer.[3]

The purpose of Hunter's speculative comments were far from clear, other than to remind the public that even biting into a barbecued chicken is not without hazard. Of course most of us will continue to enjoy these occasions, but the cumulative impact of the warnings is to diminish the pleasure we gain on a nice warm day. However, the way we perceive something as quotidian as the weather gradually alters, in response to the pressure to regard anything unusual – floods, droughts, heat waves, sleet – as 'extreme' rather than 'bad' weather.

Alarmist surveys and reports constantly intimate that a particular problem is likely to get worse and that we face a menacing future unless we immediately take decisive action. Incessant calls for precaution continually repeat the same message, which is that a particular threat is far greater than was previously supposed, and that urgent action must be taken to deal with its destructive consequences.

Prophecies of the impending apocalypse by ancient soothsayers have been displaced by a new genre of alarmist reports and studies that project yet another scenario of human extinction on the not-too-distant future.

Survey after survey claims that the situation is likely to get worse and that the future facing the generations yet unborn is likely to be far more precarious than today.[4] Predictions of an imminent ecological crisis compete with predictions of a demographic time bomb. If reports communicated through the media are to be believed, people's mental health is spiralling out of control, and children and adults are becoming more and more obese. The weather is getting steadily worse, and just when it appeared that crime was falling, it seems to be on the increase again.

A coterie of professional fear entrepreneurs are working overtime to evoke the spectre of a scary world facing young people in the years ahead. The youth are frequently forewarned that they face a future of economic insecurity and hardship. They are even cautioned that they are unlikely to live as long as their parents. According to one report, 'soaring obesity could see millennials die at a younger age than their parents'.[5] Horrific predictions of children alive today dying younger than their parents were first proposed by health professionals and then popularized by public figures such as Jamie Oliver and Michelle Obama.[6] According to the prophets of doom, not even medical science can help this unhealthy generation: as one report noted, 'doctors said the generation risked dying at a younger age than their parents, despite a host of medical breakthroughs in recent decades'.[7]

Nothing seems to get better. Even diseases for which science had found a cure in the past are said to be making a comeback. The diseases of yesteryear are now portrayed as constituting a perilous potential threat to human life in the future. Recently the public was warned that smallpox, a deadly disease that was eradicated in 1980, could return, as the thawing of ice in Siberia due to climate change could melt burial grounds, exposing corpses that died of smallpox in the past. 'Could the smallpox virus be surviving in these locations?' asks one alarmist report on the alleged reawakening of this deathly disease. Getting ready to push the panic button, the reporter coupled this hidden danger lurking in Siberia with the possibility of terrorists getting their hands on the virus. Looking to the future, he warned that, 'if smallpox were to come back, it could run rampant through the world's population that is not protected against and does not know how to deal with smallpox'.[8]

Even the plague, that scourge of the medieval era, is waiting in the wings, ready to make its comeback. A few years ago, Vic Simpson of the UK government's Veterinary Laboratories Agencies told a seminar at the British Veterinary Association's annual conference that the bacterium responsible for the Black Death, which ravaged

Europe and Asia between the fourteenth and seventeenth centuries, could find its way back to Britain. Similar fears were raised by a group of scientists from North Arizona University. They claim that a strain of bubonic plague 'as deadly as the Black Death "could return to Earth"'.[9] These days the speculative term, 'could', is inevitably used to preface the exhortation: 'Beware!'

Projections of a return of ancient diseases that have festered in the background for centuries emphasize humanity's inability to solve the problems it confronts. As Pascal Bruckner noted:

> Hardly have we dealt with one focus of pain before another springs up, making our efforts seem ridiculous. An enemy we thought we had conquered continues to hurt us; undeniable victories, the eradication of a certain number of diseases that had been relegated to the past, have been put in question by the return of old viruses or bacilli in more aggressive forms, not to mention the appearance of new, ultra-resistant bacteria against which our antibiotics are powerless.[10]

It is as if past attempts to find cures for the diseases that afflicted people have only served to inflate the perils facing humanity in the future.

The future has become a canvas on which scaremongers project their terrifying images and alarmist predictions. 'Superbugs are on track to kill 10 million people by 2050 if things don't change – fast', insists a fairly typical contribution on the soon-to-be-born superbug.[11] This rhetoric of scaremongering is both precise and visual. The superbugs are 'on track' – they are getting closer and closer to the finishing line, and unless they are stopped, 10 million will die. This alarmist prediction is reasonably restrained in comparison with the claim made in a report by DARA International that 100 million will die by 2030 'if the world fails to act on climate'[12] – and that figure is positively modest compared to the 600 million children who supposedly 'face death, diseases and malnutrition by 2040 as water resources evaporate'.[13]

In the twenty-first century, the rhetoric of fear is far more expansive regarding the perils facing society decades from now than it is towards immediate issues. Typically, a future threat is said to be already lurking in the background in the here and now. Though it is not yet visible, it will soon escalate or explode into a full-blown existential crisis. The metaphor of choice used to communicate a sense of anxiety about what lies ahead is that of the *time bomb*. This explosive image is deployed to summon up a menacing vision of fear that can effectively prey on people's disquiet about an uncertain future. Since the bomb is already said to be ticking, the metaphor connects a clear and present danger with an almost unavoidable act of destructive explosion in the indefinite future.

In the twenty-first century, time bombs come in all shapes and sizes. As I write this paragraph, today's Google Alert offers a number of warnings. 'Fast food Timebomb: Obesity fears grow as burger, fried chicken and pizza joints flood Britain's high streets', claims the headline of *The Daily Mirror*.[14] Another headline informs its readers: 'In Venezuela, Washington is ignoring a ticking time bomb' and speculates that 'if it explodes the results would be uniformly bad'.[15] One news outlet points to 'The Climate Bomb Lurking Under Arctic Permafrost',[16] while a business consultant offers a commentary on how 'businesses can defuse the workforce timebomb'.[17] 'Debt-ridden families a ticking time bomb for EVERYONE in Britain, Bank of England Warns' forms a headline in the *Daily Express*;[18] 'Men in West face fertility "time bomb"', reports the *Metro*.[19] A disturbing account of how cocaine laced with a de-worming chemical is putting users in Bristol 'at risk of their faces rotting away' remarks that people who are infected by this chemical 'may be walking around like a ticking timebomb'.[20] Other references to ticking time bombs refer to the possible closure of a mine, and a stepfather who beat a five-year-old boy to death – he, apparently, was 'to some degree a ticking timebomb'.[21]

Numerous studies have pointed to the apocalyptic tone adopted by narratives of ecological catastrophism and other end-of-the-world narratives.[22] However, what is even more remarkable than the dramatic tone adopted by prophecies of planetary destruction is that an identical language is used to frame even the most banal concerns facing society. It appears that there are an infinite variety of time bombs ticking away in every community. Mortgages, Hepatitis B, Root Canals, Transgender People in Combat Zones, the Property Market, Syrian Refugees in Lebanon, dodgy builders using foams, the cladding on Australia's buildings, and IVF treatment are just some of the time bombs ticking away according to news outlets during the last week of July 2017.

Strikingly, an individual does not have to be a suicide bomber to be portrayed as a ticking time bomb. A person's uncertain, unpredictable or uncontrolled psychological behaviour is also framed through this metaphor; indeed, anyone who has experienced a distressing experience in the past may be an unwitting bomb ticking away, ready to explode at some future date. 'Are You a Social Time Bomb?' asks the title of a blog on the website of *The Good Men Project*. The blog invites people to listen and consider if they can hear 'something ticking' in their 'ear'.[23]

The metaphor of the time bomb implicitly transforms relatively routine problems into a potential future catastrophe. The *Oxford English Dictionary* defines a time bomb 'as a person or thing regarded as likely to lead to or cause a sudden catastrophic event at some point in the future'.[24] Others define it as 'a situation that threatens to have disastrous consequences at some future time'.[25] As we shall see, the orientation of this metaphor towards the future is important since it signals the idea that it makes sense to fear, in the here and now, bombs that may explode in the decades ahead. The promiscuous application of the metaphor of a time bomb to issues that were hitherto regarded as technical or personal problems illustrates contemporary society's addiction to worst-case thinking.

Most of the time bombs that we hear about are the unintended consequence of human action or initiative. An individual described as a walking time bomb does not intend to explode. However, matters are complicated by the fact that we are also confronted by time bombs that have been intentionally designed and activated in order to threaten our future. Computer experts warn about logic bombs and time bombs that can create malfunctions and global havoc. The ease with which the time bomb metaphor has been assimilated into the language of computer security highlights the disposition of twenty-first-century society to fear the future. Time bombs that will sooner or later explode resemble ancient stories of Fate; a terrifying and unstoppable force.

THE MENACING FUTURE

Statements about a time bomb not only serve to alert society about an imminent explosion – they also offer a menacing account of time. From this standpoint, the passing of time resembles a machine, inexorably ticking away towards an explosive future. According to this scenario, the principal role assigned to people is to try to defuse the ticking time bomb. The alarmist refrain 'we face a race against time' highlights humanity's precarious status. The nail-biting movie scene of an anxious hero desperately struggling to defuse a weapon of mass destruction captures a sensibility that informs the appeals promoted by twenty-first-century fear entrepreneurs about the future.

What endows these fear appeals with significant cultural power is that they are not restricted to exotic and unlikely cases of global catastrophe. Stories of killer asteroids 'with an explosive power of 3 Billion Atomic Bombs' which 'barely misses the earth', are bad enough.[26] Such melodramatic tales of planetary destruction are often too incomprehensible to command people's attention; frequently, however, such tales of super-catastrophe are rendered more ordinary and immediate by linking them to people's immediate, personal concerns about family life. The headline of a *Forbes* commentary, 'Asteroids Are Coming: Do You Know Where Your Children Are?' serves to transform a threat to planetary survival into yet another issue for mothers and fathers to worry about.[27]

It is important to emphasize that the warning that 'we face a race against time' is not simply directed at mega-threats such as biological, genetic or climate-related time bombs. The exhortation that something needs to be done now, before it is too late, extends into most intimate domains of personal life. Authors of race-against-time scenarios often use the term 'irreversible damage' to emphasize how people's behaviour today will have destructive consequences that cannot be reversed tomorrow.

Even childrearing does not get a free pass from the race-against-time pessimists. 'Are You a Ticking Time Bomb?' is the question directed at parents by a religious commentator.[28] 'A tooth decay time bomb threatens the nation's children because *1 in 3 (33%)* Brits don't realise dental care is free for kids', claimed 'research' carried out for Europe's largest dental provider in May 2017.[29] *The Nanny Time Bomb: Navigating the Crisis in Child Care* is the title of a self-help book that self-consciously exploits parental insecurity about the future of their children. This book, which is ostensibly about helping parents make a 'well informed decision when choosing a nanny for their child', relies on provoking a sense of anxiety about the simple act of finding a babysitter. It evokes what it describes as a 'parent's most horrific, unimaginable scenario' of 'coming home to an abused, badly injured, or even deceased child'.[30] That even babysitting has been absorbed into the ticking time bomb drama indicates that this narrative is not so much a response to any specific threat but a wider statement about the future.

The sociologist Jan Macvarish has studied extensively the use of race-against-time stories by fear entrepreneurs preying on parental anxieties about their children's future. For example, she notes that parents are told that unless they learn to stimulate their baby's brain from birth onwards, a once-in-a-lifetime opportunity for helping them flourish will be lost. Parenting experts regularly claim that a child's 'first years last forever' and refer to infancy as a 'critical period', after which it may be too late to ensure that a child develops along the right lines.[31] The theme of time running out was forcefully asserted by the former British prime minister David Cameron, when he underlined the 'pivotal importance of the first few years of life in determining the adults we become'. According to Cameron's scenario, 'destinies can be altered for good or ill in this window of opportunity', after which presumably, children become victims of their fate.[32] The message that once this 'window of opportunity' is wasted a child's opportunities are undermined underlines the urgency of future-proofing the nursery.

The subjugation of the troubles of contemporary life to the tyranny of future threats is a prominent feature of the twenty-first-century culture of fear. The main message advocated by proponents of the race-against-time campaigns is that humans should behave as if the threats of the future were already present-day realities. As Svendsen points out, 'future threats become the cause of present changes' and, in effect, 'we live with a *telos* that is constantly directed towards a catastrophe'.[33] This teleology of doom dominates society's perception of the relationship between the present and the future.

Unlike a religious, philosophical or ideological project, the current teleology of doom rarely assumes an explicit and systematic form. Instead it offers an entirely negative orientation towards future uncertainty. The goal is to avoid or at least minimize the consequences of uncertainty. This defensive attitude is captured by the concept of *future-proofing*, which entered the Oxford English Dictionary in 1983. Future-proofing is a process sold by consultants to protect institutions from the shocks and stresses of future events. Though it is generally used as a response to the necessity of providing protection against rapid obsolescence, it also projects a vision of the future as disruptive, if not always destructive.[34]

It is not simply leaders of global corporations or governments who are obliged to future-proof their institutions. Future-proofing is frequently posed as a mundane activity to be embraced by responsible and sensible adults. Numerous self-help manuals advise parents on the science of future-proofing their child,[35] relying on the race-against-time scenario to legitimate their argument. Kathy Walker, the Australian author of *Future-proofing Your Child*, highlighted the 'disturbingly' high rates of suicide among young adults, before stating that she wanted to offer a model for parents to 'future-proof' their children before it is too late.[36] Advice on future-proofing relationships, marriages and friendships is also available from self-help experts.[37]

Throughout history, communities have sought to make provisions for the future. Agrarian societies understood that their survival required that they set aside seeds for the next year's sowing. Ancient urban conurbations were built with an eye to protecting their inhabitants from future conflicts. However, unlike today, the future was rarely regarded as simply an alien and unfamiliar territory. Societies feared the unknown future but they also devised rituals, myths, religions and philosophies to guide them through the uncertainties they faced.

The ancient equivalents to the twenty-first-century narratives of catastrophism attempted to balance the message of despair with that of hope. Today the word apocalypse conveys a sense of dread about the terrifying end to the human drama. In its current general usage, it means a 'disaster resulting in drastic, irreversible damage to human society or the environment, esp. on a global scale; a cataclysm'.[38] Its meaning has entirely negative connotations. However, the original biblical meaning of Apocalypse offered a positive and hopeful vision of the future. Apocalypse is the revelation of the future: a disclosure of knowledge – of a wisdom that was hitherto hidden to the human eye. From this perspective, the revelation of heavenly secrets provided enlightenment and an understanding of the human predicament.

Humanity's fear of the unknown has been a constant feature of its history. And, as with twenty-first-century scaremongering about ticking time bombs, proponents of magic and religion attempted to utilize people's fear of the future to influence their behaviour. The ancient Egyptians used people's fear of the divine 'final judgment which awaited them in a future state' to control the behaviour of the populace.[39] Nonetheless, the way in which communities responded to this fear and how they imagined the future was subject to great variations.

In one of the first explicit philosophical reflections on the nature of fear, Aristotle's *Rhetoric* directly linked the working of this emotion to the mental picture that people possessed of the future. He wrote that 'fear may be defined as a pain or disturbance due to a mental picture of some destructive or painful evil in the future'.[40] Aristotle took the view that the most effective antidote to the fear of the future was *confidence*. By confidence, Aristotle referred to the possession of a mental picture of the 'nearness of what keeps us safe' and 'the absence or remoteness of what is terrible'; this offered reassurance about an individual's capacity to deal with the future.

As Aristotle intuited, uncertainty refers to the lack of clarity and confidence about the course of events that lie ahead. Consequently, attitudes towards uncertainty are governed by the way that society regards the relationship between the present and the future. Although there are important variations in people's attitudes towards the connection between the present and the future, such individual perceptions are influenced by society's capacity to provide its members with confidence, knowledge and meaning about the challenges ahead.

Throughout history, societies have looked to different cultural resources – magic, religion, science, ideology – to provide their people with a measure of certainty about the future. Though many religious rituals and primitive magical practices strike the contemporary imagination as unhelpful superstition, they helped communities to make sense of their predicament in the future. At the very least, rituals and magic offered people rules and guidance that assisted them to get a handle on the uncertainties they faced. Belief in the impending final judgement helped connect everyday life to a future that, though unknown, certainly possessed meaning. Compared to the narrative of the ticking time bomb, the story of the impending Judgement Day bequeaths a measure of meaning about the future. When a time bomb finally explodes there is only chaos and destruction.

The cultural script that fosters the use of the metaphor of a ticking time bomb gives little guidance for people reflecting on their future predicament. Unlike past stories of a future of revelation, redemption, progress, liberation or even of more of the same, it merely hints that our lives are likely to be far worse than today. Stories of current generations having a shorter life than their Baby Boomer parents or grandparents highlight the mood of cultural pessimism that more or less gives up on the future.[41]

AN ALIEN TERRITORY

Since the beginning of modern times, cultural perceptions of uncertainty have been influenced by three important interconnected questions. These are: Will the future resemble the present? Is the future comprehensible? Can humankind influence the future? How society answers these questions determines the relationship between people's confidence about, and fear towards, the future. The following sections will argue that the answers that contemporary society provides to these questions differ in several respects from those offered in previous times.

Let us look first at the question, will the future resemble the present? The premise of the practice of future-proofing is the conviction that contemporary customs, practices, knowledge, and even the insights provided by science are likely to prove irrelevant to the needs of society tomorrow. Of course, the claim that the traditions and knowledge of the past will be quickly outdated has recurred since the emergence of modern society and the ascendance of scientific thinking. However, in recent decades the contrast between the present and the future is frequently inflated to the point that the classical tension between continuity and change has been represented as a rupture. Arguments about the absence of continuity sometimes go so far as to suggest that even as our lives unfold, tomorrow will bear little resemblance to our condition today.

Arguments for future-proofing childhood insist that young people are growing up into a world that will barely resemble life as we know it. The advert exhorting would-be customers to purchase the book, *Future Proof Your Child: Parenting the Wired Generation*, focuses on the theme of relentless change, evoking a vision of a world that has become estranged from the one we still struggle to understand:

> The future has changed. Childhood is changing. Raising children has never been more challenging – or potentially rewarding. It is increasingly obvious that the world into which our young children will enter as adults, somewhere between 2020 and 2030, will be nothing like the world their parents grew up in, or even the world

we currently inhabit. We need a better understanding of the world of the future in order to prepare our children and to 'future-proof' them.[42]

Assertions about a world that has irrevocably changed forever are not simply projected on to the canvas of the future: commentators often remind their audience that this shift has already occurred. Such sentiments were frequently voiced in the aftermath of the terrorist attacks of 9/11. The contention that after this tragic event nothing would be the same for the United States and for the rest of the world are repeatedly voiced in discussions of global affairs. The perception of hyper-change dominates conventional wisdom on the subject of the future. The title of British sociologist Anthony Giddens' book *Runaway World* captures this sensibility. The former American vice president, Al Gore, contends that we are passing through a 'new period of hyper-change', as a technologically driven revolution is 'now carrying us with a speed beyond our imagining toward ever newer technologically shaped realities'.[43] A rate of change that is said to be 'beyond our imagining' inevitably directs humanity towards a world that is unrecognizable to the contemporary eye.

The belief that the future will be an unfamiliar and alien territory has acquired the status of a cultural dogma. The future is always uncertain but when it appears totally unfamiliar, society has great difficulty in preparing itself for it. In many historical circumstances, communities at least possessed a map that roughly outlined a vision of the future; and even if the map proved to be inaccurate, it allowed people to imagine different possible outcomes. When the future ceases to resemble the present, our sense of uncertainty is no longer mediated through an explanatory framework that can help interpret it and give it meaning. In such circumstances, uncertainty may acquire unprecedented power and fuel a sense of fear.

Historically, such a sense of unmediated uncertainty tended to be directed towards the question of what happened to a person's body and soul after death. As one nineteenth-century bestselling American self-help book explained to its readers, 'That which makes the thoughts of death so terrifying to the soul, is its utter uncertainty what will become of it after death. Were this uncertainty to be removed a thousand things would reconcile us to the thoughts of dying.'[44] In the twenty-first century, people's traditional uncertainty about life after death has expanded to other spheres, fostering a disposition to equate the future with danger.

In his classic essay *On the Sublime and Beautiful*, Edmund Burke, the eighteenth-century conservative political philosopher, commented that: 'it is our nature, when we do not know what may happen to us, to fear the worst that can happen; and hence it is, that uncertainty is so terrible, that we often seek to be rid of it, at the hazard of certain mischief'.[45] Burke's comment on an uncertainty that is 'so terrible' that it leads people to fear the worst attempted to shed light on an individual's response to the unknown. It anticipated a far more comprehensive form of worst-case thinking – one that transcends the individual and permeates cultural attitudes towards the future.

In his 1998 study *A World Without Meaning*, the French political scientist Zaki Laidi highlights the loss of an explanatory framework for interpreting uncertainty in what to many appears as an unfamiliar and unrecognizable global environment. His comment that 'the need to project ourselves into the future has never been so strong, while we have never been so poorly armed on the conceptual front to conceive this future', provides the context for understanding the impoverished intellectual resources with which uncertainty is addressed in the twenty-first century.[46] The problem of an unmanaged and potentially unmanageable sense of uncertainty bears down upon public life. It has a disorienting influence on attitudes and behaviour of individuals in their everyday affairs. According to one account of the culture of fear, 'at the core of modern fear lie two essential and related causes: ontological insecurity and existential anxiety'.[47] These conditions are symptoms of the way that uncertainty towards an unrecognizable future influences human emotions.

Back in 1970, the futurist Alvin Toffler characterized Western society's cultural temperament towards the future as one of shock. His term *future shock* sought to describe a society-wide reaction, but Toffler believed that this sensibility also permeated the individual's psyche, accounting for the perception of 'too much change in too short a period of time'.[48] Toffler's concept of future shock captured the mood of an era that had become not just uncomfortable with, but increasingly alienated from, change. However, like many contemporary futurologists Toffler overlooked the fact that the perception of 'too much change' was mainly an outcome of the difficulty that society had in making sense of uncertainty. In the absence of a meaningful framework, change is likely to appear out of control, and the future will seem to be a perilous one.

A TERRITORY BEYOND COMPREHENSION

The answer to our second question – is the future comprehensible? – is also crucial for understanding the relationship between society's attitude towards uncertainty and its culture of fear. One of the most disturbing developments in recent decades is that the pessimistic disposition towards the future has run in parallel with a loss of confidence in humanity's capacity to know, understand and give meaning to its condition. Despite science's hope that humankind would be able to conquer the unknown, it appears that perceptions of uncertainty have hardened and confidence in people's capacity to manage the future has diminished. These developments continue to shape public manifestations of fearing.

The belief that humanity is involved in a race against time before a bomb explodes highlights the limitation of human science and knowledge. It often appears that the passing of time and the meaning of change continually expose the limits of the state of human knowledge and science. The constant refrain that we live in an era of unprecedented change often serves as a prelude to call into question the value and status of human knowledge. These kinds of apprehensions are even raised in relation to such basic issues as the apparent difficulty of educating children to deal with change. In the sphere of education, anxiety about the race against time is commonly vented through the mantra that the rapid pace of change has rendered many spheres of traditional knowledge redundant.

In 1972, when UNESCO issued its influential report *Learning to Be*, change was depicted as an autonomous and dramatic force that would render formal education increasingly obsolete and irrelevant. It predicted that 'progress in human knowledge and power, which has assumed such dizzying speed over the past twenty years, is only in its early stages' and that future prospects were at once 'exalting' and 'terrifying'.[49] In more recent decades, educationalists have become obsessed with the struggle to ensure that schools keep up with what they perceive as a dizzying speed of change. According to Andreas Schleicher, the coordinator of the OECD Programme for International Student Assessment (PISA), 'while the world has changed rapidly with technology, education has not kept up with the pace of change'.[50] Often the language of chaos and uncertainty is used to express anxieties about the future of education. 'The fact is that wherever we look – science, history, management, politics – systems are giving way to chaos', asserted Michael Barber, a British educationalist and former government adviser.[51]

Change has acquired a fetishized character in Western pedagogy not because the world is going through an era of unprecedented transformation, but because of society's anxiety about its capacity to educate children to deal with uncertainty. Educationalists have long been concerned with the capacity of their institutions to keep up with the demands of change; however, it is only in recent decades that these concerns have mutated into a profound sense of disorientation about the future. Mainstream pedagogy has little to say about the future other than to declare that it will be very different to the world we know today. As the innovation guru Bill Law explained, 'we may not know precisely what shape the future will take, but we do know that the futures of our current students will not much resemble those of our past ones'.[52] There is nothing new about not knowing the shape that the future will take – what is strikingly novel is the lack of confidence about our capacity to comprehend it. Society's intellectual resources must be seriously depleted if the only thing that is certain about the future is that it will not resemble the past.

For Aristotle, confidence constituted the medium through which fear could be contained. In the modern world, the main antidote to fear is knowledge and its capacity to give meaning to and manage uncertainty. Confidence in the authority of knowledge and science has, throughout history, served to diminish fatalistic attitudes towards the future. Knowledge also assists people to engage with the future because it helps convert uncertainty into probable outcomes, which can be grasped as calculable risk. Conversely, a loss of authority of knowledge excites the sensibility of uncertainty and inflates society's fear of the future. The devaluation of knowledge endows uncertainty with stability and leads to its dramatization. In turn, the dramatization of uncertainty turns it into a frightening and incomprehensible force.

What I have previously described as unmediated uncertainty is to a significant extent an outcome of a palpable mood of scepticism towards the authority of knowledge. That is why, despite the continuous advance of knowledge and science, the problem of how to deal with the unknown has acquired a force that is unprecedented in the modern era. Contrary to the widely held view that our fear of uncertainty is the product of a *failure* of knowledge, the problem is the loss of the *authority* of knowledge. In fact, knowledge and science are expanding at an accelerated rate. 'The world struggles to keep up with the pace of change in science and technology', declares a headline in the *Financial Times*.[53] What's interesting about this and other reports about the rapid pace of developments in science and technology is that it is not depicted as a testimony to the power of knowledge but as an illustration of its failure to keep up with the issues thrown up by the rapidity of scientific and technological advance.

A loss of faith in the authority of knowledge is demonstrated by the remarkable attitude of associating scientific advance with expanding the territory of the unknown. It is as if the development of knowledge is losing a frantic race against time and against a rapidly expanding foe – science and technology. As a report in the *Financial Times* laments:

> It appears that – for all the level of technology change and interest in the power of engineering to create radical shifts in how the world works – the ability of humans to make sense of it all may not be increasing at the same rate as innovation activity overall.[54]

Scepticism about the ability of humans to make sense of technological change has invariably led numerous commentators to the conclusion that knowledge may be the source of the intensification of the problem of uncertainty, rather than its solution.

As I noted in my 1997 study *Culture of Fear*, for a variety of reasons Western society has become disappointed with the promise of the Enlightenment, and its confidence in humanity's ability to know, understand and ultimately control the future has diminished.[55] The most striking manifestation of the loss of confidence in the authority of knowledge is the frequently cited argument that the advance of knowledge is itself a mixed blessing. From this perspective, the advance of knowledge serves to expand society's mood of uncertainty because it promotes innovations and technologies whose consequences cannot be known in advance.

Suspicion towards the authority of knowledge sometimes takes the full-blown form of what the French philosopher Dominique Lecourt has characterized as 'epistemophobia'.[56] Epistemophobia, which is conventionally defined as the morbid and irrational fear of knowledge or fear of wisdom, is a diagnosis that is traditionally applied to the behaviour of individuals. In recent decades, this description of individual pathology also captures the cultural mood of suspicion directed at the growth of scientific knowledge. 'Many of the uncertainties which face us today have been created by the very growth of knowledge,' wrote Giddens.[57] Echoing this view, Beck remarked that the 'sources of danger are no longer ignorance but knowledge'.[58] According to this interpretation, the application of knowledge creates both new hazards and uncertainties. So whereas in previous centuries the advance of knowledge was perceived as vital for diminishing the territory of the unknown, today it is frequently blamed for expanding it.

Suspicion towards the authority of knowledge not infrequently leads to blaming it for making the world a more uncertain and dangerous place. In his influential bestseller *Homo Deus: A Brief History of Tomorrow*, the author Yuval Noah Harari holds the advance of knowledge responsible for creating a future that is far more difficult to predict than in the past. Harari argues:

> Centuries ago human knowledge increased slowly, so politics and economics changed at a leisurely pace too. Today our knowledge is increasing at a breakneck speed, and theoretically we should understand the world better and better. But the very opposite is happening ... Consequently we are less and less able to make sense of the present or forecast the future.[59]

If indeed, as Harari suggests, the acceleration of human knowledge 'leads only to faster and greater upheavals', a more hesitant and more downbeat assessment of its potential is called for.

Society has become wary and frequently fearful when confronted with revolutionary technological innovations. Until the 1970s, the advance of knowledge and technological innovation was celebrated as the way for society to turn the unknown into the knowable. As late as the 1970s, uncertainty served as a stimulus to experimentation and the quest to master the unknown. Today, uncertainty seems to possess an ominous power and the territory of the unknown is marked off with a sign stating 'Danger: Do Not Cross' – hence the ascendancy of the influence of race-against-time theories. The scepticism about humankind's ability to anticipate outcomes is often based on the proposition that we simply don't have the time to catch up with the fast and far-reaching consequences of modern technological development. Many experts claim that since technological innovations have such rapid consequences, there is simply no time to understand their likely effects. According to their model of change, understanding always runs behind the consequences of technological change in a Faustian race against time.

The cultural script that attempts to protect society through imposing a quarantine against the toxic effects of unknown threats cannot hold back the attempt to innovate and develop science. So although its authority has been devalued, knowledge as such has not been explicitly rejected. Instead, it is frequently assigned a fundamentally defensive role. As a result, the relationship between what is known and what is unknown has altered to the point that statements acknowledging ignorance enjoy cultural affirmation and are heralded as a responsible response to uncertain threats. It often appears that the inability to comprehend the future or to understand the nature of a particular threat is represented as if this were a variant of knowledge. As a result, the boundary separating knowledge and ignorance has become inexact. In effect, it reverses the old aphorism attributed to Mark Twain: 'If you think knowledge is dangerous, try ignorance.'

Western society's cultural script of fear reflects the shifting perceptions of the relationship of the known to the unknown and of knowledge to ignorance. Fear entrepreneurs often promote human ignorance as a marker of the gravity of a threat, rather than as a problem of incomplete knowledge. The reluctance to acknowledge ignorance when confronted with a threat is then condemned as an act of irresponsibility. In numerous accounts – especially those promoted by environmental campaigners – ignorance is depicted as a permanent condition, a fact of life that requires people to behave very cautiously and fear the worst. This apotheosis of ignorance assigns the unknown a formidable autonomous power that, in effect, transcends the human imagination.

This trend is exemplified by the tendency to raise the stakes by refocusing attention from the unknown to what has been described as the 'unknown unknowns'. Public awareness of a new focus for dread – the unknown unknowns – emerged after the former American defence secretary Donald Rumsfeld used the term to describe a new species of threat; one that simply eludes humankind's capacity to grasp. At a press briefing in February 2002 he astonished his audience when he stated:

> Reports that say that something hasn't happened are always interesting to me, because as we know, there are known knowns; there are things we know we know. We also know there are known unknowns; that is to say we know there are some things we do not know. But there are also unknown unknowns – the ones we don't know we don't know.[60]

At the time many commentators responded with a mixture of amazement and cynicism to what they interpreted as Rumsfeld's convoluted attempt to avoid accounting for the absence of information or evidence regarding Iraq's alleged weapons of mass destruction programme. Others interpreted it as yet another example of dishonest double-speak. However, Rumsfeld's comments conveyed an orientation towards the problems of the future that is widely communicated through the cultural script of fear that prevails in Western societies. Since his speech, the term 'unknown unknowns' has become widely used to underline a variety of so-called existential threats.

According to one version of the call to raise awareness about unknown unknowns:

> It should be kept in mind that there also will be what have been called 'unknown unknowns'. These allude to cases where we are not even able to state the questions as we are unable to picture the possible effects. Examples of such cases cannot be supplied for the very good reason that we really do not know.[61]

The statement that we don't have the knowledge to deal with the threats that confront society serves as a warning of the perils of the future. Such as-yet incomprehensible perils pale into insignificance when society's ignorance prevents it from even knowing what it does not comprehend, and where it even lacks the knowledge to know what questions to ask. These dreadful unknown unknowns expand the terrain of fear and encourage the naturalization of worst-case thinking.

In one sense, the world has always faced unknown unknowns. However, the very invention of this term and its increasing usage by environmental campaigners, security analysts, anti-terrorism policy makers, and risk managers speaks to a model of a future where uncertainty has hardened and gained a degree of unprecedented autonomy from the human imagination. In the era of the unknown unknowns, uncertainty can no longer be interpreted as a transient state that will alter once knowledge is applied to understanding it. Nor is uncertainty a temporary prelude to the attainment of certainty. From the standpoint of worst-case thinking, the only certainty that has meaning is that the threats we face in the future are likely to be worse than we imagine – worse still, we have no idea what these threats look like.

The term 'unknown unknowns' has not acquired the status of a colloquial phrase. Nevertheless the assumptions that underpin it are continually recycled by academics, policy makers and commentators, whose rhetoric of ticking time bombs directs the public's fears towards the threats that will explode in the future. There is something quasi-mystical in the way that modern society attributes such an omnipotent power of destruction to the unknown. The very problem of not being able to see what is coming or to find a name for this unknown power is itself represented as a threat that deserves the response of fear. Bauman gave voice to this spectre of unnamed and unknown threats when he warned that 'by far the most awesome and fearsome dangers are precisely those that are *impossible* or excruciatingly *difficult* to anticipate, the unpredicted, and in all likelihood *unpredictable* ones'.[62]

Historically, the threats for which society could find no name were associated with religion, black magic and evil. 'He Who Must Not Be Named' serves as a reference to the evil Lord Voldemort in the Harry Potter series of books. A Voldemort Syndrome, of not naming or being unable to name, is symptomatic of the internalization of a rhetoric of evil by our culture of fear. Bauman pointed to the relationship between the idea of evil and a preoccupation with unnamed and unknown threats: 'we resort to the idea of "evil" when we cannot point to what rule has been broken or bypassed for the occurrence of the act for which we seek a proper name'.[63]

Incomprehension towards the unknown future has been a recurrent focus of concern in human history. However, the current preoccupation with unknown and unnamed threats is far more apprehensive and disoriented than throughout most of the post-Enlightenment eras. Accounts of this shift towards the attempt to quarantine society from the effects of uncertainty often claim that it is a sensible response to a rapidly changing world that is far more complex and dangerous than in the past. This book contends that, by contrast, the current tendency to perceive the world as a ticking time bomb has far more to do with the erosion of the authority of knowledge than with the proliferation of threats to human existence.

In historical terms, the shift in attitude towards uncertainty and the unknown from the nineteenth century to the present moment has been a spectacular one. Take the manner with which the fear of the unknown was discussed in the pages of the American review *The Public: A Journal of Democracy*, in its first issue in 1898. The author pointed to 'our victory over the *fear of the unknown* and undiscovered, over demons and witches and all the false gods which mock when our fear cometh'. This victory was described as 'the greatest triumph of all'. The article explained that unlike 'primitive man', who could not deal with the mysteries of nature and 'so he feared them', his modern equivalent has discovered laws that help him to 'cease to dread them'.[64] From this optimistic standpoint, humankind could cease to be the prisoner of the mysteries of the future and turn 'physical nature' into 'his very obedient servant'. Today such a statement would be described as outrageous, irresponsible and arrogant in its underestimation of the threat posed by the unknown. It is humankind whom our cultural script casts in the role of the 'very obedient servant' to powerful forces that it does not comprehend.

THE OBJECTIFICATION OF CHANGE

The answer to the third question posed at the start of this chapter – can humanity influence the future? – is very much bound up with the way that society perceives change and uncertainty. Today change is frequently visualized as a mechanical or objective process that works its magic behind people's backs. Observations about hyper-change are often presented as if they are incontrovertible and unalterable facts. However, statements about change are rarely based on an objective measurement of material and social reality. These statements are infused by cultural attitudes towards uncertainty and influenced by subjective beliefs about society's capacity to adapt and to manage it. The way that society interprets the relationship between the efficacy of human agency and the impact of change has great bearing on the question of whether or not humankind can influence its future. In turn, the degree to which society believes that its future is manageable dictates whether it approaches the unknown with fear or with confidence.

The rhetoric of ceaseless rapid change implicitly invites people to feel uncomfortable, if not fearful, towards it. Typically, hyper-change is portrayed in a dramatic and mechanistic manner – objectified as an omnipotent autonomous force that subjects human beings to its will. On balance, society today tends to perceive change as a damaging process that is now and again punctuated by a few positive outcomes. Popular culture, which ceaselessly feeds its audience with visions of a dystopic future, both reflects and reinforces the tendency to imagine the outcome of change as destructive. Even twenty-first-century radicalism is characteristically estranged from change. It regards innovation and new technology with suspicion and at times appears to want to quarantine the present from the ravages of change. Radicalism is often more devoted to preserving the present than advocating the transformation of the world. It is the fear of the future rather than hope for radical transformation that motivates its activity.[65]

It is useful to recall that with the ascendancy of the Enlightenment and the commanding influence of science and knowledge, belief in the creative and transformative potential of humanity played a dominant role in intellectual and cultural life. During the nineteenth and most of the twentieth centuries, these sentiments continued to enjoy considerable influence despite the anxieties and fears provoked by the catastrophes of two world wars. When US president Franklin Roosevelt stated in 1939, 'Men are not prisoners of Fate, but only prisoners of their own minds', he echoed the belief that people possessed the power to make their own way in the world. That Roosevelt could express such a positive construction of the human condition in the dark days of 1939 is testimony to an admirable quality of refusing to defer to Fate, and stands in sharp contrast to present-day attitudes on the subject.

As suggested above, the objectification of change and the tendency to regard it as an autonomous power resembles in some respects the ancient practice of evoking Fate as a terrifying and unstoppable force. Yet, though many Ancients were in awe of Fate, from time to time questions were still raised about whether or not its power foreclosed the possibility of individuals being able to influence their future. In ancient times, different gods were endowed with the ability to thwart human ambition or to bless it with good fortune. The Romans worshipped the goddess Fortuna, giving her great power over human affairs. Nevertheless, they still believed that her influence could be contained and even overcome by people of true virtue. As the saying goes: 'Fortune favours the brave.' The conviction that the power of Fortune could be limited through human effort and will is one of the most important legacies of the humanist tradition.

The belief in people's capacity to exercise their will and shape their future flourished during the Renaissance, fostering a climate that encouraged people to dream about gaining a degree of mastery over their destiny. A new refusal to defer to Fate was expressed through affirming the human potential. During the Enlightenment, this sensibility developed further, giving rise to a belief that, in certain circumstances, humanity could gain of freedom from necessity and influence its future. That was then. In the twenty-first century, the optimistic belief in humankind's ability to subdue the unknown has given way to a belief that it is powerless to deal with the perils that confront it. Today, the problems associated with the uncertainty of the future are constantly amplified and, courtesy of our own imaginations, turned into existential threats. Consequently, unexpected natural events are rarely treated as such – they are swiftly dramatized and transformed into 'threats to human survival'. At times, climate alarmists get so carried away with their rhetoric that genuine scientists have to call them out. So when Prince Charles claimed that the war in Syria was brought on by climate change, scientists declared that there was no evidence for his 'widely publicised theory'.[66]

Often the distinction between a threat to people's lives and a threat to human survival becomes eroded. Many Western governments have elevated the threat of terrorism into an existential threat and turned this menace into an issue of survival. Terrorist violence can and does inflict significant damage on its target society. But its portrayal as an existential threat erodes the distinction between a threat that causes serious damage to life, property and morale and one that endangers the survival of a society.

In contrast to the Enlightenment's conviction that knowledge could eventually solve all problems, the intellectual temper today tends to focus on the impossibility of knowing. Such attitudes even pertain to problems that are purely technical in nature, such as the so-called Millennium Bug, discussed in the introductory chapter. A problem that could be – and, in fact, was – relatively easily fixed through the application of technical knowledge was promoted as a catastrophe of biblical proportions. This pessimistic view of humankind's capacity to understand and fix problems has important implications for how society views its future. If the impact of our actions on the future is not knowable, then our anxieties about change inevitably become amplified. In a roundabout way, the devaluation of knowledge expresses a diminishing of belief in the power and influence of human subjectivity. That is why it is now commonplace to hear the Enlightenment project described as naïve, or to see scientists castigated for 'playing God'. Such criticism of human ambition inexorably leads to a reconciliation with – if not a deference to – Fate.

FROM FEAR OF THE FUTURE TO A FUTURE OF FEAR

Our discussion on the way that uncertainty is framed and perceived has important implications for understanding the way in which fear is projected towards the future. As noted previously, dread of the unknown and of the future has been a central theme in society's cultural script of fear throughout the centuries. It is evident that despite the hopes expressed by Enlightenment thinkers and optimistic commentators, humanity's fear of the unknown has not been conquered. Indeed, the sentiments expressed about the future, by the current cohort of opinion makers, scientists and politicians, often convey an alarmist frightful tone.

One of the most fascinating features of the rhetoric of fear directed at the future is the casual – indeed promiscuous – manner with which prophecies of global catastrophes are hurled at the public. Even respected scientists feel relaxed about adopting the mantle of a professional scaremonger. In his book, tellingly titled *Our Final Hour*, the astronomer Martin J. Rees informed his readers that the odds of humanity surviving to 2100 are about 'even'.[67] The chilling assertion that there is a good chance that humankind is likely to be extinct in the not-too-distant future implies that it would be foolhardy to place a wager on the survival of the human species. Historically, prophecies of human doom were promoted through a grave, momentous and sombre tone. But Rees, like many twenty-first-century fear entrepreneurs, conveys his apocalyptic vision of the future in a matter-of-fact fashion. In his *Our Final Hour*, Rees states that he bet $1,000 on the proposition that 'by the year 2020 an instance of bio-error or bio-terror will have killed a million people'.[68]

Rees is not the only prophet of doom who conveys his message with a light-hearted touch. During the flu pandemic of 2005, Dr Copperfield, a professional 'media doctor', wrote in *The Times*:

The big numbers being thrown around the press at the moment refer to the 'inevitable' worldwide outbreak of the avian influenza virus, which is limbering up to leap across the species barrier and to start picking on human beings.

Yes, folks. Forget about your evaporating pension, you're all going to die in the upcoming flu pandemic. But look on the bright side; it's 20 years overdue, so we're lucky to have survived this long.[69]

Copperfield's homespun and jokey treatment of mass death illustrates the current tendency to treat catastrophes in a casual and light-hearted manner. Even celebrities who do not possess any scientific status feel empowered to adopt the tone of an easygoing scaremonger. So in 2013, former pop star, Bob Geldof, predicted that humankind might have as little as 17 more years until a 'mass extinction event'.[70]

The proliferation of prophecies about human extinction, planetary destruction or a mass die-off is often interpreted in academic studies as the most important symptom of the power of the culture of fear over the human imagination. There is little doubt that the regular diet of doom-mongering has some effect on people's view of life in the present and in the future. But it is important not to confuse the rhetoric of fear with people's actual beliefs and response to scaremongering. From a sociological perspective, statements such as those made by Rees, Copperfield or Geldof should be interpreted as performative – as a performance of fear. Statements conveying fear, such 'I am afraid', do not simply mean that one is really scared. Such a statement often serves to draw attention to an issue. It can also signal that one is an aware and responsible person who – unlike others – takes a specific threat seriously. As the historian William Reddy notes, 'saying that one is afraid' is 'itself a performative action of individual agency'.[71]

A common example of the performance of fear is the voice-over at the end of a disturbing television programme. They come across as a public service message, offering a help-line to those who have been scared, upset or traumatized by the programme. However, the main point that this message communicates is that you should be scared by this programme.

In some circles, the utterance of fear is used as a form of affectation to signify great sensitivity to the many hidden perils facing people. To acknowledge fear is to demonstrate awareness. This self-conscious affectation does not mean that people are necessarily more scared than previously. It merely signals the idea that they *ought to be*. The performative signalling of anxiety and fear is highly valued by campaigners who believe the seriousness of their cause requires them to use drama to gain attention for their message. From this perspective, scaring the public is equated with an act of civic responsibility. For example, the American political scientist George Marcus asserts that anxiety assists individuals to be more informed citizens. 'Most Americans do not know very much about politics in general or where candidates for office stand on the sundry issues of the day', he argues – but 'anxious citizens are well informed because the emotional incentives have caused them to grasp the importance of issues in uncertain times.'[72]

It is unlikely that most fear performances are actually inspired by an unshaken conviction regarding apocalyptic prophecies of the future. Fear appeals are often used as a tactic to raise attention to an issue and to scare people into action. They are now widely recognized by publicists, campaigners, politicians and fear entrepreneurs as a legitimate instrument for influencing behaviour. According to one study, a fear appeal 'is recognized as a distinctive type of argumentation by empirical researchers, who see it as a kind of argument used to threaten a target audience with a fearful outcome (most typically that outcome is the likelihood of death) in order to get the audience to adopt a recommended response.'[73] Like Plato's *Noble Lie*, fear appeals are justified on the grounds that regardless of the facts, they reveal a higher truth. Fear promotion is advocated because 'fear could be beneficial not only for the way it encouraged people to act in safer ways: it could also promote more "civilised" behaviour. For instance, drink-driving and anti-smoking campaigns used the fear of death to discourage anti-social or self-destructive behaviour.'[74]

A similar attitude has been adopted by some campaigners committed to raising awareness about global warming. Stephen Schneider, a climatologist, justified the distortion of evidence supporting his cause in the following terms: 'Because we are not just scientists but human beings as well … we need to … capture the public imagination.' He added that, 'we have to offer up scary scenarios, make simplified dramatic statements, and make little mention of any doubts that we have'.[75] His colleague David Viner took a similar approach, noting that the film *The Day After Tomorrow* 'got a lot of the detail wrong' but the fact that it 'raises awareness about climate change must be a good thing'.[76] A typical Hollywood fantasy film about the mother of all super-storms setting off a series of catastrophic disasters is harnessed to the project of 'raising awareness'!

Whether or not fear appeals actually work is a matter of controversy. There is a continuing debate about whether frightening 'cyber-doom scenarios' educate or motivate people to take cyber-security seriously. Critics argue that 'fictional cyber-doom scenarios' have 'the potential to undermine productive debate aimed at addressing genuine cyber security challenges'.[77] Similar arguments have been advanced by critics of campaigners, who exaggerate the destructive consequences of climate change. They argue that the ceaseless prophecies of doom about the future of the planet switch people off instead of motivating them to take sensible steps to mitigate the effects of climate change. In contrast, a study of fear appeals in the sphere of public health contends that 'strong' – that is, alarmist – fear appeals are more 'persuasive than low or weak ones'.[78]

The cumulative outcome of fear appeals and the non-stop production of narratives of doom is not so much their direct impact on individual behaviour as their indirect influence on wider cultural attitudes and perceptions. The regular circulation of negative claims about the future inevitably influences people's mind-sets and expectations about their future prospects. As Chapter 4 observes, this undermines confidence in people's capacity to deal with the risks that confront them. When even individuals are described as ticking time bombs, it is evident that the association of an explosion with the vision of a future has become subconsciously internalized and normalized. In an unstated and implicit manner, a teleology of doom has imprinted itself on public deliberations.

The most significant role of the teleology encapsulated in society's cultural script about uncertainty is that it gives the phrase 'fear of the future' a distinct twenty-first-century feel. References to the fear of the future during the eighteenth and nineteenth centuries tended to focus on religious themes such as future punishment or future Hell. Decade by decade during the twentieth century, the fear of the future was redirected towards more earthly matters and significantly acquired a more personal form. Look, for example, at how fear of the future has been framed by providers of life insurance. In 1949, the American insurance industry publication *The Weekly Underwriter* offered a down-to-earth secular and exclusively personalized version of the fear of the future to its readers:

> Actually, to start with, let us consider why most men buy life insurance. They do so because of fear of the future, both for themselves and their families. Fear of disability, fear of lack of funds when needed, fear of death, fear of living too long, fear of not completing plans for education ...[79]

Since this publication perceived the fear of the future as a business opportunity, it rhetorically posed the question: 'Do you use "fear" to close your business?'

The secular version of the fear of the future presented by *The Weekly Underwriter* was focused on unanticipated personal troubles and crisis, and on individual plans not realized or disrupted. These were not fears of the unknown but of instantly recognizable risks faced by the members of society. This version of the fear of the future persists to this day but it sits alongside a narrative where future threats are also far less specific than the ones outlined by *The Weekly Underwriter*. Consequently they raise a problem that goes beyond the conventional notion of the fear of the future, one that is directed at some unknown threat. In the present age, the future itself – and not merely some unanticipated threat – is portrayed as a *source of fear*.

The idea of a fearful future is most dramatically depicted in frightening dystopias about environmental calamities. Yet the more mundane stories about a future that will be far worse than the present era have the greatest impact on society. Stories about the 'collapse of the American Dream' or the probability that the millennial generation will be far worse off than their parents or grandparents distract us from adopting a positive future-oriented approach to life. Such narratives do not so much produce fear as weaken society's confidence. The lowering of expectations for the future promotes attitudes that even interpret what ought to be seen as good news from a suspicious and negative perspective.

Take life itself. Throughout most of the world, life expectancy continues to expand. In most Western societies, the population is healthier and lives longer than in previous times. The latest generation of young people is likely to live 20 years longer than their grandparents.[80] Yet there has never been so much propaganda warning the public about yet another danger to its health. Since the turn of the century, public health campaigners and their political allies have ceaselessly warned people that their unhealthy lifestyles will increase the level of illness and early death. Such scare stories take an odious turn when they target parents with the threat that unless they adopt a healthy lifestyle, their children might die before them. As Dr Steve Field, a former chair of the Royal College of General Practitioners. asserted:

> Parents need to act as role models from early on and take control of their children's eating habits by providing sensible, appropriate portion sizes and by not feeding them rubbish ... Unless parents exert more control over their children's diets, they are risking a lifetime of health problems and even premature death – death before their parents, which is almost too sad to contemplate.[81]

Scare stories of children dying before their parents appear to have acquired a life of their own. The British Heart Foundation published what it called a 'wake-up call' to parents, which claims that the unhealthy lifestyles of their children could see them 'dying younger than their mothers and fathers because of heart disease, diabetes and other medical conditions'.[82] Prophecies of children dying earlier than their parents are sometimes coupled with the claim that they will also be far poorer than the older generations. Professor John Ashton, former president of the Faculty of Public Health, commented: 'we've got used to the idea that our children aren't going to be as well off as us, but we haven't got used to the idea that they won't be as healthy'.[83]

Did we really get 'used to the idea that our children aren't going to be as well off as us'? The answer to this question is difficult to answer with any degree of scientific precision. But the fact that this disturbing statement can be stated in such a matter-of-fact manner serves as testimony to the influence of the rhetoric of generational despair. And if, indeed, 'we got used' to this assessment of the prospects facing young people then it suggests that society has more or less given up. The call to get used to a grim and austere future is often staged in an exaggerated theatrical manner. The French essayist, Guillaume Faye, lectures his readers in the following manner:

> You need to get used to the idea that the relatively comfortable individualist consumer society, in which you are living, will probably not last for a very long time. Your middle class way of life is perhaps experiencing its last days ... The present young generations are going to experience the return of history, that is, the return of tempests.[84]

The call to 'get used to it' is not always raised in such an explicit manner as this statement, but the constant barrage of stories about a generation without a future implicitly conveys the same message. This narrative of despair reinforces society's disillusionment with the potential for positive change.

In highlighting the precarious economic position of young people, numerous surveys and reports predict that this is not merely a temporary phenomenon. Since there is no accurate way of predicting the economic position of young people in the future, forecasts of doom are based on speculation. Typically such statements are based on people's off-the-cuff answers to opinion polls. So a 2016 report finding that 56 per cent of Americans think the next generation will be worse off than them financially represents little more than a statement about people's instant view of the future.[85] Similarly, a survey of 5,000 working millennials, published by *Fortune*, found that 80 per cent indicated that their generation will be 'much worse off' in retirement than their previous generations.[86] In the current climate, such statements of opinion are fatalistically converted into hard facts about a future foreclosed to today's youth.

Encouraging people to become used to the idea of the pointlessness of hoping for too much from the future is possibly the most destructive consequence of the current narrative through which ideas about uncertainty are framed. The feeling of hope is intermeshed with those of trust and confidence. It signals expectations of achieving aims and desires. Cultural and political forces that restrain society's hope for the future provide opportunities for the feeling of fear and resentment to gain momentum.

It is worth noting that in many contexts the word 'future' is used to serve as a synonym for hope. Throughout history, the prospects for humankind were frequently portrayed as subject to the influence of the relationship between Hope and Fear. As the eighteenth-century poet Alexander Pope explained, the 'balance of happiness amongst mankind is kept even by Providence by the two passions of hope and fear'.[87] 'Hope springs eternal in the human breast', wrote Pope in a reassuring and optimistic vein. Today's teleology of doom constitutes a striking counterpoint to Pope's optimistic philosophy. Religious figures still preach the message that hope is always stronger than fear, but their words often come across as a desperate attempt to put a positive gloss on what is a pervasive mood of disorientation. The statement 'I have a future' is a roundabout way of stating that 'I have hope'. Taking away people's future strikes a blow at hope.

The relationship between fear and hope is not simply determined by individual psychological attributes. Nor are feelings of hope a direct response to the opportunities available to people in society. Hopeful attitudes towards the future are interlinked with the possession of a system of meaning with which people can tackle the unknown. It is to the relationship between fear and meaning that we now turn.

3

Moral Confusion – the Main Driver
of the Culture of Fear

One of the least understood features of the culture of fear is the significant influence of moral uncertainties on society's reaction to threats. Although the term *moral panic* is frequently used to characterize the way communities 'over-react' to threats, there is little attempt to explain what is moral about these reactions. Often the word moral is misused to highlight the irrational or superstitious feature of the reaction. The term is frequently deployed to signify that a particular reaction should not be taken seriously.[1] The association of morality with prejudice, irrationality or false consciousness leads to a failure to take seriously the moral dimension of fearing.

Experience indicates that what endows a panic with the character of the moral is its genesis in the perception that the moral order is under threat. A moral order refers to the deep structures of moral life through which people and their community make sense of their circumstances. It signifies 'the latent and typically unspoken frameworks of authority, teleology, anthropology and narrativity that tend to define meaningful order and continuity in a culture'.[2] What makes a panic moral is that it disrupts and serves to unravel the web of through which individuals and communities understand their experience.

Originally, in everyday language the term moral panic tended to be attached to anxieties that were related to uncertainties about values, specifically religious ones. The first use of the term in an English-language publication – found through searching Google Ngram – was in *The Quarterly Christian Spectator* in 1830.[3] It was used to highlight the religious confusion and disorientation of the individual. The meaning conveyed by moral panic was analogous to that of a moral paralysis. A year later *The Biblical Repertory and Theological Review* used the term in a similar manner in relation to a religious experience that paralyses 'the soul' to 'strike it through with a moral panic'.[4] In these publications, as well as others, the term was utilized to highlight the moral uncertainties regarding a person's relation to God and religion, and its attendant upheavals, that serve as a catalyst for a panic-like reaction.

In 1906, the Church of England bishop, Mandell Creighton, characterized the despair and doubt of a biblical figure as a moral panic. 'Then he realized that the prevailing scepticism was really a moral panic, and had to be regarded as such,' he stated. Elsewhere he wrote that 'there was, in fact, a moral and religious panic, which swept away many well-intentioned persons by the gathering force of the counsels of despair'. Creighton discussed in some detail the working of this panic and its disruptive impact on an individual's system of meaning, which he claims are the 'results of a sudden alarm in the outward surroundings of life'. He argued that, inwardly, such reactions are particularly destructive to those who have 'no wiser impulses to fall back upon'. In contrast 'those who have moral or intellectual impulses to fall back upon' succeed in restoring their mental equilibrium and realize that 'the danger no longer seems so imminent as it did at first'.[5] For Creighton the ability to minimize the destructive consequences of being overwhelmed by panic-like impulses was the possession of wisdom and character.

Creighton believed 'that moral panics are not rare' because 'religious difficulties have never ceased to weigh upon the hearts of men'.[6] For Creighton, panics that are moral are inextricably linked to the anxieties and fears provoked by the crisis of belief that haunted Christianity in the modern era. Others used the term in ways that focused on reactions and movements motivated by powerful moral sentiments. Evidence laid before the Royal Commission on the Liquor Traffic in Canada in 1895 by a witness observed that 'prohibition had been carried by a kind of wave of moral panic'. In response to this evidence a member of the Commission asked, 'Do you understand, then, that prohibition does represent something of moral sentiment?' The answer offered by the witness was an unequivocal 'undoubtedly'.[7] It was during this exchange on the relationship between moral sentiment and moral panic in relation to the Temperance Movement that we have probably the first attempt to grapple with a phenomenon that would be referred to in the twentieth century as a moral panic.

The attempt to capture the relationship between moral turmoil and a 'wave of moral panic' is important because it allows this experience to be understood as an expression of a threat to values and meaning rather than as a direct response to a specific perceived problem. Historical studies of the relationship between social anxiety towards threats suggests that its intensity is inversely proportional to the authority of the prevailing system of meaning: 'the system of rules, principles, and the assumptions which are taken for granted'.[8]

Throughout history, the unknown constituted a dominant theme in the fear cultures of different societies. The words usually associated with the unknown – strange, unfamiliar, secret, mysterious, hidden, concealed, dark or invisible – have always incited concern. In the previous chapter it was noted how, in the current era, uncertainty and the unknown seem to have acquired an independent existence. This version of the unknown does not readily yield its secrets to the inquiry of science; rather than waiting to be charted or discovered, it is as if it has a power of its own.

Though we live in a world of science, commentaries on this subject describe the unknown in a language that implies a quasi-mystical quality. Even secular commentators and scientists articulate the sentiment of mystification when addressing the threats of the future. Listening to the thoughts of Ulrich Beck on the catastrophic threat facing humankind, one can almost draw the conclusion that these hazards lurk in a shrouded, parallel universe:

> The world of the visible must be investigated, relativized and evaluated with respect to a second reality, only existent in thought and not concealed in the world ... Dangerous, hostile substances lie concealed behind the harmless façades ... Those who simply use things, take them as they appear, who only breathe and eat, without an inquiry into the background toxic reality, are not only naïve but they also misunderstand the hazards that threaten them, and thus expose themselves to such hazards with no protection ... Everywhere pollutants and toxins laugh and play their tricks like devils in the Middle Ages.[9]

Toxins produced by high-tech industry are represented not simply as risks: like the devils of the Middle Ages, they constitute the embodiment of evil, from which there is no escape. Pointing to the laughing devils, Beck laments that 'people are almost inescapably ... bound to them'.

Throughout history, the language of evil was usually associated with threats that elude humankind's capacity to understand them. Understanding is not simply the accomplishment of science and knowledge – it is the outcome of the capacity to give meaning to the problems and threats facing society. The previous chapter suggested that one reason why the prevailing cultural script finds it so troublesome to give meaning to the unknown is because of the scepticism and lack of confidence that surrounds the authority of knowledge. Knowledge is not only contested; its power to illuminate and solve the problems of humanity carries less conviction than throughout most of the twentieth century.

Similar problems afflict the position of moral authority. Like the status of knowledge, moral authority is also subject to contestation. It is widely acknowledged that there is a manifest absence of consensus on the norms and values that ought to govern people's conduct and attitude to the problems confronting society. A paucity of agreement on this issue has profound consequences for the way that communities interpret the threats they face and how they respond to them. One of the most important drivers of the culture of fear is a lack of agreement and clarity about how to make sense of and respond to threats. Confusions concerning what threat to worry about also amplify the problem and bestow on fear an arbitrary and increasingly divisive dynamic.

It is difficult to live in an uncertain world. Fear of the unknown has traditionally been restrained by a system of meaning that afforded people with guidance and reassurance. Through their systems of meaning, communities develop customs, practices and attitudes towards engaging with the unknown. In the current era, it sometimes appears that in the absence of a robust system of meaning that offers a perspective for guiding fear, fear itself has become a stand-alone perspective.

As we note below in our discussion of witch-hunts in the fifteenth century, at times of moral confusion communities find it difficult to deal with uncertainty. During periods of social upheaval and disruption people sometimes discover that their assumptions and conventions fail to give them direction or explain the predicament they face. In such situations, fear can break free from institutional control and guidance, and acquire an unpredictable and unrestrained dynamic. In this form, fear is neither rooted in folk culture nor guided by a generally accepted narrative of meaning. When fear assumes a morally unrestrained form, communities responding to threats often seek refuge in simplistic black-and-white answers to their predicament. Unease with uncertainty can encourage the attitude of 'Certainty At Any Cost', and intolerance towards those who question dogma is often one of the regrettable outcomes of this cause. The recent re-emergence of the fear of the heretic and of hostility to scepticism is symptomatic of the difficulty that our culture of fear has in engaging creatively with uncertainty.[10]

An absence of a consensus on moral issues has profound consequences for the way that communities interpret the threats they face and how they respond to them. *This is one of the most important drivers of the culture of fear.* Confusion as to what threat to worry about also amplifies the problem, and has led to a free-for-all between competing interests and fear entrepreneurs who hold different ideas about what threats should preoccupy society the most. Contrary to the age-old claim that fear unites people, in the current climate it has become increasingly divisive.

This chapter explores the way that today's society attempts to provide explanations of the threat it faces and the meaning of the unknown. It argues that because the prevailing script has failed to develop an adequate system of meaning for the processing of the threat of the unknown, fear has become stripped of many of the cultural resources that can restrain or guide it in an effective and rational manner. Detached from a system of meaning, fear itself has become a perspective for interpreting human experience.

FEAR AND MORALITY

Although the fear response is fundamentally a psychological one, it is both mediated and regulated through moral norms. Historically, fear constituted a fundamental element in the development of moral authority. Religion has always been interwoven with guidelines about what and what not to fear. Secular fear appeals concerning health, the environment, food or terrorism continue this tradition and are also often conveyed through a moral tone. However, in the absence of a master-narrative that endows the unknown and the threat it poses with shared meaning, people's response to threats has acquired an increasingly confusing and arbitrary character.

By historical standards, moral authority in Western society possesses a relatively weak and continually contested status. Not surprisingly, the absence of a solid consensus on moral issues deprives people of the guidelines they need to deal with threats. That is why in the current era fearing appears to be such a volatile and directionless activity. It seems as if one threat begets another, only to be contradicted by yet another newly discovered target of fear. Ominous claims that insist that the scourge of obesity is an even bigger threat than terrorism compete with scares about the threat posed by stereotypes of thin models to the body image of teenage girls. Young people are given the choice of fearing being fat or being anxious about starving themselves to look thin. The proliferation of competing advice on health, dieting, parenting, alcohol consumption and risk taking renders the fear response volatile and unstable. In many instances, fear becomes decoupled from its original concern and effortlessly attaches itself to a very different issue.

Narratives of fear appear to emerge out of nowhere and can fasten themselves on to human experiences that were considered to be the natural or routine features of childhood or of growing up. What used to be described as children playing 'doctors and nurses' is today often described as 'peer to peer sex abuse'. An activity hitherto perceived as harmless has acquired ominous and dark connotations. In Britain, children as young as four have been excluded from nurseries and primary school for their supposed sexual misbehaviour. Until recently, the fear of exams in school was considered to be a normal feature of education; in recent decades this reaction to testing has been rebranded as a psychological syndrome, and fears directed at children's mental health and wellbeing have become a topic of constant discussion in education.

This volatile fear response is often voiced through a moralizing rhetoric that elevates relatively routine issues into a problem of evil. There is an unconscious impulse at work that attempts to raise the moral stakes and treat technical problems as the fault of malevolent forces. In the UK, recent governments have been accused of creating a mental health crisis because of the system of examinations that they imposed on schools.[11] With each report on the threat of exam stress, the scale of the problem appears to be ramped up. The UK-based charity Childline reported a 200 per cent increase in counselling sessions relating to exam stress from 2012–14. In its review for 2015–16, it claimed to have found an 11 per cent increases in exam worries and 12 per cent increase in children and young people reporting problems in school.[12]

The testing of children is often denounced as a mild version of a crime against humanity. The British tabloid newspaper the *Sun* captured the panic-like spirit in which the threat of exams is publicly discussed: *'THE CRISIS IN OUR CLASSROOMS. As a mum tells how exam stress gave her 14-year old child PANIC ATTACKS, we reveal our life-changing campaign taking on the mental health epidemic in Britain's schools.'*[13] The article claims that 'we're' at a crisis point, and appears to communicate the conviction that the expectation of academic achievement was responsible for what it described as a 'mental health epidemic'.

Fears about subjecting pupils to 'impossible pressure' by schools and ambitious parents are habitually articulated in a moralistic tone. One exemplar of this trend is the histrionic language that surrounds the controversy over reading pedagogy. The debate surrounding the pros and cons of teaching children to read by using the phonics method is often conducted through a crusading spirit that resembles a contemporary version of a medieval religious war. Both sides accuse one another of using teaching methods that create grave health problems for children. Writing of 'phonics toxicity and other side effects', US neurologist Steven Strauss asserts that phonics turns off children from reading and leads them to become 'emotionally damaged' and to 'all sorts of emotional and phychological distress'.

The Durham University academic Andrew Davis, who claims that imposing synthetic phonics on children who can already read when they start school is 'almost a form of abuse', echoed a similarly moralistic approach.[14] Some proponents of phonics teaching are also happy to condemn their opponents' pedagogy as an instrument of child abuse in order to justify their claims, condemning whole-language pedagogy for 'destroying the innocent' child, or asserting that their opponents are 'killing the hopes, and the potential, and the mental health of the children who are victims of the reading disability epidemic'.[15]

The competing rhetoric of fear that surrounds the debate on teaching children how to read illustrates a problem that is far more significant than a matter of pedagogy. That both sides interpret each other's behaviour as a moral hazard to the child's wellbeing exposes the ease with which the conflicts of everyday life are communicated through the vocabulary of evil. One consequence of our unsettled fear culture is its spontaneous tendency to transform hitherto uncomplicated problems like anxiety over exams into grave threats.

At times, the deliberation over newly moralized threats reveals a tendency to blur the line that divides perception and fantasy. Take the recent discovery of the threat of so-called modern slavery. During the past decade, fear appeals about this newly discovered global peril have gained widespread prominence on both sides of the Atlantic. Campaigners insist that this worldwide threat and crime against humanity is on the rise and constitutes a moral evil comparable with slavery in the past. Politicians and even governments have jumped on the bandwagon, and are busy promoting high-sounding resolutions and new laws against this recently constructed crime.

According to the reports published by campaigners, the global scale of modern slavery simply beggars belief. Jimmy Carter, the former US president, accompanied the promotion of his book *A Call to Action: Women, Religion, Violence and Power* with the dramatic claim that not only was slavery a 'serious problem in the US', but that it was also 'more prolific now than during the eighteenth and nineteenth century'.[16] From Carter's worldview, the transatlantic slave trade, which was responsible for the brutal enslavement of 12 to 15 million Africans, is merely a less prolific version of the 'modern' variety of the twenty-first century. That Carter's fantasy history of slavery was not seriously interrogated by commentators serves as testimony to the supremacy of a *zeitgeist* that readily authorizes newly invented threats with legitimacy.

The narrative of fear surrounding many newly perceived perils relies on the language of invisibility to highlight the gravity of this threat. Paradoxically, at a time when scientific evidence serves as the sole legitimator of an argument, its absence can also offer justification for underlining the seriousness of a threat. Carter and other campaigners insist that it is not possible to know the full scale of the danger modern slavery represents. Like the hidden toxins 'playing their tricks' – discussed above – modern slavery is not visible to the eye. Typically, its hidden victims are said to be invisible and, therefore, the number of cases that have been actually detected are only the 'tip of the iceberg'.

In 2013, during the course of the Parliamentary discussion on the newly enacted Modern Slavery Bill, the then UK Home Secretary Theresa May acknowledged that she had no idea whether her claim that slavery is a rising crime was actually supported by evidence. Parliamentarians were reluctant to call her out. Many of them joined in this speculative crusade of scaremongering and threw around the figure of 10,000 victims, as a guestimate. In this melodrama, what is not seen carries greater weight than what the eye can perceive. According to the advocacy campaign aptly named *Unseen*, the fact that modern slaves are unseen only reinforces the campaigners' certainty that the prevalence of this threat is far greater than previously feared.[17] As in ancient and medieval times, the unseen has become an important site for the flourishing of a new species of malevolent threat.

According to Jeff Nesbit, a former White House communications director, 'No one knows the numbers. That's what's so scary!'[18] In fact, it is campaigners' ignorance of the facts that makes it 'so scary'. Ignorance liberates the anti-modern-slavery campaign from assuming responsibility for the burden of proof. A campaign devoted to a higher truth need not let the absence of visible or tangible facts stand in its way. Nesbit notes: 'It could be more than at any time in human history. It might be less (though that's doubtful). What is true is that there are millions who are trapped, with virtually no recourse.'[19] Almost imperceptibly, the hesitant remark 'it could be more' turns into the unassailable truth that there are 'millions who are trapped'. This assertion is based on the conviction that what matters is what you cannot see or know, rather than the visible facts. As Nesbit explains: 'We don't know the number of global victims; criminal enforcement is virtually non-existent; and hidden populations may be so vast that what we *do* know is just the tip of the iceberg.' That's another way of repeating the old religious exhortation, 'Believe!'

Modern slavery serves as an all-purpose portmanteau category into which every kind of brutal and unpleasant form of exploitation and oppressive labour-related practice can be inserted. For example, cheap labour in a developed society, especially when it involves young people, is now frequently classified as slavery. Undoubtedly many people are tricked into working in unspeakable and degrading conditions. They often feel trapped by vile and violent employers. Such exploitative practices should be condemned for taking advantage of poor and powerless people. But harsh and even brutal labour conditions do not constitute slavery. In some instances, people working in difficult conditions have protested against being labelled as slaves. In Cornwall a crowd of more than 100 workers protested at a police station after officers 'rescued' them from an 'alleged slave form'.[20]

The term slavery serves as a rhetorical device to support a claim that 'something must be done' to ameliorate a situation. Arguing in this vein, a lawyer accused British immigration detention centres of slavery for paying those detained one pound an hour instead of the minimum wage. Toufique Hossain stated that 'if this isn't slavery, I don't know what is'.[21] Someone should acquaint him with what slavery looked like in the seventeenth, eighteenth and nineteenth centuries.

The campaign against modern slavery constitutes an attempt to appropriate a symbol of evil with which to excite the public's fear. Because of its highly charged association with human evil, the term 'slavery' has been hijacked to draw attention to a cause that has little to do with it. Without a moral grammar to express ideas about right and wrong, ethical guidance often has a forced and artificial character. In recent years, more and more interpersonal problems and issues have been discussed using highly sensationalist analogies with slavery.

The former American vice presidential candidate Sarah Palin has argued that America borrowing money from China is like slavery, because 'we are going to be beholden to a foreign master'. The former Arkansas governor Mike Huckabee has adopted a similar rhetoric and sought to fire up supporters of an anti-abortion bill in Texas by claiming that abortion is like slavery. Scotland's former most senior Catholic, Cardinal Keith O'Brien, has condemned gay marriage as an 'aberration' that is akin to slavery and abortion.[22] In the past, numerous American Republicans have claimed that their fight against

Obamacare was a twenty-first-century version of the nineteenth-century struggle against slavery. Similar claims are sometimes made by campaigners against climate change: they insist that anyone who opposes them resembles the 'slave-owners in the nineteenth century who opposed the abolition of slavery'.[23] The inappropriate use of the term slavery is particularly rife in discussions about the plight of migrant workers, particularly women who have been brought into Western nations by organized gangs.

The opportunistic rediscovery of slavery as a contemporary problem is integral to the quest for developing a language of good and evil that can endow threats with meaning. Like the Holocaust, slavery has been plucked out of its tragic historical context and transformed into a generic metaphor of evil. The very few examples of unambiguous evil – paedophilia, Holocaust, pollution – are constantly seized upon to reinforce the message that what is at issue is not just a physical, but also a moral, threat. As in the past, the project of securing the moral order has had to draw on the unseen and invisible territory of the unknown to evoke an evil demonic force. This land of the unknown, which was formerly inhabited by Satan and his helpers, continues to offer a fertile terrain for the flourishing of fear.

Commentaries on the culture of fear tend to overlook and underestimate one of the most significant elements of the experience of fearing – its moral dimension. Yet, as the experience of history reveals, responses to perceived threats are underwritten by beliefs regarding values, and uncertainties about the boundary that separates the moral from the immoral. Policing this border is a task that has always relied on the use of fear. But unlike in the past, when communities possessed a shared meaning about what constituted moral transgression, in the twenty-first-century fear itself is tasked with constructing a contemporary version of moral hazards.

FEAR AND MORAL REGULATION

Fear is both mediated and regulated through moral norms. Historically, fear constituted a fundamental element in the development of moral authority. Religion has always been interwoven with guidelines about what and what not to fear. Today, secular fear appeals about health, the environment, food, or 'modern slavery' continue this tradition and are also conveyed through a moral tone.

The present-day conflict of values – best expressed through the idiom of the Culture Wars – is but the latest example of conflicts over moral authority that periodically recur in history. There are numerous historical moments when the prevailing moral norms become exhausted and fear loses its power to guide people's behaviour. The philosopher, Thomas Hobbes interpreted the English Civil War in the seventeenth century as the outcome of the weakening of his culture of fear to maintain the social order, blaming religious preachers and intellectuals for promoting dissent and moral conflict, and thereby undermining people's fear of disorder.

In his discussion of the plague that ravaged Athens during the second year of the Peloponnesian War, Thucydides offered one of the earliest accounts of what happens when fear becomes uncoupled from a grammar of morality. Thucydides noted that as fear spread, 'anxious citizens disregarded civic authority and violated laws and customs' that were previously dutifully observed.[24] What really worried Thucydides was not that people became too fearful but that they ceased to fear the authority of their old traditions. When many citizens abdicated their traditional responsibilities, Athenian society unravelled. Thucydides wrote that many Athenians no longer feared God since they felt that because they were living under a death sentence, they had little to lose. He observed: 'fear of gods or law of man there was none to restrain them.'[25]

In years to come, this account of the decline of the custom of fearing gods in Athens served as a cautionary tale of what occurs when this emotion ceases to be guided by moral norms and traditions. For Thucydides, the problem was not fear as such but a fear that was not contained by respect of customs, laws and traditions. During the Athenian plague, people simply stopped fearing gods, and their behaviour contributed to the diminishing of the authority of moral norms.

During modern times, the relationship between fear and moral norms has become rationalized. Fearing is acceptable so long as it is based on rational grounds and the assessment of the threat is founded on scientific evidence. The old superstitious fears of the past are believed to have no place in the modern world of reason and science, therefore controversies about which threats are worthy of fear are couched in language that gives pride of place to reason, science and empirical evidence. That's why, for example, campaigners against 'modern slavery' are so devoted to discovering the evidence for their beliefs. A United Nations Report acknowledges the problem of evidence thus:

> At present, there is no sound estimate of the number of victims of trafficking in persons worldwide. Due to methodological difficulties and the challenges associated with estimating sizes of hidden populations such as trafficking victims, this is a task that has so far not been satisfactorily accomplished.[26]

Of course, the absence of evidence does not inhibit advocates from asserting their beliefs. And in many cases the absence of evidence is reinterpreted as proof that the threat is actually far greater than previously believed. This point was reiterated time and again by some of the supporters of the invasion of Iraq, who asserted that the very fact that UN inspectors could not find Saddam Hussein's weapons of mass destruction implied that he was a far greater threat than they had previously imagined. The failure to detect these weapons did not deter the former US defence secretary Donald Rumsfeld from advocating the invasion: his response was to state that 'the absence of evidence is not evidence of absence'.

Cavalier attitudes towards the status of evidence show that arguments about threats are often founded on a prior conviction, rather than discoveries made by science. That is why it is so difficult to distinguish the scientific from the moral in the language of fear. Nonetheless, in a modern society people are upbraided for the irrational prejudices that lead them to fear what is often described as the 'wrong things'.

Historically, the relationship between rational and irrational fear has been a perpetual focus of controversy. It was the topic of a fascinating lecture delivered by the social reformer and historian Reverend Charles Kingsley at the Royal Institution in London on 24 April 1866, titled 'Superstition'. Kingsley defined superstition as the fear of the unknown, which is not guided by reason. He explained that he had no problem with fear as 'long as it is controlled by reason', and contrasted such fear, which he described as 'wholesome', with what he labelled 'blind fear'. Kingsley claimed that blind fear feared the unknown, 'simply because it is unknown',[27] and was scathing about the destructive consequences, proclaiming that blind fear led people to 'be afraid of the wrong object'. 'When he dreads beyond all reason, he will behave beyond all reason,' he stated, concluding that, 'left unguided', blind fear will lead 'him into terrible follies'.

Kingsley, who was a friend and regular correspondent of Charles Darwin, was uncompromising in his denunciation of superstition. He 'hoped, that science and superstition will to the world's end remain irreconcilable and internecine foes'. Yet despite his fervent condemnation of superstition, he intuited that irrational fears could not always be kept separate from rational ones. In his review of humankind's irrational response to the unknown, Kingsley pointed to the tendency for societies to infuse their superstitions with coherence and explanatory power. He believed that people *rationalize* their superstition, and 'erect' it 'into a science'. In this manner, man creates 'a whole mythology out of his blind fear of the unknown'. Kingsley argued that the infamous book *Malleus Maleficarum*, along with the rest of the witch-hunting literature produced between the fifteenth and seventeenth century, was the outcome of the attempt to transform superstition into a science.

Kingsley believed that when superstition is framed through a science, fearing gains coherence and force and is, therefore, likely to have particularly destructive consequences. He perceived the terrible cruelty of the campaign of fear directed against witches in early modern Europe as an illustration of this trend. At first sight it is far from evident why Kingsley chose *Malleus Maleficarum* as an illustration of the project of transforming superstition into a science. *Malleus Maleficarum* (The Hammer of Witches) was published in 1486 in Germany, and was one of the first examples of a printed publication that was devoted to promoting the fear of witchcraft. On re-reading this text from the standpoint of today, it is evident that the principal concern of the authors was not so much the threat of witches, but the apprehension that the public did not fear them enough. In targeting its energy at the absence of fear, *Malleus Maleficarum* resembles the approach adopted by fear appeals in the twentieth and twenty-first centuries.

The aim of *Malleus Maleficarum* was to challenge directly those who were sceptical of the existence of witchcraft, through a carefully organized presentation of the evidence. The book, authored by Heinrich Kramer and Jacob Sprenger, attempted to provide a comprehensive manual for witch-hunters. What was significant was that it offered a relatively sophisticated and theologically informed framework through which traditional popular prejudices about witches could be reframed through an intellectually coherent doctrine. Moreover, the way in which witches were represented lent these demons an intensely sinister dimension. Witches were no longer portrayed as individuals practising their sorcery and magic; they were heretics who were actively assisting the work of Satan.

As was the case with most demonological texts, *Malleus Maleficarum* communicated a zealous sense of intolerance towards anyone who questioned the existence of dark demonic forces. When this manual was published, it declared on its title page the epigraph *Haersis est maxima opera maleficarum non credere* – 'not to believe in witchcraft is the greatest of heresies'. This point was echoed by Jean Bodin, the famous sixteenth-century French political theorist and jurist whose text *On the Demonic Madness of Witches*, published in 1580, played a crucial role in the promotion of the witch scare. Bodin asserted that those who denied the existence of witches were themselves witches. Denial of and scepticism concerning witches were portrayed as the point of departure for embracing atheism and ceasing to fear God.

Although Kingsley did not develop his observations about the attempt to transform superstition into a science, the case study of the campaign of fear directed against witches illustrates the ease with which, at times, the irrational can assume the mask of the rational. In such circumstances, the distinction between superstition and science is far from clear. The attempt to use the status of science to legitimate demonology offers an early example of how non-moral resources could be deployed to assist the project of moral regulation.

In the early modern era, science and belief in the threat of witchcraft were not seen as polar opposites. Bodin was one of the most important European intellectuals of the sixteenth century, and seen at the time as the leading French legal humanist of his era. He is still regarded as 'one of the originators of modern approaches' to the field of political and economic theory.[28] That Bodin played such a ferocious role in the bloody campaign against witches appears at first sight to be puzzling. However, as one study explains, 'the authors of demonological tracts were not simply zealous propagators of old traditions or cynical oppressors of free thought and popular peasant culture' – they 'developed the science of demons as sincere embattled defenders of faith'.[29]

The term 'science of demons' may strike the twenty-first-century reader as odd. The belief in and fear of demons is considered to be inconsistent with the scientific mind. Such ideas, however, were not always thought to be contradictory. Many early modern adherents of scientific thinking believed in the existence of witches. Joseph Glanvill's 1666 booklet, *A Philosophical Endeavour towards the Defence of the being of Witches and Apparitions*, announced in its title page that it was written by a 'Member of the Royal Society' – a leading institution promoting science and natural philosophy. Glanvill was an enthusiastic defender of the 'new science', regarded himself as a rationalist, and vigorously defended the Royal Society in his writings. Nevertheless this upholder of rationalistic principles also felt compelled to write a robust defence of a medieval superstition.[30]

Glanvill was by no means the only well-known advocate of science to believe that it was necessary to develop arguments for the need to fear witches in order to uphold the moral authority of belief in God and religion. Many of his colleagues – such as Richard Baxter, Meric Casaubon and George Sinclair – were committed to the pursuit of the research project of finding evidence to counter scepticism in the belief in witchcraft. From their viewpoint, the resources of science had to be deployed to combat the threat posed by atheist sceptics. Though most leading scientists did not get involved in the science of demonology, they shared many of Glanvill's sentiments. Sir Francis Bacon, Sir Thomas Browne, Henry More and Robert Boyle appeared to accept the existence of witchcraft. According to one study, the 'only English thinker of first-rate importance during the seventeenth century who unmistakably and emphatically opposed the belief in witches was Thomas Hobbes'.[31]

The use of science to advocate the necessity for fearing witchcraft shows how concerns with the moral order and moral authority intertwine with cultural attitudes towards fearing. Demonologists were not simply worried about the power of Satan – they were also apprehensive about a public that at times seemed less than enthusiastic about fearing the right things. It is likely that their fear of the rise of scepticism was as much of a motivating force for developing the science of demonology as their fear of witchcraft. Heresy-hunting was not simply about defending the moral order. It also assisted the project of imposing a degree of certainty on an otherwise uncertain world.

The work of early modern demonologists offers a textbook example of the way in which, at a time of moral uncertainty, hostile narratives of meaning fuel the flame of fear. With the rise of the Reformation, the sixteenth century saw the disintegration of Christian unity in Europe. Competing interpretations of the truth led to the outbreak of violent conflict. Violence, underwritten by struggles over the constitution of moral authority, ensured that a pervasive sense of fear and disorder dominated sixteenth-century European society. Paradoxically, the era that saw the steady advance of science and reasoning was also a time when Europe was plagued by an outbreak of panic about heresy and witchcraft. The fears surrounding witchcraft exploded into mass hysteria around 1550, and witch-hunting continued well into the seventeenth century.

FEAR AND THE IMPERATIVE OF MORALIZATION

The eruption of religious war between Catholics and Protestants, and the conflict between traditional moral authority and science during the sixteenth century, were paradigmatic instances of conflicts caused by humankind's search for meaning. The problem of meaning tends to acquire a feverish intensity at times when moral authority is contested and there is little agreement on what to fear.

Meaning directly touches on the purpose of life and provides the cultural resources used by humankind to deal with the unknown. Human beings have always been meaning producers and have attributed meaning to such natural phenomena as plagues, comets, hail storms, earthquakes and floods. Twenty-first-century society continues this practice, and unusual weather and natural conditions are often carefully examined for signs that it is caused by human-induced climate change.

In medieval times, unusual climatic episodes were seen as the handiwork of wicked demonic forces. Witchcraft was used to account for virtually every misfortune and distressing event. One compelling interpretation of the rise of witch-hunting highlights the significance of climatic change brought by the so-called Little Ice Age in the sixteenth century: from 1380 onwards, magic and weather-making 'became increasingly prominent in inquisitorial trials'.[32] According to this interpretation, the resurgence of witch-hunting in the late sixteenth century was 'accompanied by a debate on weather-making, because this was the most important charge against suspected witches'.[33] It was widely believed that witches possessing demonic powers could 'interfere with elements and climate to achieve especially hurtful and unseasonable reversals'.[34]

Throughout history, people have sought to blame unusual climatic conditions on demonic forces. They have 'always been capable of constructing narratives of fear around their direct or vicarious experience of "strange", unknown or portended climates', argues one review of this subject.[35] The association of witchcraft with weather-making turned such fears into a frenzied and violent reaction. Scaremongering about witchcraft promoted the idea that its demonic powers could literally dominate nature. Father Friedrich Spee, a Jesuit critic of witch-hunting, noted sarcastically that 'God and nature no longer do anything; witches, everything'.[36] But such beliefs were no joke. A late winter in the district of Treves in the fifteenth century led to over a hundred people being burned at the stake.

Secular thinkers have often argued that fear ought not to constitute the foundation for morality. As early as the seventeenth century, John Locke wrote that 'we should not obey a king out of fear' but for 'conscience's sake'.[37] Similar arguments were proposed by humanist and liberal commentators during the past two centuries. In an idealistic vein, Albert Einstein stated:

> If people are good only because they fear punishment, and hope for reward, then we are a sorry lot indeed. The further the spiritual evolution of mankind advances, the more certain it seems to me that the path to genuine religiosity does not lie through the fear of life and the fear of death, and blind faith, but through striving after rational knowledge.[38]

Einstein, like many other scientists and philosophers, hoped that fear could be detached from the grammar of morality. Instead of relying on fear to motivate people's behaviour, it was hoped that an ethics based on rationality, education or sympathy could serve as the foundation for morality.

At least formally or rhetorically, the rejection of fear as a tool of moral or political regulation resonates with the outlook of contemporary society. Today, the word 'witch-hunt' carries entirely negative connotations. Even many religious fundamentalists regard fear as an inappropriate instrument for moral regulation. Yet paradoxically, despite the tendency to depict fear as a 'negative emotion', it has acquired an unprecedented influence over public discussion and debate. In part, the reason why fear narratives are so prevalent is because society lacks a consensus or a web of meaning through which people can engage with the threats of uncertainty. Fear has become stripped of many of the shared moral and cultural resources that restrain it, guide it and above all, make it comprehensible.

Outwardly, the promotion of twenty-first-century fear avoids a moral tone. In line with Kingsley's injunction, the evidence of reason and science provides the motivation for fearing threats. Fear directed at all the high-profile existential threats of our time claim the authority of science and justify their warnings by underlining the force of their (scientific) evidence. Warnings about obesity, flu epidemics, SARS and superbugs all draw on the authority of science to legitimate their case. Some of society's greatest anxieties, such as global warming, are directed at threats that we do not yet see but whose consequences we only understand through the research of scientists. Time and again health warnings and scare stories begin with the phrase 'Research shows ...' The term 'Research shows' has the character of a ritualistic incantation. It is the modern equivalent of the mandate offered by the Holy Scripture.

Every day, the public hears stories about how research has discovered that this or that food may cause cancer, that cancer will increase because of the rise of obesity, that obesity will rise because people are eating dangerous food, or that in any case food is becoming more dangerous because of a growing use of carcinogenic additives and other polluting substances. Often 'new research' need not be more than a perfunctory marketing survey to provide copy for a scare. A marketing survey carried out by a pharmacy chain showing that 17 per cent of 11- to 14-year-olds have chocolate before school every day was linked to the warning that obese children in the future could die before their parents. 'We could be looking at a generation with shorter life expectancies than their parents, which is an alarming prospect,' stated Colin Ware, chair of the National Obesity Forum.[39]

Though fear appeals draw on the authority of science they are not simply dispassionate statements. Paradoxically, the contestation of moral authority, and the weakening of the moral consensus about what to fear, intensify the tendency to moralize threat. The imperative of moralization plays an important role in the culture of fear. Moralization seeks to interpret problems and threats symbolically, giving a moral quality to problems that may otherwise seem to be relatively trivial technical matters. Consequently a health issue such as obesity is seamlessly transformed into a moral failing. Some public health professional have no inhibitions about this, since allegedly 'the social stigma attached to obesity is one of the few forces slowing the epidemic'.[40] Their message is: change the way you live, get on your bike or walk, eat less, cut out meat and you will save yourself and the planet. One campaigning researcher claims that 'given the crushing burden of obesity on individuals and society, all potential sources of motivation need to be stressed'.[41] As ever, fear is harnessed to the project of motivating people to change their diet.

In the absence of a compelling moral code that can guide people's lives, the temptation to moralize fear appeals has proved irresistible. We live in an age where the policing of people's lifestyles works as the functional equivalent of moral regulation. Uncertainty encourages a climate where people's behaviour is governed by health warnings, danger signs and rituals of risk management. Instead of denouncing moral transgressions, fear appeals are more likely to castigate 'risky behaviour', 'unhealthy choices' or 'green sins'.

The line that separates the rational and scientific from irrational moral regulation can be easily breached. The public health campaigns directed at the threat posed by the sun offers an illustration of the trend to moralize the 'wrong' lifestyle choices. Often, value judgements that used to be conveyed in a self-conscious moral tone are expressed in the apparently neutral language of health. The statement that smoking is bad for your health, for example, frequently serves as a prelude for condemning a smoker as a bad person. Similarly, expositions of the health risks of junk food are often connected to the denunciation of 'bad parents' who feed their children on such an evil diet. Statements on the health problems associated with obesity sometimes implicitly question the moral status of the unhealthy people responsible for their weight problem.

The displacement of the moral by the narrative of health for making judgements of value is most striking in the domain of sex. The widely used term, *sexual health*, designates a domain of human life that was for thousands of years a central focus of moral concern and regulation, as a health issue. Instead of applying categories of good and bad or right and wrong to the sphere of sex, this medicalized concept uses the language of health. According to the World Health Organization, 'sexual health is a state of physical, mental and social wellbeing in relation to sexuality'.[42] This definition indicates that the attainment of sexual health 'requires a positive and respectful approach to sexuality and sexual relationships'. Though it does not explicitly explain the meaning of non-positive or non-respectful approaches to sexuality, the WHO is no less judgemental about 'unhealthy sex' as old-school religious figures were about 'immoral behaviour'.

The seamless meshing of health advice and moral regulation is clearly illustrated through the scary narratives about the health risks of basking in the sun. There was a time when warnings about avoiding the sun like the plague were confined to the world of vampires – and Dracula's aversion to daylight and sunshine symbolized the malevolent and unnatural dimension of his perverse personality. But thanks to years of scare stories about the threat of sunshine to human health, Dracula has become something of a role model for all of us. 'There is no such thing as a safe sun tan' is the message of zealous campaigns, and it seems that most people have got the message. In nurseries and schools, one of the first things that children learn is that the sun is bad for them and that they must cover their skins so as not to be exposed to its deathly rays. 'Covering up' has acquired the character of a sacred ritual, and the sun hat has become part of children's survival kit, a hallmark of responsible parenting. Companies now incite parents to purchase special sun suits that cover the entire body of their youngsters, and massive Legionnaire or Wide Brimmed Cricket-type hats are available for the offspring of anxious parents. As is the case with most forms of scaremongering, businesses operating on the fear market soon claim a piece of the action. The sales of special UV protective suits pale into insignificance compared to the hugely lucrative sun cream/sun block industry.

Those who questions the wisdom of treating the sun like a dangerous carcinogen face incredulity and condemnation. The moralistic tone directed at parents who allow their children to enjoy sunshine is illustrated by an exchange on the discussion board of the Netmums website, in which one angry parent noted: 'I know people who let kids burn to get their skin some colour – it makes me sick. Just plain laziness, and totally thoughtless and irresponsible. Our little ones need protected [sic] while they are so vulnerable, and that includes the awful pain of sunburn.'[43] For the responsible parent, protecting 'the little ones' from sunburn is not merely a matter of looking after their health, but a moral imperative. It matters little that, until recently, it was believed that the sun is actually good for our health. Today the mere mention of the dreaded word CANCER ensures that we take the words of scaremongers very seriously. So when health campaigners in the 1990s insisted that sunbathing was a highly dangerous activity, conventional attitudes towards sunshine changed very rapidly. 'In an ideal world we would stay out of the sun all the time', was how the July 1995 issue of *Top Santé* magazine summed up the new wisdom. Some ideal world that would be!

It is worth reflecting on the radical transformation of our attitude towards the sun because it shows how health warnings and fear appeals can alter some of the most taken-for-granted aspects of daily life. Throughout most of the twentieth century, many people went out of their way to ensure that their body was 'kissed by the sun'. It is claimed that it was Coco Chanel who glamourized the sun tan in the 1920s. However, even in ancient times the Greeks regarded the sun-tanned body as both desirable and beautiful, and referred to sun tanning as helio (sun) therapy. For centuries the sun was regarded as a source of healing. For example, in 1903, Auguste Rollier opened the 'sunshine clinic' in the Alps for the treatment of tuberculosis; in the 1930s and 40s, the medical profession promoted sunbathing as beneficial for children. Until the 1980s, despite warnings from a few killjoys, exposure to the sun was embraced by the vast majority of people in Western societies. One notable exception being puritanical Victorian ladies, who frowned on sun tans and whose repressed and fragile sensibilities anticipated the sentiments of anti-tan crusaders today.

Of course the liberating and sensual appeal of the sun continues to exercise its influence over society. People haven't gone so far as to regard gloomy grey skies as aesthetically pleasing, and advocacy organizations that are in the business of stigmatizing sunbathing are continually complaining that people still regard a tanned body as pleasing to the eye. One of their leaflets warns that 'a sun tan is not a sign of good health, in fact it's the body's attempt to defend itself against sunburn and is evidence that the skin has already been damaged'. Anti-sunbathing campaigners do not simply use medical arguments but also seek to morally condemn. In particular, they aim to displace the image of the tanned body as a healthy and outdoor type with that of the personification of irresponsibility.

Sara Hiom, described by the *Observer* as 'the pale-skinned information manager at Cancer Research UK', has launched a 'struggle against the tanning culture'. She ran the SunSmart campaign, aimed at educating sunbathers about the allegedly mortal danger they are putting themselves in. Hiom argued that we need to 'get back to that Victorian way of thinking where the sun is something to be avoided'.[44] Some of her co-thinkers have suggested that parents who allow their children to get sunburned should be prosecuted for neglect. In this criticism of parents who let their kids out to 'burn', it is easy to detect distinct moral undertones to what is presented as medical advice. However, it is easier to scare than to totally change people's behaviour and sense of beauty. It was with a note of regret that the American Academy of Dermatology reported in 2002 that '81% of Americans still think they look good after being out in the sun ... even though they know the risks'.[45]

There is little doubt that the anti-sun lobby has succeeded in altering people's behaviour: not least by consolidating a mood of anxiety about exposure to the sun through grossly exaggerating the danger it represents to children. However, the very success of this campaign has raised new fears. Numerous experts have pointed out that humans get over 90 per cent of their vitamin D from the sun, and that therefore some unblocked exposure to the sun is necessary to prevent vitamin D deficiency.

MORALIZING THREATS

Though justified on the basis of scientific evidence, most fear appeals adopt moral exhortation to promote their objective. Dangers are often framed as threats unleashed by malevolent forces, and those who do not heed the warnings of experts are frequently castigated as irresponsible if not evil. The moralizing of threats is pervasive in areas of life as disparate as childrearing, pregnancy, the environment, terrorism, eating and public health. Those who do not follow the 'advice' of public health experts are criticized for their irresponsibility, while people who are sceptical of the advice they are offered are depicted as morally irresponsible.

As in the age of witch-hunting, the sceptic is frequently cast in the role of a purveyor of evil. Writing on the BBC News Ethical Man blog, Justin Rowlatt expressed his concern that the word 'sceptic' was in danger of becoming a term of abuse, whereas since it was 'the foundation of good science', scepticism should be praised.[46] Rowlatt is very much in a minority and scepticism is fast losing its positive connotations as an essential ingredient of open inquiry. This has gone so far that sceptics who question the prevailing consensus on climate change can find themselves depicted as morally akin to Holocaust Deniers. As one angry article explained, 'because climate change denial supports, by default, future catastrophic social and environmental outcomes – despite overwhelming agreement about the existence of global warming and its likely consequences – the comparison with Holocaust denial seems appropriate'.[47] It is evident that, for this writer, the debate on climate change involves a morally charged conflict between good and evil. Therefore, from this standpoint opponents can be appropriately castigated as morally inferior evil agents.

The aspiration to conduct debates supposedly based on scientific evidence in the language of 'right or wrong' is symptomatic of the tendency to lend claims about scientifically charged threats a moral significance. As in the past, so today the narrative of fear is frequently devoted to raising concern about evil. The conviction that threats touch directly on good and evil influences what outwardly appear as secular fear appeals. The narrative through which warnings about the threat of epidemics are communicated resembles the moralist language used in the medieval era to describe the Black Death. Warnings about the 'revenge of the superbugs' or the 'revenge of nature' convey the sense of a supernatural punishment being visited on a sinful and arrogant humankind.

Anxieties about immoral behaviour threatening human survival are as old as human history itself. Through catastrophes such as the Deluge or Sodom and Gomorrah, the religious imagination fantasized about the end of the world. More recently, apocalyptic ideas once rooted in magic and theology have been recast as allegedly scientific statements about human destructiveness and irresponsibility. As Philip Alcabes notes in his cultural history of epidemics, 'prominently, ancient suspicions of contamination, divine punishment, and moral correction have permeated humanity's awareness of disease and continue to influence our grasp of the epidemic'.[48]

The transformation of the Black Death into an epidemic of evil in the Middle Ages continues to excite people's fears today. According to one study, it was 'only after Europeans had experienced this epidemic' that 'they were ready to accept witchcraft as a real threat'.[49] The moralization of AIDS indicates that modern 'plagues' still possess the potential to convey a culturally meaningful message of evil. However, the moralization of illness is not confined to any one disease. Today, the so-called epidemic of obesity is depicted as the dangerous consequence of bad behaviour: 'junk food' is denounced as 'evil', and the obese are portrayed as irresponsible if not immoral inferior beings. Companies that target children with their dangerous food products frequently face the kind of moral condemnation hitherto reserved for drug dealers and petty criminals.

The scientist James Lovelock poses as a prophet-scientist when he states: 'I take my profession seriously, and now I, too, have to bring bad news ...'⁵⁰ Today, the future of the earth is said to be jeopardized by human consumption, technological development or by 'man playing God'. And instead of original sin leading to the Fall of Man, we fear the degradation of Nature by an apparently malevolent human species. All of today's various doomsday scenarios, from oil depletion and global warming to the Millennium Bug or avian flu, emphasize human culpability. Their premise is that the human species is essentially destructive and morally bankrupt. 'With breathtaking insolence', warns Lovelock in his book *The Revenge of Gaia*, humans 'have taken the stores of carbon that Gaia buried to keep oxygen at its proper level and burnt them.' From this perspective, the physical threat to our planet is the consequence of immoral human conduct.

In the twenty-first century, scaremongering works most effectively when it enjoys the authority of science. The authority of science is so powerful that its warnings are taken very seriously even by God-fearing religious people. That is why at a New Baptist Covenant meeting, the green crusader Al Gore claimed not only a scriptural but also a scientific mandate for his warning about global warming. He cited Luke 12:54-57 for biblical support and stated that it was dishonest for anyone to deny that global warming was a scientific fact. 'The evidence is there,' he said. 'The signal is on the mountain. The trumpet has blown. The scientists are screaming from the rooftops. The ice is melting. The land is parched. The seas are rising. The storms are getting stronger. Why do we not judge what is right?'⁵¹ The image of scientists screaming from the rooftops conveys the impression that they must be speaking the truth, and can only be ignored at one's peril. So although Gore is happy to receive the acclamation of his fellow Baptists, his vision of the impending catastrophe is communicated through appeals to scientific authority.

Fear appeals work best when they are able to draw on both the authority of science and the language of good and evil. This trend is clearly visible in the domain of sex, where it is difficult to draw a line that divides scientific claims about what is safe from moral exhortation and stigma. Indeed, some of the most morally charged crusades about sexual behaviour have been promoted as scientifically validated truths. To gain a historical perspective on this subject it is worth revisiting the campaign of stigmatization directed at masturbation during early modern times. The ascendancy of widespread anxiety about the perils of masturbation was at least in part due to the authorization that this panic received from science.

It was not that long ago that zealous moral entrepreneurs sought to frighten generations of schoolboys with alarmist stories about how masturbation would make them blind. Frightening descriptions of the sin of 'self-pollution' would dwell on the horrifying physical and moral consequences of so-called 'post-masturbation disease'. In his *Onanism: Or a Treatise Upon the Disorders Produced by Masturbation: Or, the Dangerous Effects of Secret and Excessive Venery*, the Swiss physician Simon-Auguste Tissot produced a veritable catalogue of horror stories about the appalling consequences of this dangerous practice. He recalled visiting a patient suffering from post-masturbation disease, where what he found

was less a living being than a cadaver lying on straw, thin, pale, exuding a loathsome stench, almost incapable of movement. A pale and watery blood often dripped from his nose, he drooled continually; subject to attacks of diarrhea, he defecated in his bed without noticing it; there was a constant flow of semen; his eyes, sticky, blurry, dull, had lost all power of movement; his pulse was extremely weak and racing; labored respiration, extreme emaciation, except for the feet, which were showing signs of edema. Mental disorder was equally evident; without ideas, without memory, incapable of linking two sentences, without reflection, without fear of his fate, lacking all feeling except that of pain, which returned at least every three days with each new attack. Thus sunk below the level of the beast, a spectacle of unimaginable horror, it was difficult to believe that he had once belonged to the human race ... He died after several weeks, in June 1757, his entire body covered in edemas.[52]

In 1760, when this influential treatise was published, Tissot's description of his patients resonated with prevailing opinion on this subject. Indeed, for some time to come Onanism would do for the policing of sexual behaviour what *Malleus Maleficarum* did for witchcraft. In the eighteenth and nineteenth centuries, popular fears about a non-existent disease were mobilized to terrorize people to practise a 'healthy' and moral lifestyle. Tissot himself advocated the medical intervention of 'treatment by terror': unlike witches, Tissot's patients were not burned at the stake – they merely faced a form of moral and psychological torture.

At its inception, apprehension about the perils of masturbation were promoted on moral and religious grounds. In medieval times religious officials condemned it as a 'sin against nature'. By the seventeenth century, moral condemnation was accompanied with terrifying accounts about its debilitating physical consequences. With the publication of the anonymously authored text *Onania* in 1716, masturbation became increasingly conceptualized as much as a medical as a moral failing.

Onania still relied on biblical sources, but it also sought to mobilize medical claims about how masturbation was the outcome of dysfunctions that caused disease and physical impairment. The text put forward a coherent medical diagnosis of the illness, describing the symptoms and their progression, and offered a frightening prognosis. From this point onwards, science was increasingly used as the authority for promoting fear about masturbation. The belief that masturbation was the cause of a real and deadly disease was widely accepted by leading figures of the Enlightenment such as Voltaire and Rousseau, as well as the leading medical doctors of the eighteenth and nineteenth centuries. For Rousseau, the curbing of solitary sex constituted something of a crusade. 'Whatever we may do, a young man's worst enemy is himself, and this is an enemy we cannot avoid,' he warned.

It appears that the early modern medical profession looked upon the campaign against masturbation as a 'welcome opportunity' to 'demonstrate the importance of medical expertise for promoting individual as well as social welfare'.[53] With the publication of Tissot's *Onanism*, the moral problems associated with masturbation became gradually more and more medicalized. Tissot, too, preached the moralist message that warned of the hazards of sex undertaken for pleasure rather than procreation. But his moral objection to masturbation was justified on the grounds of the destructive physical and social causes of the disease, rather than moral prohibitions.

In the decades that followed the publication of *Onanism*, masturbation became increasingly seen as a disease that robbed young men of their vital energies, contributed to physical deterioration and led to insanity. In the popular imagination of the nineteenth century, it was directly connected with the latter. Its association with mental health problems continued into the next century and it was often portrayed as a form of psychological defect.

With hindsight, it is evident that anxiety about masturbation exercised an exceptionally powerful influence. So how do we account for the unusually significant impact of this scare on Western societies? One observer notes that other 'similarly plausible and often-repeated warnings about the dangers of tobacco, chocolate, or the reading of novels never achieved the same kind of impact', and claims that the reason why fear-mongering about masturbation worked so effectively was because it succeeded in synthesizing traditional moral concerns with the validation of scientific authority. Stolberg writes that:

> The disorders ascribed to masturbation were described and perceived as particularly threatening. In addition, their highly charged, evocative imagery mediated successfully between what happened to be empirically validated, medico-scientific concepts on the one hand and widespread religious, social and political concerns on the other.[54]

The high point of the anti-masturbation panic was probably the second half of the nineteenth century. According to one study, there was a sharp rise in the practice of repressive and surgical interventions against masturbation from 1850 onwards. Spitz argues that 'sadism becomes the foremost characteristic of the campaign'.[55] It was only around the turn of the twentieth century that medical opinion began to question the causal connection between masturbation and disease. By the middle of the century the fear of masturbation ceased to haunt the popular imagination, and parents begun to understand that it was a normal part of childhood and human development. Sections of the Church continued to condemn the practice: in 1976 the Vatican published a *Declaration on Certain Questions Concerning Sexual Ethics* that condemned masturbation as an 'intrinsically and seriously disordered act'. But by this time very few people were listening. Without the support of scientific authority, the moralization of this practice failed to provoke people's fears.

Contemporary warnings about sex are no less subject to moralizing than in previous times. However, morally driven anxieties tend to be couched in a medical language. Warnings about 'safe', 'responsible', 'negotiated', 'risky' or 'unsafe' sex are transmitted through a medical idiom. Young people are rarely warned about the perils of recreational sex on moral grounds: instead, medical arguments are used to warn of the emotional and physical damage that such behaviour can cause. Not infrequently, young people are told that the emotional trauma caused by early experience can 'damage them for life'. And in contrast to the wisdom of the eighteenth and nineteenth centuries, masturbation is frequently recommended as an ideal form of safe sex.

The policing of people's conduct through frightening them about the health consequences of their behaviour is accomplished through the process of medicalizing individual behaviour. 'Health' has come to operate as a 'moral framework' for society, emphasizing 'individual responsibility and … compliance with the appropriate medically-sanctioned standard of behaviour', argued Michael Fitzpatrick in his important study on the workings of medicalization.[56] Medicalization provides a system of meaning through which people's conduct is transformed into both a moral and physical problem. In the twenty-first century it is frequently used by moral entrepreneurs to frighten people into accepting what they consider to be appropriate behaviour.

THE MORALIZATION OF INFANT FEEDING

The moralization of parenting practices is an important feature of the culture of fear. In recent decades, the feeding of infants has captured the attention of advocacy organizations who are zealously committed to the virtues of breastfeeding. Of course there are some powerful health-related arguments about the benefits of breastfeeding children, especially during the first three months of their lives; however, the practical question of how best to feed your child has become moralized by campaigners who regard breastfeeding as a quasi-religious or moral obligation that a mother has towards a child. The moralization of breastfeeding as the symbol of maternal responsibility has been a recurring theme in modern history. Jean-Jacques Rousseau had strong faith in the virtues of breastfeeding, writing in *Emile*:

> Do you want to bring everyone back to his first dutie? Begin with mothers ... Everything follows successively from this first depravity [wet-nursing]. The whole moral order degenerates, naturalness is extinguished in all hearts ... But let mothers deign to nurse their children, morals will reform themselves, nature's sentiments will be awakened in every heart, the state will be repopulated.[57]

According to Rousseau, the failure to breastfeed is the 'first depravity', a moral failure that has serious repercussions for the life of a community.

In the twenty-first century, this moral tone has given way to more crude attempts to stigmatize those mothers who use formula milk to feed their babies. The language used aims both to frighten and to morally condemn its target, denouncing such mothers for their 'unnatural' and 'selfish' practice, for risking the health of their babies, and for opting out of a once-in-a-lifetime opportunity to achieve emotional closeness with their offspring.

The language used to castigate errant mothers typically assumes the tone of moral superiority. 'What's stopping you breastfeeding?' asks a *Prima Baby* journalist in disbelief. In a hectoring voice it insists that 'it's perfectly natural and will help protect your baby from many illnesses from asthma to diabetes'. From this perspective, those who opt to bottle-feed are complicit in an act of neglecting their children's need. The statement 'it's perfectly natural' communicates the message that the alternative is unnatural and therefore morally inferior. 'Breastfeeding, by its very nature, requires the sort of skin-to-skin contact that babies need', and therefore it is 'a uniquely bonding experience', claims one advocacy organization.

Pat Thomas, writing in *The Ecologist*, denounces formula milk as 'junk food', which she compares unfavourably to the 'miraculous substance' which is breast milk. From this perspective, anyone who opts for 'artificial milk' and rejects this 'miraculous substance' violates the natural order of things. A sense of moral zeal encourages a rhetoric of scaremongering that verges on the hysterical. She claims that 'newer data from the West clearly show that babies in otherwise affluent societies are also falling ill and dying due to an early diet of convenience food', and adds that 'the health effects of sucking down formula day after day early in life can be devastating in both the short and long term'. Cultivating the well-worn approach of the conspiracy theorist, Thomas blames the widespread practice of such unnatural feeding practices on a highly orchestrated plot by the forces of darkness. Her article is introduced with the portentous statement: 'Pat Thomas uncovers a world where predatory baby milk manufacturers, negligent health professionals and an ignorant, unsympathetic public all conspire to keep babies off the breast and on the bottle.'[58]

One of the consequences of the moralization of infant feeding is that it gives permission to zealous campaigners to adopt a highly inflammatory language to denounce the evil they see. The strap line across the web page of one advocacy group, Baby Milk Action, screams that: 'Every day 40000 babies die from unsafe bottle feeding.'[59] Not to be outdone, the International Baby Food Action Network (IBFAN) warns on its website that 'Bottle feeding can kill' and that a 'baby dies every 30 seconds from unsafe bottle feeding'. Official campaigns adopt a similar approach. An alarmist, US advertising campaign, 'Babies were born to be breastfed', compared bottle feeding with a heavily pregnant woman taking part in a log-rolling competition, and riding a mechanical bull. Its strap line is: 'You wouldn't take risks before your baby is born ... Why start after?'[60] Such scare campaigns are not without effect. According to research carried out by the sociologist Professor Ellie Lee, 'mothers who formula feed do worry, sometimes to a great degree, about the harm they might have done to their child'.[61]

THE FEAR PERSPECTIVE

Though fear is no longer accepted by many as the foundation for morality, it still plays an important role in moralizing the problems of everyday life. Thus the disassociation of fearing from the grammar of morality has not reduced the significance of this cultural force in public life: quite the contrary. In the absence of a script offering a perspective on how to fear, *fear itself has become a perspective* through which life is interpreted. Its emergence as a perspective is one of the most important features of the contemporary fear culture.

As a perspective, fear is not merely a response to a threat but a viewpoint or disposition towards the world in general. It often sets the tone for deliberations about high-profile existential global threats – such as flu pandemics, global warming or terrorism. But arguably this perspective plays a far more significant role in influencing ordinary forms of personal behaviour. Fear appeals directed to support breastfeeding, avoidance of the sun or maintaining positive body image indicate that even the minutiae of life are informed by this perspective. As Svendsen concludes, 'we seem to see *everything* from a perspective of fear'.[62] The tendency to approach the problems of life from this outlook can turn the most banal or routine of experiences into a potential target of fear.

The term 'perspective of fear' – a cultural outlook for explaining and understanding reality – accurately captures this relatively new trend. The emergence and consolidation of the fear perspective is implicitly recognized by the remarkable expansion of the usage of the term *politics of fear*. Often it appears that fear is not simply a perspective but a powerful medium through which society makes sense of itself.

The rhetoric of fear is used to convey a variety of different objectives. It is used to draw attention to a particular problem or a cause. Fear continues to guide and influence people's attitudes and behaviour. At the same time, the rhetoric is critically directed to condemn those who use fear. Constant criticisms of those guilty of adopting the politics of fear or of 'playing the fear card' highlight the divisive consequences of espousing this perspective.

The influence of the fear perspective is illustrated by the fact that people of all shades of opinion rely on it to make sense of their circumstances. This is a perspective that citizens share across the political and cultural divide. Parties, movements, campaigns and individuals often distinguish themselves from one another through their competing claims about what to fear. It seems that people are so imbued with this perspective that in the very attempt to expose an act of fear-mongering they resort to a counter scare. One critic of this perspective pointed to the jacket of Barry Glassner's book, *The Culture of Fear*, to illustrate his concern. The educator Glen C. Altschuler noted that for each 'scare' that Glassner debunked: 'he substitutes something Americans should be afraid of. Road rage is not a "growing epidemic", but traffic congestion is a serious and sometimes lethal problem. Trick-or-treating isn't dangerous … but violence by family members against children is pervasive.'[63] Altschuler concluded that 'like the scares it seeks to expose', the book 'actually heightens anxiety'. Altschuler's argument has a wider relevance for understanding how the transformation of fear into a perspective has encouraged the tendency to turn disputes into a series of claims and counter-claims about what constitutes a legitimate focus for feeling scared. In these disputes, the perspective of fear is implicitly accepted by all the key protagonists. What divides the different parties is how they use these perspectives, and for what purpose.

As a perspective, fear has acquired qualities that are unique to our times. Historically, fear has played a significant role in reinforcing the moral order. In a world where that order is continually contested, fear itself acquires a new role. It cannot just sit still and regulate. Freed from its mooring in a stable moral order, it continually circulates and looks for more targets to moralize. The influence of this perspective over public life is recognized in times of political controversy and conflict, where fear has been explicitly attributed the quality of a project. In debates on this subject it is not always clear whether Project Fear serves a higher purpose or merely its own object. In Chapter 4, we look more deeply at how the fear perspective influences public life.

THE ZERO TOLERANCE TOWARDS SCEPTICISM

History shows that moral uncertainty creates conditions where the emotion of fear can acquire a menacing and coercive cultural form. The very condition of uncertainty often provokes a defensive response of attempting to assert certainty by any means necessary. Kingsley's reflections on blind fear indicated that superstition itself looks for solutions to the problem of uncertainty. The so-called science of demonology appeared to offer a provisional solution to the moral uncertainties thrown up by scepticism towards belief in witchcraft, and the campaign of fear promoted by witch-hunters should be seen as an attempt to eliminate critics of the prevailing moral dogma.

At first sight, it appears that the fear culture of today has little in common with the practice of demonology. The modern secular imagination has left Satan behind, prides itself on its evidence-based approach, and explicitly relies on science to justify its claims about threats. However, despite the great advances in science and technology, society remains intensely uncomfortable living with uncertainty. Consequently the professional proponents of fear appeals resemble old-school demonologists in one important respect: their response to uncertainty is often to close down criticism and debate. The moralizing of hazard works as an argument for silencing sceptics and critics.

The development of science relies on an open-ended orientation towards experimentation and the testing of ideas. Science is an inherently sceptical enterprise and its findings are provisional, open to reinterpretation. That's the theory. But in public controversies over policy and related matters, science often comes across as a moralizing project. The language used by Al Gore constantly leaps from the scientific to the moral, which is why he could assert that scientific evidence offers 'Inconvenient Truths'. Gore's version of science has more in common with the art of divination than with genuine experimentation. Gore and many others have adopted a defensive version of science that constantly targets doubts and uncertainties, and their moralized interpretation of science is one where findings have a fixed, unyielding and unquestionable quality. Frequently, they prefix the term science with a definite article, using 'The Science' to assert claims about a variety of threats. Statements like 'The Science says' serve as the twenty-first-century equivalent of the exhortation 'God said'. Unlike science, the term 'The Science' serves a moralistic and political project. It has more in common with a pre-modern revealed truth than with the spirit of experimentation that emerged with modernity. The constant refrain of 'Scientists Tell Us' serves as a prelude for a lecture on what threat to fear.

The use of the term 'The Science' in public debates expresses its advocates' insecurity with the absence of certainty. This leads to a defensive posture where scientists are reluctant to entertain the possibility that they might be wrong and that their critics might have a point. Sadly, a science that cannot work with the assumption that it might be wrong has more in common with a religious dogma than with open-ended experimentation. Such moralization of the imperative of fear has important implications for the conduct of public life. By representing scepticism and criticism as a threat that deserves to be feared, disciples of The Science set in motion a cultural dynamic that is inherently hostile to the free and open exchange of views. As we explain later, a palpable sense of intolerance towards freedom, particularly towards free speech, is intimately connected to the working of the culture of fear.

4

The Perspective of Fear – How it Works

In its extended usage, a perspective refers to a mental outlook towards the future, conveyed through expectation and anticipation. Perspective as an anticipatory stance has both an individual and wider cultural significance. Fear has emerged as an influential perspective that shapes thoughts towards uncertainty, and today it is unquestionably more influential than the perspective of hope. Fear informs feelings and behaviours, and because of its influence it is readily used as a medium through which problems – old and new – are interpreted and given meaning. As discussed below, given the relative weakness of positive sources of inspiration, the perspective of fear works as the principal motivational force in twenty-first-century society.

The importance of the perspective of fear is illustrated by the readiness with which it is adopted as an explanatory framework for making sense of public affairs. This is illustrated by the explosion in the use of the term 'politics of fear'. The belief that fear has become politicized and that this emotion constitutes an important influence over public affairs is widely held at all levels of the social hierarchy – yet extensive public interest in the politics of fear is a relatively new development. Google Scholar listed 339 academic texts that had the term 'politics of fear' in their titles between 2000 and mid-2017: almost a ten-fold increase over the 38 titles published in the previous 17 years.[1] Its increased usage in the mainstream media is even more spectacular. Nexis cites just one media source in 1980 using the term in its headline: this increased to 216 citations for 2016.

Headlines containing the term 'politics of fear' cited in Nexis

1980–90: 15 hits

1990–2000: 79 hits

2000–10: 338 hits

2010–16: 571 hits

Those who use the idiom 'politics of fear' assume that the meaning of the term is self-evident: it is not explained, and is deployed as a statement of condemnation. In the midst of political conflicts and controversies, opponents habitually condemn one another for 'using' the politics of fear.

The fear perspective offers a viewpoint through which society makes sense of itself and the problems it confronts. However, it is not merely an outlook: fear has become an interpretative instrument with the power to turn the objects of its concerns into real problems. For example, policy makers have come to regard the fear of crime as a threat in its own right. That the fear of crime now has a separate, stand-alone existence that is distinct from the incidence of crime is widely accepted. Law enforcement agencies have developed policies and practices for managing the fear of crime. The destabilizing and destructive outcome of the fear of crime for public life ensures that resources are devoted to measuring it and managing it.

The aim of this chapter is to discuss the different dimensions of the perspective of fear with a view to illuminating how it works. I argue that this perspective has been so thoroughly internalized that many who adopt this outlook are not aware of its influence on their behaviour. For most people, such a perspective comes across as common sense. This does not mean that people are perpetually scared or fearful; rather, the perspective of fear works by sensitizing people to focus on potential threats and dangers while distracting attention from the probable positive outcome of engaging with uncertainty. Consequently, people are encouraged to anticipate the worst, and thereby to lower their expectations about the outcome of their experience.

THE PERSPECTIVE OF FEAR

Accounts of the perspective of fear tend to fall into the trap of interpreting its influence in a one-sided subjective manner. Instead of addressing the question of 'how it works', the analysis of fear tends to focus on the issue of 'how it is used'. An emphasis on the conscious creation of fear detracts attention from the logically prior existence of the fear perspective. The fears that resonate with people's imagination are not created in a vacuum: a disposition to interpret issues and problems as dreadful exists prior to the act of playing the fear card. Individuals or groups may well decide to adopt scare tactics to realize a particular objective, but the success of this project depends on the availability of cultural resources that they can draw on. In the current age, the cultural affirmation of the fear perspective constitutes a ready-made, valuable resource for fear entrepreneurs.

One of the most fascinating and also disturbing aspects of the way that the fear perspective works is its capacity to recast the normal features of life as a threat. As society is drawn into adopting this perspective, the way people lead their lives alters. People are not always aware of the effect of this perspective on their lives, since these changes occur in an imperceptible manner. In the previous chapter we noted how hitherto taken-for-granted activities such as sunbathing have been reinterpreted as a threat to our health. Another example is the transformation of a routine activity like drinking water into a source of anxiety and concern. There was a time when people did not walk around holding different brands of bottled water in their hands; they drank tap water unless they lived in areas where tap water was considered to be unsafe, in which case water was boiled. In the past two decades, the sight of people clutching their bottles of water has become an everyday urban spectacle. Though this is motivated in part by ceaseless health advice to drink more water, warnings about the safety of tap water have led to a boom in the sales of the bottled variety.

Since the late 1970s, as the perspective of fear attached itself to water, people's drinking habits have changed. In 2016, bottled-water consumption in the US reached 39.3 gallons per person. The journey towards the normalization of bottled-water consumption began in 1976, with the launch of Perrier water in the US. In the subsequent four decades, the consumption of bottled water in America rose from 354 million gallons in 1976 to 11.7 billion gallons in 2015: an increase of more than 2,700 per cent in four decades.[2] A similar surging rise in the consumption of bottled water is evident throughout the Western world.

Numerous critics have pointed out that the fears directed at tap water are not based on an objective evaluation of the risks of drinking it. From a health perspective, the consumption of bottled water makes little sense. Unfortunately, the sensible message that tap water is in most places safe to drink and that paying for the bottled variety is unnecessary is often distorted through a narrative of fear. Instead of merely stating 'Let's get real and drink tap water', opponents of the bottled-water fad frame their argument through the perspective of fear.

In recent years, the perspective of fear, which originally incited millions to abandon drinking tap water, has shifted its focus to the supposed threat posed by bottled water. Environmental and consumer lobby groups often argue that not only is bottled water very expensive but it is also not as safe as tap water.[3] One website features an article titled '6 Scary Facts about Bottled Water'. Aside from informing the public that bottled water is a rip-off, it suggests that it 'can be more harmful than tap water', because tap water is more regulated than the bottled variety. For good measure, it warns that 'plastic bottles can be toxic', and condemns bottled water for being 'lethal for the environment'. This article contends that the 'production and disposal' of bottled water 'consumes and destroys resources at an astounding rate'. Not surprisingly it advocates joining a campaign to 'Ban the Bottle'.[4] Due to environmental concerns over the disposal of plastic bottles, many people are returning to drinking tap water.

Supporters of the bottled-water industry have responded to their critics by launching a public information campaign, claiming that 'myths about bottled water' are 'confusing consumers', and that many people have become influenced by the fear campaign against bottled water.[5] The controversy over drinking water indicates how effortlessly the perspective of fear can turn a routine activity into a target of competing fear appeals. That this perspective has great bearing on the behaviour of people is shown by the rapidity with which many altered their former habit of drinking tap water. That anxiety about the threat posed to the environment by plastic bottles has also changed some people's drinking habits illustrates the disorienting effect of competitive fear appeals.

As a perspective, fear has acquired a taken-for-granted quality. The fear card does not have to be consciously 'played': people's attitudes towards uncertainty are infused with it. Consequently, the most significant feature of this perspective is not that people use it but that they live it. The term 'playing the fear card' conveys the assumption that the people involved in this activity are dishonestly manipulating the public's emotions, and often supposes that the people playing the fear card do not actually believe their own warnings. That may be the case in some instances – but in most cases, even self-conscious manipulators are not immune to the influence of the culture of fear.

There are, of course, dishonest peddlers of fear who attempt to scare people with threats that they themselves know to be untrue. Though these individuals may cause suffering and distress, they are actually marginal to the workings of the culture of fear. The perspective of fear is a cultural resource that they draw on, voice, magnify, expand and sometimes manipulate. Typically, people using fear are themselves influenced by a society-wide outlook, disposing them to view the future from this perspective. The acting out or the performance of fear is not simply a personal statement but also a cultural act. It is a form of behaviour that flows from the understanding that one is expected to draw on the narrative of fear in both public and private communication. The use of fear is a valuable resource, for it lends legitimacy to an argument.

As a perspective, fear does not simply guide people's attitudes and feelings: it offers a coherent, and deeply embedded, outlook. Society expects its citizens to be fearful and actively promotes the values of caution, risk aversion and safety. Those who ignore the advice of health professionals and experts are regarded as irresponsible and their behaviour is sometimes represented as a threat to the community. Consequently, as Chapter 6 explains, the aspiration for safety has emerged as the principal virtue in Western society.

Playing the fear card has a long history, but the *perspective* of fear is a unique feature of the present era. Since the ancient Greeks, it has been recognized that fear was an important motivating force driving human behaviour. William Graham Sumners, one of the founding figures of American sociology, claimed that 'fear as a motive rules the lives of primitives'.[6] His analysis of how fear acquired influence as a motivational force emphasized the institutionalization of its sublimated manifestations, such as pilgrimages and rituals of witchcraft. Through its internalization via cultural practices, the motivating force of fear has gained traction. Sumner argued, 'when fear becomes firmly established in the folkways, it acted as an ever-ruling tyrant', adding that 'in the *mores* it became firmly entrenched and was a leading factor in molding character'.[7] For Sumner, the mores of a community referred to the cultural habits, traditions and conventions that have great moral significance in relation to the conduct of members of a community.

Unlike the communities analysed by Sumner, contemporary society is far less bound by cultural habits, customs and traditions. In contrast to the settled system of customs with clearly defined moral norms and taboos, twenty-first-century society is self-consciously post-traditional. On balance, Western societies tend to regard the customs of the past as irrelevant and, in many cases, inappropriate to their needs. Fear, too, is far more unsettled and unstable today than in traditional communities, where it was explicitly guided by dogma and religious practices. Arguably, it is precisely its unsettled dimension that informs the manner in which fear works as a motivational force.

THE PROBLEM OF MOTIVATION

In a complex post-traditional setting, motivation constitutes a constant challenge. In different times and contexts, a wide range of motivational factors such as fear, hope, greed, loyalty and ideology influenced people's actions. People contribute to society because they identify with their community or nation. They are also motivated by a variety of impulses, such as an aspiration for financial gain, religious convictions or ideological affiliations. Society relies on these motivational influences to realize its objectives and maintain stability and order.

Since the 1960s, it has been widely recognized that Western societies suffer from a motivational deficit. Values that have inspired citizens in previous times – patriotism, loyalty, religion, ideology and so on – appear to have lost much of their import. More significantly, values that touch on everyday behaviour are themselves a focus of constant debate and contestation. The absence of the commanding influence of moral authority created a condition where traditional values lost much of their influence over the outlook and behaviour of the younger generations.

During the 1960s, this development was diagnosed as a temporary problem. Half a century later, the problem has endured and there has been little progress in establishing a system of values to replace those that have lost their authority. Especially since the 1980s, Western societies have found it difficult to generate values with which to motivate people to identify with the social order. The scale of this problem was recognized by the German social theorist Jürgen Habermas, in his 1973 essay *The Legitimation Crisis*. Habermas argued that the problem of legitimacy was underpinned by a 'motivation crisis', which was the outcome of the failure of the 'socio-cultural system' to supply the values required for the maintenance of the social order.

The implication of Habermas's thesis was that society lacked the spiritual or cultural resources necessary for maintaining its authority. His analysis suggested that Western capitalist institutions, which have historically relied on traditional values to legitimate themselves, were now forced to find new sources of validation.[8] Since that time, the crisis of legitimation has become increasingly expansive and governments are continually in search of a 'new narrative' or a 'big idea'.

From the 1970s onwards, the problem of motivation has expanded into all dimensions of social life. The motivational influences of communist, socialist and liberal ideology, or identification with the nation and the belief in the efficiency of capitalism, have significantly diminished. The authority of science has also lost some of its lustre, and the formidable hopes invested in its potential to benefit humankind now compete with pessimism about its future trajectory. In this cultural landscape, the perspective of harnessing people's beliefs and hopes to motivate their loyalty and gain their commitment has lost much of its weight.

By default, the motivational influence of fear has gained momentum and influence. One symptom of its growing appeal as a motivational force is the readiness with which fear has been absorbed into the narratives of competing movements and campaigns. In this context, fear is not simply a motivational influence but offers a wider perspective that touches on the different dimensions of people's lives.

The emergence of the perspective of fear is intimately linked to the motivational crisis that stems from the feeble status of moral authority. As I note elsewhere, 'the shift from positive affirmation to a negative conception of authority is one of the most significant developments in the cultural history of modernity'.[9] A negative conception of authority does not communicate or rely on upbeat and confident ideals about the future. Instead it depends on motivating people through appealing to their sense of vulnerability, existential insecurity and anxiety about the future. This is a form of authority that relies almost exclusively on protecting people from the negative influences that threaten their lives. The absence of positive ideals and objectives that could constitute a focus for unity and legitimacy has led to the emergence of a fear-based negative conception of authority.

Outwardly, the perspective of fear resembles the outlook of Thomas Hobbes, who saw people's fear of death as the foundation for establishing the authority of the sovereign ruler and for maintaining social order. Yet Hobbes's embrace of the fear of death as a sentiment that could underpin the stability of political authority has little in common with the workings of the perspective of fear in the twenty-first century. This perspective is detached from the momentous struggle for human survival that preoccupied Hobbes. Hobbes offered a big picture that depicted the fear of death as a motive for converting individual aspirations into a single unifying force – ultimately the secular state. In the twenty-first century, warnings about death touch on the minutiae of existence, and possess a matter-of-fact, banal quality. They have little to do with the affairs of the state or with providing legitimacy for authority of a political ruler. So, something as mundane as dietary advice can effortlessly mutate into a warning about life and death, with headlines such as: 'Low-fat diet could kill you, major study shows'.[10]

RISK AS AN OBJECT OF FEAR

The study informing the public that a low-fat diet 'could kill you' does not actually say that people who avoid butter and cheese will die. This study, published in *The Lancet*, claims that 'low-fat diets could raise the risk of early death by almost one quarter'.[11] The key word in this statement is *risk*. Conventionally, the term 'risk' refers to the probability of damage, injury, illness, death or other misfortune associated with a hazard. Hazards are generally interpreted as threats to people and what they value. In this instance, the hazards threatening people are low-fat foods. If low-fat diet is a risk, than why not a high-fat one? 'Although high-fat diets may have some merit for weight loss, they also present some serious risks', warns one expert.[12]

One of the accomplishments of the fear perspective is that it continually expands the number of issues that constitute a hazard and are therefore represented as risk. Since the 1980s numerous commentators have commented on the explosion of risks. Every food product, toy, cosmetic item, or experience is evaluated from the viewpoint of a risk manager. Even activities that are directed at improving people's health – such as a low-fat diet – are portrayed in these terms. People are made aware of the risk of exercising too hard. Claims are made about the risk of jogging and about the risk of children participating in school sports. An ever-expanding obsession with risk is one of the most striking features of the culture of fear. Indeed risk talk, risk assessment and risk management often provide the narratives through which the perspective of fear is communicated. The mere intimation that a toy might pose even a tiny risk is sufficient to produce an explosion of outrage, leading to the recall of millions of products.

Although risk is historically defined as exposure to the probability of loss, harm or some kind of misfortune, through its current expanded usage it has been reinterpreted as the *possibility* of such adversity. This shift in meaning from probability to possibility has led to a fundamental revision in the conceptualization of risk. A lack of confidence about managing uncertainty has altered society's understanding of the meaning of risk. Throughout most of the modern era, people conceptualized things as good and bad risks. In some instances, risk taking was perceived as an admirable enterprise; in others, as an evil. For example, in 1908, a commentator in the *Northwest Mining Journal* objected to miners using the term 'good gamble', to mean a 'good risk', by stating: 'Mining men should rebel against the synonymous use of these terms, because the word gamble undoubtedly only refers to an evil risk.'[13] What this writer objected to was the equation of risk with the term gamble. For him, as for most early twentieth-century commentators, risk was not about gambling but involved rationally calculating probable outcomes. From this vantage point, the meaning of risk was neutral – whether it was considered to be good or bad depended on the outcome of the calculation of probabilities.

The potential for gaining or losing something of value is central to the modern outlook on risk. Risk itself is a neutral category. Whether, in a specific circumstance, it is considered good or bad depends on the calculation used to determine the outcomes. Since the 1980s, under the influence of the perspective of fear, this neutral and technical version of risk has given way to a tendency to equate it with a loss or a danger. The weighing up of gain and loss, or of opportunity and threat, which was an integral part of risk assessment, has been displaced by an outlook that associates risk with hazard, and invites the response of fear. Once risk acquires a reputation for conveying bad news, it becomes a hazard to be handled with care. That is why risk managers often use a language that attempts to 'minimize risk' or 'reduce it' or 'avoid' it altogether. In its most irrational version, some people demand 'zero risk' – a project that would require abolishing uncertainty completely.[14]

Risk has absorbed the narrative of fear, and its contemporary meaning has little in common with the project of attempting to understand the likely outcome of uncertain events. In present times, one of the principal objectives of a risk manager is to 'reduce risk'. Since risk is not a fixed quantity but a concept that expresses the outcome of the calculation of probabilities, the term risk reduction is an illogical one. Though it is possible to mitigate against undesirable outcomes, a risk cannot be quantitatively reduced. Discussions on the topic of risk reduction explicitly acknowledge that its object is to reduce danger rather than risk. Hence risk reduction tends to be defined as measures designed to reduce the frequency or severity of losses: it is another name for 'loss control'.

Now and again it is still possible to read risk-related statements that regard the calculation of risk as an instrument for managing uncertainty and negotiating a future that consists of both opportunities and threats. However, the prevailing cultural mood continually signals the message that risk taking is tricky and dangerous. An aversion to risk pervades controversies on this subject. Once upheld as an exemplar of courageous behaviour, the act of taking a risk no longer enjoys automatic cultural valuation. The risk-taker is often depicted as an irresponsible and foolish person, whose activity is likely to court social disapproval. On the other hand, risk avoidance – which in practice means drawing back from embracing uncertainty – is widely praised as a form of responsible behaviour.

At one time, one of the definitions of the word *risky* was that of 'bold, daring; adventurous'. According to the *OED*, this manner of defining risk is now rare.[15] Terms like 'risky sex', 'risky love' or 'risky teen behaviour' refer to practices that do not possess any redeeming qualities. A discussion on 'risky parenting advice' referred to forms of guidance that were likely to damage a baby's health. Examples of risky parenting advice included 'exposing a baby to hot tarmac fumes to "strengthen its lungs"' and telling mothers that 'under ones don't need sun cream because they can't get sunburnt'.[16]

Throughout most of the modern era, the science of risk assessment tended to provide society with an important instrument for restraining and guiding fear. It relied on using knowledge to transform uncertainty into calculable risks. Through gaining a handle for dealing with uncertainty, risk calculation assisted the project of rationalizing the fear of the future. With the rise of the perspective of fear, the meaning of risk has become subjugated to the narrative of fear. A disposition to anticipate negative outcomes permeates attitudes towards risk. The emergence of what I have previously characterized as *risk consciousness* – the tendency to perceive the different aspects of life through the prism of danger and loss – highlights the influence of the fear perspective over people's lives.

Reality dictates that the classical interpretation of risk continues to prevail in the work of scientists. People involved in the innovation of technology, in the financial markets, or in industry rely on precise calculations of risk to manage their affairs. Even sections of the policy-making community – especially in the sphere of security – need to take seriously the calculation of risk. No doubt the tools used for such calculations have become more sophisticated and complex, but the imperative of working with probabilities continues to influence their work.

However, the diminishing influence of the classical version of risk, within wider culture and public life, is palpable. A growing body of opinion, consisting of campaigning groups, lobbyists, academics, political activists and policy makers, argues that holding on to the classical version of risk is irresponsible. From their perspective of fear, they claim that humankind does not possess the knowledge that is necessary for the calculation of probable outcomes. Arguments against the conventional definition of risk are often supported by the claim that the long-term irreversible damage caused to the environment cannot be calculated and therefore a probability-based risk analysis is irrelevant. 'The term "risk" is very often confused with "probability", and hence used erroneously', writes one opponent of genetic modification.[17] From his perspective the threats faced by humankind are so enormous that they are beyond the power of rational calculation. Critics of probabilistic thinking prefer to rely on their intuition and imagination and speculation.

In popular culture and public life, speculative thinking often trumps attempts to deal with uncertainty through probabilistic calculation. Although twenty-first-century society is often characterized as the Knowledge Age, speculative thinking towards the future is based on the principle that what we do not know is far more significant than what we do know. The fear of the unknown serves as justification for policing anyone – scientists, companies, explorers, risk takers – who wish to leap beyond the territory of the known. New innovations and new technology are habitually resisted on the ground that we do not know their side effects and long-term consequences, and society's fear of change is refracted through a palpable mood of suspicion towards experimentation and innovation.

From the perspective of fear, society must be protected from the consequences of innovation and change, even if there is no evidence of potential harm. Once this perspective grips the imagination, any new technology – nanotechnology, genetic modification, fracking, artificial intelligence – will be evaluated from the perspective of its fearful consequences. Scientific innovations are perceived as ticking time bombs, largely because they are new. A few alarmist statements directed at a new technology are all that is needed for it to become a source of dread. The ease with which the moniker 'Frankenstein Foods' displaced the term 'genetically modified crops' in the public imagination of the late 1990s shows how swiftly an exciting new technology can become a target of outrage and condemnation.

The cultural script of fear often relies on the metaphors that highlight the unintended dangerous consequences of new technology. The metaphors 'opening a Pandora's Box' or 'letting the genie out of the bottle' intimate anxiety towards the irreversible damage caused by experimentation and innovation. These metaphors convey a warning about the danger of trespassing into the domain of an uncertain future. As Beck put it, 'with the technologies of the future – gene technology, nanotechnology and robotics – we are opening a new Pandora's Box.'[18]

The perspective of fear encourages society not only to fear, but to fear the worst. It exudes a cultural temper that rejects probabilistic risk analysis because this approach is far too open to the possibility of positive outcomes and opportunities in the future. Opponents of probabilistic risk analysis assert that the world today is so dangerous and complex that society can no longer afford to act on the basis of what is probable; instead, it needs to worry about what is possible. Since in principle just about anything is possible, worst (and least likely) fears become qualitatively indistinguishable from far more likely threats.

The perspective of fear is most coherently expressed through the growing influence of *possibilistic* thinking. Possibilistic thinking invites speculation about what can possibly go wrong. In our culture of fear, what can possibly go wrong is frequently equated with what is likely to happen. This constitutes a uniquely one-dimensional and unimaginative approach towards the uncertainties of the future, which has some direct and disturbing consequences for the trajectory of policy making.

The important role assigned to worst-case thinking by policy makers is often justified on the grounds that the impact of new innovation cannot be calculated. The mantra of 'we simply don't know' is sufficient to eliminate all but the worst-case scenario. Although often linked with environmental concerns, worst-case thinking has emerged as a distinct orientation to the future, which serves as a guide to behaviour in a variety of social settings. As I argued in my 2001 study *Paranoid Parenting*, virtually every childhood experience now comes with a health warning. Parents are expected to assess each experience from the point of view of worst-case scenarios; and once this approach is adopted, the world of children appears as a perilous place. So a playground is seen not as an open space where children can run around, mess about and have fun but as a hostile alien territory, where youngsters face pollution, accidents, bullies and paedophiles.

Parents, of course, have always been concerned about the need to protect their children from harm. Asking what can go wrong is a sensible way of dealing with the numerous experiences that children encounter. But asking what can go wrong is qualitatively different from acting on the assumption that things *will* go wrong. The impact of worst-case thinking on childrearing has had a dramatic effect on the way that children are raised. Fear of the outside world has led many parents to confine their offspring indoors, but fear of threats confronting children online showed that young people are not even safe in their digital bedrooms. The expansive logic of worst-case thinking in relation to the dangers of childhood now dictates the message that children should not be allowed out of their parents' sight. The reorganization of childhood around the anticipation of the worst possible outcome demonstrates that the perspective of fear has a profound influence on how people lead their lives. As most parents intuitively know, the redefinition of risk as a marker for danger has enormous implications for the conduct of family life.

Unfortunately, worst-case thinking encourages the public to perceive a growing range of stuff as harmful. As harm becomes attached to a variety of new phenomena, its very meaning alters. With the rise of speculative thinking, harm has acquired an expansive and boundary-less character. Claims are not confined to toxic contamination and pollution: the pain caused to people through experiencing psychological distress or trauma is represented as a lifelong harm, and people are described as scarred or damaged for life. This expansive definition of harm extends the time span between a distressing episode and its lasting harmful effects.

The expanding timescale of the consequence of a harm turns it into a fearful object from which there can be no escape. Nor is harm confined to the people who directly experience it. A group of scientists has recently concluded that the children of Holocaust survivors are not only psychologically and culturally disoriented, but also genetically altered, by the trauma suffered by their parents 60–70 years previously. A paper published in *Biological Psychiatry* in 2015 concluded that there is evidence of the 'transmission of pre-conception parental trauma to child [sic] associated with epigenetic changes in both generations'. The authors claim their research provides a 'potential insight into how severe psychological trauma can have intergenerational effects'. That's another way of saying that the trauma experienced by Holocaust survivors led to genetic changes in their children. As researcher Rachel Yehuda noted, 'the gene changes' observed among the children of the 32 Jewish men and women studied 'could only be attributed to Holocaust exposure in the parents'.[19] When harms suffered by a parent are seen to alter the genes of their children, this reminds the world that there is no escape from the injuries inflicted a lifetime ago: fear is the only sensible option.

The perspective of fear is tacitly endorsed by most of the main institutions of society. In practice, fear has acquired the status of *a first-order value*. It is a value that legitimates the shift from probabilistic to possibilistic thinking and drives the new narrative of boundless harm. It is a perspective that promotes the spirit of suspicion and mistrust – especially towards science and innovation. As discussed in the following section, it also encourages the emergence of a political culture in which appeals about fear serve to authorize policies and calls for action.

Worst-case thinking is not simply a form of abstract thought. Its approach to risk and to future uncertainty has been transformed into the doctrine of the *Precautionary Principle*. The Precautionary Principle states that when confronted with uncertainty and possible destructive outcomes it is always better to err on the side of caution. As Stern and Wiener explain, 'the Precautionary Principle holds that uncertainty is no excuse for inaction against serious or irreversible risks' and that the absence of evidence should not bar preventive action.[20] This perspective informed the approach of the

European Environment Agency, when it insisted in January 2002 that 'forestalling disasters usually requires acting before there is strong proof of harm.'[21] The exhortation to act without any proof of harm conveys the sentiment that it is sensible to imagine the consequences of change as threatening. But acting on the basis that change constitutes a threat has harms of its own – not least in the extent to which it undermines people's belief in their capacity to influence their destiny.

NEGATIVE THEORY OF AUTHORITY

Commentaries on the politics of fear are far better at pointing the finger of blame at others than exploring this troubling practice in a balanced fashion. Many commentaries only notice evidence of this practice when performed by others. The politics of fear is always a practice conducted by 'them'. Many commentators who deride and criticize others for 'playing the fear card' would be surprised to learn that they, too, are fully involved in this practice. An interesting illustration of the selective approach that many adopt in their deliberation of the politics of fear was provided by a conference held at the New School in New York in February 2004. A host of papers transmitted the sentiment of frustration and anger towards the institutionalization of the politics of fear by the Bush administration in the immediate post 9/11 era. The editor of a special issue of *Social Research*, which published the conference proceedings, was in no doubt that fear was 'encouraged by our government and exacerbated by our media'.[22]

That the journal's editor, Arien Mack, did not have any principled objections to the use of fear as a political instrument was made clear when he stated: 'Fear, of course, also has its positive side, which can be seen when we are asked to be afraid of not only terrorism but also second-hand smoke, bioengineered food, or even diseases, such as SARS or AIDS.'[23] In this naïve and simplistic account, the characteristic double standard applied to the politics of fear was laid bare. For Mack there are two types of fears – positive and negative ones. The 'positive side' of fear relates to causes that the editor supports, and the negative side pertain to policies that he opposes. In his paper titled 'A Life of Fear', George Kateb, Professor of Politics at Princeton University, explicitly endorsed the instrumental use of fear against governments and causes that he opposed. He stated that he did not want 'to direct fear away from terrorists, but to expand the scope of fear to include the American government and its close collaborator Israel'. Calling for 'suspicion and vigilance' against the Bush and Sharon administrations, Kateb conceded that he has no problems with accepting conspiracy theories: 'I would never rule out *a priori* the existence of conspiracy in political life.'[24] From his standpoint, expanding 'the scope of fear' was a legitimate tactic used to support a good cause.

Though concerned with the coercive influence of the politics of fear on public attitudes, the participants at this conference appeared to be more worried about citizens' failure to fear the right things. The critic John Hollander hinted that his fear of the ignorance of the masses matched his concern about the politics of the Bush administration: he asserted that 'one might personally confess to feeling more and more afraid that more people are not afraid that they are being kept in ignorance by a government that rejoices in, and employs, engines of ignorance'.[25] It is likely that Hollander, like his colleagues at the conference, would react with horror if they were reminded of their complicity in the promotion of the politics of fear. No doubt they were convinced that the promotion of fear for their just cause was qualitatively different and morally superior to the politics of fear of their opponents. But imprisoned within the parameters set by the perspective of fear, they only differed on the tactic of how fear ought to be used.

Hollander's aside on his fear that people are not more afraid of being 'kept in ignorance' by their government speaks to a paternalistic mistrust of the American people. In a similar vein, a book titled *The Politics of Fear* by Ruth Wodak is as much devoted to the fears that haunt society as her fear and loathing of populist political movements.[26] In his important study *The Populist Persuasion*, Michael

Kazin noted that in the US during the Cold War, populism became the 'great fear of liberal intellectuals'. These intellectuals blamed mass democracy and an 'authoritarian' and 'irrational' working class for the rise of McCarthyism.

A unique feature of the manner in which anti-democratic sentiments are expressed today is their one-sided reliance on precisely the thing that they criticize: the politics of fear. During the Cold War, liberals within the Democratic Party did not adopt a perspective that explicitly endorsed fear as an instrument of motivation – they made an effort to project a hopeful future. The American president Lyndon B. Johnson's 'Great Society' speech to students in May 1964 offered an outlook of hope that comes across as distinctively alien to the current moment. Johnson stated: 'And with your courage and with your compassion and your desire, we will build a Great Society. It is a society where no child will go unfed, and no youngster will go unschooled.'[27] Johnson's appeal to the motivational force of courage and his idealism about the future indicated that early 1960s liberalism was still invested with hope. In current times, the emphasis has shifted to cultivating people's fears in order to motivate them to adopt desired behaviours.

The politics of fear is often associated with the practices of racist and xenophobic politicians and movements. Alternatively, as portrayed in the discussion at the New School conference above, it is linked to the behaviour of police states or the scare tactics promoted by the right-wing media. But while fear is indeed often politicized by these institutions, the most apologetic and explicit version of the politics of fear comes from other quarters. Since the late 1970s, fear promotion and its politicization has come to be represented as an ethically justified activity, on the grounds that people need to be made afraid of the risks they face in order to get them to act against future threat. Worst-case thinking has led many, especially in the environmentalist movement, to draw the conclusion that, since the activity of people today threatens the future of the planet, the use of fear to restrain their ambition and consumption is a principled endeavour.

This convergence of cultural pessimism and distrust of the masses is most strikingly affirmed by the Precautionary Principle. The philosophical rationale for the Precautionary Principle was most systematically outlined in the works of the German philosopher Hans Jonas, whose influential 1979 text *The Imperative of Responsibility* advocated the instrumental use of fear – what he calls the 'heuristic of fear' – to promote the public's acceptance of a dreadful view of the future. Jonas offers what he perceives to be an ethical justification for promoting fear, which is that through its application, this emotion ought to be used to avoid humankind's infliction of an ecological catastrophe on the planet.

Throughout most of human history, religion played an important role in regulating behaviour and drawing moral boundaries beyond which people could not transgress. To ensure that people behaved according to the moral code, the different religions sought not only to inspire righteous behaviour but also to scare people, particularly the wayward, into submission. That is why holy texts like the Bible can also be seen as a manual of health warnings. As noted in the previous chapters, fear of God, fear of Hell and Damnation, and fear of the Apocalypse provided religious leaders and scaremongers with plenty of material with which to strike terror into the hearts of common folk. Following this tradition, *The Imperative of Responsibility* offers a secular theology designed to tame irresponsible human behaviour.

The Imperative of Responsibility develops a teleology of doom based on the premise that modern technology threatens the world with an imminent threat of disaster. Jonas recycled the classical anti-Enlightenment condemnation of human arrogance, and developed it into a theory of caution. According to his account, people utilizing the power of science have set in motion a chain of events whose destructive consequences cannot be calculated or known. He claims that in these circumstances, the restraint of human activity is the only prudent course of action. But how can human ambition be restrained? Jonas's answer is straightforward: the moralization of fear.

There is no alternative to a dark future of ecological catastrophe, unless humanity fundamentally alters its ways and adopts a culture of austerity. To realize this objective, humankind must abandon its faith in the principle of hope and learn wholeheartedly to embrace the principle of fear. Jonas argued:

> Consequently, an imaginative "heuristics of fear," replacing the former projections of hope, must tell us what is possibly at stake and what we must beware of. The magnitude of those stakes, taken together with the insufficiency of our predictive knowledge, leads to the pragmatic rule to give the prophecy of doom priority over the prophecy of bliss.[28]

In Jonas's prophecy of doom, Freud's concept of expectant fear is transformed into a doctrine.

One of the most conspicuous features of the teleology of doom developed by advocates of worst-case thinking is their reliance on a negative justification for political action and for authority. The claim that people are more likely to be inspired by fear than hope has led to an emergence of a political style that regards scaremongering as the only realistic instrument of political mobilization. Jonas had no doubts on this point, stating that people are much more likely to be moved by the evils that threaten them than by their hopes for a virtuous future: 'We know much sooner what we do not want than what we want. Therefore, moral philosophy must consult our fears prior to our wishes to learn what we really cherish.'[29] This 'fear first' approach highlights the foundational status that Jonas ascribes to this perspective. The logical priority that Jonas attaches to fear is linked to his assertion that what is at stake is nothing less than human survival. He believes that fear must be deployed by any means available, and that the duty of ecologically aware individuals like himself is to construct, through both 'reason and imagination', future scenarios that can 'instil in us the fear whose guidance we need'.[30]

For Jonas, the elevation of ecological survival into an immediate pressing issue had profound implications for public life. He took the view that ecological problems are far too important to be left to the unpredictable outcome of democratic decision-making. His sceptical attitude towards democracy and popular sovereignty was informed by an elitist disdain; he rejected liberal democracy because he was convinced that people would resist attempts to restrain their ambition or accept the lowering of their living standard through the imposition of a regime of austerity.

To realize his project of institutionalizing a regime of austerity, Jonas opted for the rule of a benevolent elite, one that he saw as akin to an ecologically aware Marxist tyranny. But his tyranny would be only Marxist in name, since Marxism is classically associated with developing science, production and consumption. Jonas understood that Marxism was fundamentally alien to his project, but wanted to maintain a Marxist façade while keeping secret the noble elite's commitment to a world organized around restraint. In his advocacy of the promotion of deception by an enlightened elite, Jonas's treatise comes across as a caricature of Plato's *Republic*.

In his *The Imperative of Responsibility*, Jonas is at times aware of the depressing and dehumanizing qualities of his embrace of dishonesty and deception. But he explained: 'perhaps this dangerous game of mass deception (Plato's noble lie) is all that politics eventually have to offer to give effect to the principle of fear under the mask of the principle of hope'.[31]

In this tortured logic, lying acquires the quality of a virtue, and promoting the principle of fear under 'the mask of the principle of hope' is represented as an exercise in ethical responsibility. Jonas argued that in twisting the truth, his noble liars had conjured up a higher truth: 'we are also saying that in special circumstances the useful opinion may be the false one; meaning that, if the truth is too hard to bear, then the good lie must do service'.[32] No doubt Plato would have approved of this latter-day version of the noble lie.

From a sociological perspective, what is most remarkable about the publication of *The Imperative of Responsibility* is not its content but its reception in Western societies. Jonas is frequently regarded as a profound thinker, something of a philosophical saint, whose writings energized the environmental movement in Germany. He is widely promoted as the personification of sensitive and responsible behaviour towards the planet. Astonishingly, his promotion of the principle of fear, his elitist contempt for people, and his advocacy of deception and tyranny, are rarely held to account. Some of his supporters suggest that Jonas's statement of support for eco-tyranny was merely a form of musing about how to deal with the world in case of ecological collapse.[33] Their lack of concern with Jonas's politics of fear and promotion of the noble lie indicates that they, too, accept the view that the politicization of the principle of fear constitutes an exercise in moral responsibility. The very same people who condemn Donald Trump for practising the politics of fear feel that they are exempt from this charge, because their own promotion of doom is for a good cause.

Since the publication of *The Imperative of Responsibility*, the idea that the promotion of fear can serve the legitimate objective of raising awareness about a variety of different ends has been widely endorsed. The politicization of the principle of fear is also frequently advocated on the grounds that it constitutes a singularly important focus for social solidarity. Cynical ideas about negative solidarity – unity based on a common fear of a threat – are advocated on the grounds that it is the most effective way of bringing people together, when society lacks the resources to inspire and mobilize people for the achievement of positive ends. So, despite the numerous criticisms hurled against the politics of fear, there is now a substantial body of opinion that regards the principle of fear as a vital asset for building social solidarity.

The acceptance of the proposition that the use of fear is a legitimate option for raising awareness of a noble cause is increasingly noticeable in academic circles. Some academics who perceive themselves as critical intellectuals are prepared openly to advocate the legitimacy of the politicization of fear. Stanley Cohen, a UK-based criminologist, who elaborated the concept of moral panic to expose the tendency to promote anxiety directed at so-called 'folk devils', personifies the trend towards the embrace of a double standard. At the end of his career, he explored the possibility of using moral panics for positive ends, believing that they could help to bring wrongs denied by the powerful to public attention. Moral panics directed at those who deny torture, injustice, climate change or acts of abuse are often deemed a helpful approach towards motivating people to fear the right problems. In this view, a 'good moral panic' can help to put right moral wrongs.[34]

AVOIDING EVIL

The morally commanding status that supporters of the principle of caution have assigned to the promotion of fear does not simply illustrate the power of this perspective. It also exposes the relative ineffectiveness and irrelevance of other sources of motivation. The reason why so many interests and parties are drawn towards the politics of fear is because, in many circumstances, they are not able to frame their arguments in a more positive language. Invariably, politicians and campaign groups issue ultimatums rather than argument. Their insistence that 'there is only one choice' or 'there is no alternative' is followed by ominous hints of terrible scenarios if their proposals are rejected.

The adoption of the politics of fear by so many different groups and interests is often mistakenly attributed to the autonomous ascendancy of an unprincipled Machiavellian political style. However, such accounts tend to overlook the context within which this has emerged. As discussed previously, the corollary of the rise of the politics of fear was the exhaustion of belief in the principal ideologies and causes of the twentieth century.[35] In the absence of a credible positive vision of the future, society is much more responsive to calls arguing for the avoidance of evil than to appeals of hope.

It was the lack of belief in the capacity to positively motivate undecided citizens that led all sides to adopt a version of Project Fear during Britain's 2016 referendum on membership of the European Union. Both sides criticized each other for playing the fear card, while seemingly oblivious to their own complicity in practising fear politics. Arguments about who lied, what they lied about, and which fear appeals could be validated by empirical evidence, only muddy the waters. Typically, the fiercest arguments revolved around the question of which option – staying in or leaving the EU – would lead to a greater loss. Both sides held back from expounding positive arguments and relied on producing a stream of scare stories.

The recent surfacing of concern about the 'post-truth' and 'post-fact' style is the inexorable consequence of sentiments generated by the politics of fear. The new preoccupation with 'fact checking' is not simply a response to the discovery that politicians sometimes lie, but a statement about the debasement of public language. Suspicion and mistrust have become the default attitude with which political statements are now assessed. The presumption of dishonesty that pervades public life is indirectly an accomplishment of the corrosive effect of the fear perspective.

In most instances, it is unlikely that public figures perceive themselves as the practitioners of the black arts of the politics of fear. They have come to adopt the perspective of fear without very much thought. Their experience has taught them that drawing on people's insecurity is a far more effective way of winning support than appealing to their confidence in the future. As the Canadian commentator and academic Michael Ignatieff explained:

> in the twentieth century, the idea of human universality rests less on hope than on fear, less on optimism about the human capacity for good than on the dread of human capacity for evil, less on a vision of man as maker of his history than of man as the wolf towards his own kind ... A century of total war has made victims of us all, civilians and military, men, women and children alike.[36]

It is difficult to disagree with Ignatieff's assessment of the commanding influence of fear on Western political culture. However, it is important to realize that the pervasive sense of the 'dread of human capacity for evil' is itself a feature of our culture of fear, rather than simply the outcome of a century of total war. As we pointed out earlier, the advent of the authority of fear as a key motivational force occurred in the late 1970s, when pre-existing ideals about positive future possibilities began to give way to the mood of cultural pessimism. The mood of cultural pessimism that arose during this time was preoccupied by the question of survival and in some cases viewed the future as an evil to be avoided. It was in this context that the argument for embracing fear as a positive value, one that could create a consensus on the need to avoid the evils of the future, began to gain traction.

This virtuous representation of the politics of fear was rarely elaborated in an explicit form. The politics of fear had, and continues to have, a bad name – so in most cases, justifications for this political style have tended to be implicit. Even Hans Jonas's call for a 'New Machiavelli' was communicated in an esoteric form, and relied on deception.

The work of the political theorist Judith Shklar stands out for her explicit and unambiguous attempt to develop a positive normative foundation for the politics of fear. Her wholehearted endorsement of the motivational power of fear is based on a secular reconstruction of ancient religious and philosophical ideas about the commanding influence of the fear of death. In adopting the fear of evil as a potential source of unity, Shklar's argument resonates with some of the arguments that Hobbes put forward in defence of using fear to construct social order. However, Hobbes's project was far more ambitious: fear served as a political instrument for the construction of a radically new conception of authority. In line with the temper of the times, the main objective of Shklar's theory is to lower the public's expectations, and encourage them to focus on avoiding evil rather than take risks for the sake of a positive ideal.[37]

Shklar argues for what she calls the 'liberalism of fear', on the grounds that in an uncertain age of terror, fear can unite people against cruelty and injustice. She states that, 'because the fear of systematic cruelty is so universal, moral claims based on its prohibition have an immediate appeal and can gain recognition without much argument'. The proposition that the fear of evil constitutes the moral basis for unity comes across as a justification for avoiding political experimentation and the taking of risk. Shklar justifies her teleology of evil in the following manner:

It does not to be sure offer a *summum bonum* toward which all political agents should strive, but it certainly does begin with a *summum malum*, which all of us know and would avoid if only we could. That evil is cruelty and the fear it inspires, and the very fear of fear itself.[38]

Shklar makes no attempt to acquaint people with the motivational potential of *summum bonum* – the highest good. Instead, her philosophy is directed towards the fear of the *summum malum* – the highest evil – which she perceives as possessing the motivational power to mobilize the public. In a one-dimensional manner, fear is charged with the responsibility of establishing solidarity against the threat of terrorism and cruelty.

It is likely that Shklar would be scandalized by the assertion that her argument for the 'liberalism of fear' represents a coherent version of the politics of fear. She does not see a contradiction between relying on fear as an instrument for mobilizing solidarity, and genuine liberal democratic politics. Her principal preoccupation is with the evil of cruelty afflicting the world, and she believes that the use of fear to get rid of the threats we fear is a legitimate enterprise. Like other versions of the politics of fear, she regards it as a means to the achievement of a higher purpose. But what such high-minded attempts to moralize fear overlook is that the use of this emotion to realize a desired objective does not leave society and its people untouched. People who are rendered fearful are far more likely to withdraw from public life than struggle to achieve active solidarity; and the bonds constructed through fear appeals are unlikely to resemble a public ethos that can override division and fragmentation.

The politics of fear has adopted risk avoidance as one of its key values. Consequently, many policy makers and managers regard high-impact risks as the functional equivalent of Shklar's *summum malum*. The normalization of the fear of risk is continually reinforced and perpetuated through a narrative that depicts risk avoidance as an act of moral duty.

Those drawn towards the project of unifying society around the common project of avoiding evil are convinced that people's anxieties and fears are an important resource for achieving their ends. That is why Beck concluded that the threat of global terrorism has great potential for cultivating solidarity. He contends that, 'in an age where trust and faith in God, class, nation and progress have largely disappeared humanity's common fear has proved the last – ambivalent – resource for making new bonds'.[39] The argument that posits the transformation of 'humanity's common fear' into the 'last' instrument for forging bonds conveys an unashamedly dispiriting message. It forecloses the possibility of humankind evolving a positive vision of the future, and dismisses the possibility of society constructing social bonds around forward-looking goals. Beck articulates this pessimistic sentiment unreservedly, when he asserts that 'basically, one is no longer concerned with attaining something "good" but rather with preventing the worst'.[40]

Yet humanity can only prosper if it strives to attain something that is good. That is why challenging the negative attitudes conveyed by the perspective of fear is so important for our future. Understanding, why this perspective has gained so much traction is the first step towards tackling this problem. As we argue in our final chapter, defying the current regime of fear can liberate the human impulse towards attaining the *summum bonum*.

THE DIVISIVE IMPACT OF THE PERSPECTIVE OF FEAR

Despite the numerous claims that social solidarity can be forged through fear appeals, the pervasive influence of the fear perspective has failed to motivate or galvanize society to unite against the *summum malum*. It has certainly not led to the crystallization of social bonds and of solidarity. Its main achievements are periodic outbursts of fear directed towards specific threats. Short-lived mobilizations in response to an act of pollution compete with campaigns inspired by the fear of fracking. An explosion of anger targeting immigrants vies for attention with displays of outrage directed at criminals and paedophiles. In the current climate, 'evils' come in many shapes and

THE PERSPECTIVE OF FEAR

sizes and people's reaction to them does not follow the same pattern. We do not always fear the same threats and we certainly react to them with varying degrees of intensity. There are a few notable exceptions to this trend – such as the universal fear of the child predator – but by historical standards, the consensus on the meaning of evil is conspicuously fragile.

The idea that the politics of fear is a formidable weapon for mobilizing support and gaining unity often draws on the achievements of strong dictators and totalitarian regimes in the past. There is little evidence that governments that 'play the fear card' today are able to realize their goal and foster a mood of common purpose and solidarity. President Bush and his administration were often accused by their critics of playing the fear card after the destruction of the World Trade Center. Both the Administration and its critics anticipated an enduring phase of public solidarity, yet this proved to be short-lived, and within a few years, a ferocious debate erupted about the conduct of the War on Terror and the invasion of Iraq. In August 2006, a survey of 1,010 adults found that 36 per cent of the American public suspected that federal officials assisted the 9/11 attacks, or took no action to stop them, so that the US could justify going to war in the Middle East. According to this Scripps Howard/ Ohio University poll, a significant number of respondents refuse to believe the official version of events.[41]

The one-dimensional emphasis on avoiding evil that is presented by the politics of fear can foster a climate of risk aversion, but it lacks the motivating force necessary to encourage people to come together. Its main effect is to render people passive rather than to activate them. Indeed, it is the divisive legacy of the perspective of fear that ought to worry those concerned with the problem of social solidarity. The perspective of fear reinforces pre-existing social and cultural patterns, encouraging the privatization and segmentation of social experience.

The most immediate and corrosive side effect of the perspective of fear is the way it unsettles informal relations. The fear perspective does not only provide an outlook for interpreting the big issues of our times – terrorism, the environment, the global financial system – but also for making sense of relationships between people. That is why the climate of suspicion, which is created and sustained by the perspective of fear, has also enveloped the sphere of intimate life.

The crystallization of fear into a distinct perspective has altered the way that human relations – especially close, intimate ones – are perceived. This perspective perpetually invites society to dwell on the theme of the 'human capacity for evil', to which Ignatieff alluded. Such concerns extend into the way that this capacity to inflict harm plays out in the family, friendship groups and other informal settings. Consequently, the decades since the 1980s have witnessed an unprecedented degree of interest directed at the threats that people face from each other in their private lives. Difficulties in a relationship, which would have been categorized under the rubric of 'problems of life', are today designated as 'toxic', 'abusive' or 'dysfunctional'. The widely used metaphor, the 'dark side of the family', invokes a sense of dread about the evils that occur behind closed doors.

The current obsession with the human capacity for evil has led to a fundamental revision of the way that crime is perceived. It is striking how, in the contemporary period, the most high-profile crimes are those most associated with interpersonal relationships: rape, date rape, child abuse, elder abuse, bullying, stalking, harassment, trolling. This grim toll of online and offline crimes reminds us to beware of those closest to us. It is worth noting that many of these behaviours – stalking, harassment, bullying – were not defined as crimes until the 1980s. It was the application of the 'prophecy of doom' towards human relationships that led to the 'discovery' of these crimes. In turn, the discovery that evil stalks interpersonal relationships has had a profound influence over the way that people understand and deal with the problems that arise in their personal life.

The perspective of avoiding evil has acquired its most compelling cause in relation to the threat posed to childhood by sexual predators. People's understandable revulsion against paedophilia has been harnessed by campaigners and transformed into a permanent focus of moral outrage, which features prominently as a theme in popular culture. The paedophile has become the symbol of evil in twenty-first-century society.

According to the cultural script of virtually every Western society, the abusers of children are ubiquitous. Moral entrepreneurs cite large numbers to support the argument that 'all children are at risk'. England's former Deputy Children's Commissioner, Sue Berelowitz, communicated this claim when she declared that 'there isn't a town, village or hamlet in which children are not being sexually exploited'.[42] The moral weight of such claims is rarely contested, since anyone who questions the doctrine of the omnipresence of abuse is likely to be denounced as an appeaser of the child predator.

This script invites the public to regard all strangers – particularly men – as potential child molesters. The concept of 'stranger danger' and the campaigns that promote it have the explicit objective of educating children to mistrust adults that they do not know. This narrative of 'stranger danger' helps to turn the unthinkable into a threat that preys on our imagination, and demands perpetual vigilance. In this perverse way, paedophilia has been turned into a normal feature of life.

The normalization of paedophilia as an existential threat haunting childhood provides a rare example of the mutation of what first emerged as a moral panic in the 1980s into a coherent ideology of evil.[43] Relations between generations are now carefully regulated and policed, to contain the threat of paedophilia. The assumption of 'guilty until proven innocent' provides the foundation for intergenerational relations. Children are often advised not to trust adults and to be wary of 'strangers'.

The subjugation of intergenerational relations to the imperative of 'better safe than sorry' indicates that the Precautionary Principle extends to the most intimate sphere of people's lives. As we explain in the next chapter, the internalization of this outlook on life has led to the cultivation of a fearful mind-set.

5

Creation of the Fearful Subject

The ascendancy of the fear perspective does not only have consequences for the way society approaches uncertainty and the future. It also influences behaviour and ideas about what it means to be a person. People are socialized into internalizing precautionary cultural attitudes, which influence how they regard themselves and their place in the world. Through this process of socialization, people's relationship with the world alters. As suggested earlier, precautionary cultural norms work towards the *expansion of the meaning of harm*. The proliferation of harms, and their representation as far more perilous than previously thought, is consistently recycled in the public domain. Inevitably, people subjected to this expansive version of harm have become disposed towards looking at the world from the perspective of fear. The cultivation of the disposition towards being fearful is incessantly reproduced in all areas of life.

From an early age, people are educated to become preoccupied with their safety, and to regard being fearful as a sensible and responsible orientation towards the world. We are expected to respond positively to fear appeals because it is assumed that fearfulness is our normal state. Paradoxically, socialization into a state of fearfulness coincides with the widely held view that individuals are unlikely to be able to handle their fears. In particular children, but also adults, are not expected to cope with their fears. In recent decades, people's insecure relationship to a world of harms has led to the ascendancy of the assumption that *vulnerability* is the defining feature of the human condition.

Policy makers, opinion formers, and advertisers act on the basis that people are risk averse and feel powerless, and their messages normalize the perception that people are vulnerable. The way society understands harm influences not only the way that they fear, but also the awareness of *who they are*. As such, the metaphor of being 'at risk' has become a self-conscious form of identity. As the sociologist Donileen Loseke explains, the conditions that demand and influence the attention of the public 'often simultaneously construct the types of *people* who inhabit' such conditions.[1] The emergence of the fearful person as the personification of the trends that define the spirit of our times is the subject of this chapter. I argue that the culture of fear is underpinned by a far-reaching redefinition of the meaning of personhood.

PRECAUTIONARY ATTITUDES TOWARDS PERSONHOOD

The expectations that society communicates about human virtues and capacities play a decisive role in the ways that people define themselves and conduct their affairs. As individuals emerge from the womb, become socialized, and develop their sense of self, they incorporate into their behaviour culturally sanctioned notions about what it means to be human. Personhood offers an account of the 'quality or condition of being a person',[2] offering guidance on questions such as, 'are we expected to be scared or brave?', 'should we encourage risk taking and experimentation?' or 'how much distress and disappointment are we expected to manage on our own?' As an account of what constitutes the quality of being a human, the meaning of personhood evolves and alters in accordance with the values that matter to a particular community.

From an early age, the conception of personhood communicated to children shapes the way people interact with the world throughout their lives. Through the process of socialization and education, including the messages transmitted by the media and popular culture, ideas about personhood become crystallized. Views about what people can expect from one another, and how they should respond to uncertainty and change, have important implications for understanding how fear works.

Historically, the attitudes and values pertaining to personhood were based on principles based on morality. These principles were founded on the assumption that people had a moral obligation to respond to threats in accordance with virtues such as wisdom, courage, moderation and justice. Until the early twentieth century, accounts of personhood dictated that people respond to adversity and pain with courage. As Alasdair MacIntyre explains in his influential study, *After Virtue: A Study in Moral Theory*:

> We hold courage to be a virtue because the care and concern for individuals, communities and causes which is so crucial to so much in practice requires the existence of such a virtue. If someone says that he cares for some individual, community or cause, but is unwilling to risk harm or danger on his, her or its behalf, he puts into question the genuineness of his care and concern. Courage, the capacity to risk harm or danger to oneself, has its role in human life because of this connection with care and concern.[3]

As MacIntyre suggests, courage was valued not simply as a character trait but as a form of behaviour that was consonant with the assumption of responsibility for the welfare of others. The expectation that people would respond to harm and danger with courage was integral to the ideal of what constitutes moral behaviour.

The account of personhood offered to people in the twenty-first century is sceptical of the 'capacity to risk harm or danger to oneself'. It certainly does not affirm the value of behaviours that 'risk harm'. Instead of risking harm, people are expected to assess the risks they face before deciding how to respond to them. The obligation to respond to risks by adopting the technique of risk assessment works as a form of technocratic virtue. The obligation to adopt this technique affects the conduct of even the police and the military – the UK-based College of Policing argues that: 'Risk assessments should be completed for all pre-planned operations and should identify hazards that could cause harm to police officers and staff.'[4]

The implication of this approach is that the police are not expected simply to respond to a threat – their action is dictated by the outcome of their risk assessment. However, the College of Policing recognizes a downside: that the negative connotation ascribed to 'risk taking' has 'led to the police service becoming risk averse with some officers and staff afraid to make decisions in case things go wrong'.[5] In effect, the prevailing culture of policing discourages personnel to act on their judgement or to respond to threats on the basis of what they believe is the 'right' course of action. A similar trend is evident in the armed forces. An analysis of casualty aversion in the US military points out that 'as emphasis on risk avoidance filters down the chain of command, junior commanders and their soldiers become aware that low-risk behavior is expected and act accordingly'.[6] The author of this study observed, 'recent studies have revealed the existence in the services of a degree of safety consciousness and focus on risk assessment that reinforces risk aversion in general'.

An aversion to risk is clearly communicated by the guidance on risk assessment offered by the West Mercia Police, which advises its officers: 'Only deliberately enter the water to protect a saveable life and then only after a suitable and sufficient dynamic risk assessment. Consider all other options and relevant factors such as local knowledge and immediate water / waterside conditions.'[7]

Unfortunately, risk-averse attitudes towards saving lives, such as the ones advocated by the West Mercia Police, can have tragic consequences. In May 2007 Jordon Lyon, a ten-year-old boy, died after jumping into a pond to rescue his step-sister from drowning. Two police community support officers failed to help the child. They justified their inaction on the ground that they lacked training in 'water rescue': a decision supported as 'proper' by Great Manchester Police.[8] Official endorsement for the decision to stand by while a child drowned indicates the extent of the police force's preference for the value of risk aversion over courage and a sense of duty.

If two police community support officers draw the conclusion that they are not able or prepared to deal with the risk posed by saving a drowning child, it is likely that the general public will be even more hesitant and fearful about dealing with a risky situation. In this respect, contemporary society has a uniquely low threshold for experiencing harm. The amplification of our fear of harm is paralleled by the normalization of the view that people are powerless to overcome the threats they face. Powerlessness, fragility and vulnerability are the characteristics that resonate with the current representation of personhood.

Society's low threshold for experiencing harm is best captured by the redefinition of the word *uncomfortable* or the expression 'I am not comfortable'. Until recently, this word simply signalled a state of discomfort, unease or disquiet; and a state of discomfort was considered a normal and unexceptional feature of life. It is only lately that people have adopted the view that feeling uncomfortable is unacceptable, and that those people who make them feel this way pose a threat to their wellbeing. This sentiment is currently gaining institutional validation in universities. Support for the introduction of trigger warnings of potentially upsetting texts indicates that sections of the Academy believe that uncomfortable ideas should come with a health warning.[9] In this way, books, ideas or criticisms that make a student feel uncomfortable are portrayed as harmful. Consequently, some students believe that the statement 'I am uncomfortable with your views' constitutes a legitimate argument for closing down discussion and debate.

Contemporary accounts of personhood often convey the assumption that vulnerability constitutes the essence of what it means to be human. The theme of human fragility dominates popular culture. Such sentiments are conveyed in a therapeutic language that suggests that people are 'fragile', 'damaged', 'scarred for life' or 'broken'. 'How did we arrive at this moment in history, in which humanity is more technologically powerful than ever before, and yet we feel ourselves to be increasingly fragile?' asks Claire Colebrook, a Professor of

English at Pennsylvania University.[10] We could re-pose this question by asking, 'Why have we become fearful of hitherto taken-for-granted activities, such as allowing children to walk to school on their own, hitchhiking, sunbathing or drinking tap water?' Probing more deeply, we could explore the question of why problems that were perceived as existential issues in the past – shyness, stress, low self-esteem – have been rebranded as damaging medical pathologies.

Historically the virtue of courage was regarded as the most effective antidote to the corrosive effect of fearing. Western society still holds courage and the display of heroism in high regard. But in everyday practice, we have become estranged from this ideal and do very little to cultivate it. In effect, the ideal of courage has become downsized. In everyday discussion, the term courage has acquired the status of an instrument of self-help. The phrase 'courage to survive' communicates the ideal that the act of living with distress and existential pain is in itself an act of heroism. From a therapeutic cultural worldview, the very ordinary experience of surviving a loss earns the designation of being courageous: indicated by an advertisement for the self-help video *The Courage to Survive: Facing the Loss of Your Soul Mate*.[11]

The contemporary version of courage negates its classical equivalent. The classical virtue of courage rooted it within moral norms that emphasized responsibility, altruism and wisdom. The twenty-first-century therapeutic version is not based on an unshakable normative foundation; it has become disassociated from moral norms and is adopted instrumentally as a medium for achieving wellness. *Mindfulness Pocketbook: Little Exercises for a Calmer Life*, contains a chapter on 'Building Courage', and offers the following self-help tips:

> **Start something new.** It takes courage to learn something new. Take an exercise class, even though you don't know the moves.
>
> Go somewhere you've never been before … 'go to a different restaurant from the ones you usually choose'.
>
> 'Build your courage. Do one thing every day that scares you and feel your courage grow.'[12]

The advice of going to a new restaurant to build 'your courage' would have struck Aristotle and other philosophers as flaky and weird.

For Aristotle, a courageous act had as its aim a noble goal. On this point there is an important divergence of view between the classical and contemporary versions of courage. In an insightful essay, Andrei G. Zavaliy and Michael Aristidou point out that 'there is very little, if any, discussion of the noble goal of an allegedly courageous action by the contemporary authors'. The noble goal is one of the 'constitutive features for the Aristotelian holistic account of this virtue'; yet in current times courage is 'evaluated on its own terms' and 'divorced from the goal that it strives to achieve'.[13]

The claim offered by *Mindfulness Pocketbook* that banal activities such as taking an exercise class or going to a new restaurant are acts of courage communicates the belief that people are naturally fearful, that they have every right to consider going to a new gym or restaurant to be threatening. Other self-help books illustrate how our culture of fear offers a very thin account of courage, where the mere act of looking after oneself is branded as an act of bravery. Titles such as *Courage to Change: One Day at a Time*, *The Courage to Act*, *Courage to Grow*, *Courage to Teach*, *Courage to Shine*, or *Courage to be Chaste*, use the concept of courage as an instrument of therapeutic validation to reward anyone who is prepared to deal with their personal problems. Zavaliy and Aristidou explain that 'the increase in the number of courageous agents is accomplished by widening the category of fear-instilling objects, situations and conditions that can be properly confronted by an agent'.[14] In other words, the representation of the stuff of life as fearful turns its response into heroic acts of courage.

Zavaliy and Aristidou point out that, today, there is a two-fold approach to courage. It is either perceived as the property of the fearless superhero or alternatively as a relatively normal character trait:

There are two extreme approaches to courage that are prevalent in the present cultural mainstream. On one approach, the virtue of courage is seen as a somewhat mysterious vestige of the mythic past, whose proper place is in the epic poems of the ancients, or, perhaps, in movies featuring daring superheroes. The other position sees courageous people filling every police department, fire brigade or professional union, sometimes expanding the attribute to cover whole cities, or even countries. The inflationary tendency of the current media and popular culture, which issues the certificates of courage in bulk quantities, is quite obvious. Both views, we submit, are misguided.[15]

The first of these approaches represents courage as an impossible ideal, while the second debases the idea of courage to the point that it loses its exceptional, virtuous and noble qualities.

Precautionary attitudes towards personhood do not expect fearful people to be able to do much more than deal with the challenges of everyday existence, assuming that the mere act of accepting oneself 'requires the courage to be'. In offering advice on 'How to Have the Courage to be Yourself', Rob Fajardo, a self-styled thought leader, argues that 'the fear of judgment to be one's true self is the most common fear'.[16] The contemporary version of personhood conveys the belief that the fear of judgement can have such a menacing impact on people's emotional wellbeing that it should have no place in civilized society. Thus the fear of judgement is legitimated and, in many circumstances, people are protected from the threat of being criticized. Since the 1960s, the principle of not being judged has been elevated to the status of a core value. In Anglo-American societies, the ideal of non-judgementalism is celebrated as one of the fundamental values of our time.

As one comprehensive survey of American political culture concluded, 'Thou shalt not judge' has become the eleventh commandment of middle-class Americans. Alan Wolfe, the study's author, noted that 'middle-class Americans are reluctant to pass judgment on how other people act and think'.[17] As I explain in the next chapter, the current clash of values in education, and especially in universities, is fuelled by a crusade against judgement, which has come to be portrayed as a threat to the people's sense of self.[18] In order to assuage the fear of judgement, students are offered safe space and speech codes that aim to criminalize 'hurtful' words.

The explicit devaluation of the ideal of judgement can be interpreted as a symptom of society's estrangement from exposing its citizens to uncertainty and risk. Being open to the criticism of others requires that people are prepared to take a risk. In ancient times, judgement was associated with the act of gaining wisdom – not least because of its potentially distressing outcomes. The Roman Stoic Marcus Aurelius remarked that 'if you are distressed by any external thing, it is not the thing that disturbs you, but your own judgement about it', and advised that it was in 'your power to wipe out that judgement'. By contrast, the current claim that students should not have to deal with judgement is based on the proposition that they are too fragile to be expected to deal with its threatening effects, and the advice is to avoid judgement altogether.

In recent times, the harms caused by criticism and judgement have become medicalized, and offensive words are condemned as vehicles of a psychological disease. The claim that language offends is not new; what has altered is the manner in which the state of being offended is portrayed. According to the paradigm that informs university guidelines on speech, offensive language does not merely insult, but also constitutes a risk to the wellbeing of people. 'We always knew that words could hurt our *feelings*, but it turns out that words have a profound effect on our *bodies* as well', claims life coach Linda Pucci in her discussion of 'toxic words'.[19] Fearful attitudes towards words indicates that in our culture of fear, the regulation of language becomes essential for the maintenance of public health.

The contemporary account of personhood pours scorn on stoicism and the ideal of the Stiff Upper Lip. From the standpoint of a medicalized worldview, the Stiff Upper Lip, as a metaphor for the display of fortitude in face of adversity, is ridiculed as a symptom of emotional illiteracy rather than endorsed as a model of strength. The refusal publicly to acknowledge fear and anxiety is often portrayed as the cause and result of psychological problems. Writing in this vein, a group of researchers argued that one reason why the UK lagged behind other countries in the fight to beat cancer was because of its 'stiff upper lip culture'.[20]

SOCIALIZING PEOPLE TO BECOME FEARFUL

The transformation of the meaning of courage and the devaluation of judgement was intimately bound up with changing attitudes towards fear. In the United States, this shift became visible around the turn of the twentieth century; by the 1920s and 30s, it also began to acquire influence in Western Europe. New attitudes towards fear gained momentum in the interwar era and came to dominate the cultural landscape from the late 1970s. Again, it was in the US that the appearance of new rules of fear was first visible, enveloping the rest of the Anglo-American world in the early 1980s.

Stearns believes that this new fear culture stood in sharp contrast to the early nineteenth-century version.[21] Our study of historical sources, including periodicals and advice literature, concurs that the downgrading of the status of courage, and the transformation of the meaning of personhood, gained momentum from the turn of the twentieth century onwards. At this point, unlike in the twenty-first century, the justification for modifying the pre-existing rules of fear was not mainly grounded on the claim that the world had become more dangerous than in the past. The main argument for this change was the belief that most people – especially children – lacked the psychological resources to handle and manage fear. Whereas in the previous century, fear was posited as a state to be overcome, it was now seen as a threat to be avoided. These sentiments were most systematically elaborated by the new, and increasingly fashionable, science of psychology.

Throughout most of the nineteenth century, the prevailing narrative of fear was dominated by the influence of philosophers and theologians. From the late nineteenth century onwards, psychologists gradually began to establish a hegemonic influence over this narrative, and contested the prevailing view. During the Victorian era, young people were taught that in embracing the virtue of courage, they would learn to manage and overcome their fear, and use it to develop their character. In 1848, the Boston based *Christian Register* advised parents that:

> There is nothing in which children differ more than in their capacity for Fear. But every child has it more or less – or ought to have it: for nothing can be made of a human being who has never experienced it. A child who has never known any kind of fear can have no power of imagination:- can feel no wonder, no impulse of life, nor awe or veneration.[22]

The *Christian Register*'s outlook on fear signalled the belief that through character education, the acquisition of moral virtues could overcome the disorienting effect of fearfulness. With its strong moral overtones, character education extolled the virtue of assuming a responsible and disciplined stand in the face of fear.

Around the turn of the twentieth century, the moral authority of character began to be challenged by the discovery of the idea of personality. This development occurred gradually, and it was not until the 1920s and 30s that a psychologically informed concern with personality began to displace the authority of character.[23] Instead of idealizing moral responsibility, personality psychology focused on the emotions of the individual self – and its verdict was that people, especially children, could not be expected to deal with the emotion of fear on their own. The cultural shift from character to personality was influenced by a view of human nature that highlighted the threat posed by the power of the emotions. Fear, in particular, was singled out as a threat whose management required the intervention of psychologically informed experts. The new psychological approaches to childhood depicted children as far more fragile than had previously been thought, and their fear as a serious problem that needed to be carefully controlled. Stearns points to a new tone of advice, 'in what became a more systematic effort to portray children as emotionally vulnerable'.[24]

By the 1920s, a psychologically informed narrative of fear began to influence the mainstream of society. The most significant impact of these changes was on society's approach to the socialization of children, but it gradually moved to embrace adults too. Stearns notes that in the 1920s, 'fear became a major problem', its elimination a 'major goal' first 'for children then for adults'.[25]

Guidance on the socialization of children suggested that fear was a complex and dangerous problem, and charged adults with the task of ensuring that children did not have to face fearful situations. This new approach towards childrearing often adopted the stance of explicitly repudiating the previous rules of fear, arguing that their methods were scientific and modern. One London-based publication adopted this approach in its article titled, 'The Conquest of Fear: Modern Methods in the Nursery'. This informed 'mother and nurse' to 'avoid all reason for rousing fear', and that 'while they are still small more harm than good is done by insisting that small boys, as opposed to small girls, must be brave and bold'.[26] As an object of socialization, the cultivation of the virtue of courage became less and less important during the succeeding decades.

'Modern' parenting advice stressed the importance of protecting children from situations that might frighten them. A discussion on 'Nerves in the Nursery' warned that 'even children are now "Suffering from Nerves"'. It advised that 'nervousness can be cured but never by ridicule, anger, or sternness', and added that parents should ensure 'never to "suggest" fear in children'.[27] Scare stories about the danger of parents failing to protect children from exposure to experiences that might frighten them often concluded with the warning that they risked inflicting lifelong emotional scars on their offspring. One of the most prominent behavioural psychologists of the era, James Watson, asserted that 'the main job of the parent should be to prevent fears, since some fears are extremely difficult to cure'.[28] Parents were also instructed not to show their fears lest their children internalize this emotion.

Criticism of traditional approaches towards the management of children's fears was characteristically unrestrained. Its fire was particularly directed at incompetent mothers. One advice columnist asked:

Why will some mothers persist in the senseless practice of frightening little children into obedience? One would think that in this day of enlightened motherhood, and a day when mothers can learn by reading and observation of the proper method to adopt in childrearing, that this practice would cease.[29]

Criticism of parents' mismanagement of their children's fears often acquired the character of scaremongering, accusing parents of failing to understand their children's fragile emotional state. 'The average mother of to-day understands these mental and spiritual enemies, these psychological foes lurking to prey upon her child as little as her grandmother understood the physical danger of germs', wrote a commentator in December 1922.[30]

As this new narrative of childhood vulnerability gained influence in the 1920s and 30s, threats to children's mental health were highlighted as the principal problem of childrearing. One of these threats allegedly came from parents' incompetent behaviour. After noting that a 'new disease has made its appearance in our midst', George Draper observed that 'it is not the crippling of the muscles but of the spirits of children'. Draper criticized parents for putting too much pressure on their children, warning that 'at various points along this thorny pathway which leads from the nursery to the college degree, children and adolescents are breaking down under the strain'.[31]

The calls for isolating children from fear were integral to a fundamental reorientation towards the practice of childrearing. Parents were told to validate their children, to encourage them rather than reprimanding or putting them under pressure. These attitudes were also embraced by a section of the educational establishment, who argued that too much pressure on pupils would heighten children's sense of anxiety and fear. Indirectly, the 'modern' advice on childrearing often had the effect of making parents anxious about their competence to bring up a child successfully, leading them to offer validation of their child's behaviour while reducing pressure and discipline.

The ascendancy of a new orientation towards insulating children from their fears often raised the concern that modern practices spoiled children, and made them unnecessarily fearful of facing the challenges they faced. Bertrand Russell counselled parents to adopt a more nuanced approach: in his essay 'Your Child and the Fear of Death', written in 1929, he wrote that, 'The place of stoicism in life has perhaps been somewhat underestimated in recent times, particularly by progressive educators.' Russell regarded the Stoic ideals of relying on courage to negate the power of fear as offering an important legacy, and tried to find a middle way between the harsh disciplinary practices of the past and the indulgent tactics of childrearing advocated by the 'modern experts'. 'Whoever has to deal with young children soon learns that too much sympathy is a mistake,' he wrote – arguing, on the other hand, that 'too little sympathy is, of course, a worse mistake, but in this, as in everything else, each extreme is bad'.[32]

At first, it was only a minority of mainly middle-class parents who took on board the call to soften discipline and constantly reassure their children. But gradually, the adoption of therapeutic techniques to deal with children's fears instead of relying on the cultivation of courage became equated with the practice of responsible parenting. In public rhetoric, bravery, risk taking and courage were still celebrated, but the old rules of fear gradually unravelled in the face of the challenge posed by a new therapeutic orientation. From the 1940s onwards, the new emotional culture of fear entered the mainstream and its ideals were frequently communicated through sections of the media and popular culture. At least in the United States, according to Stearns, by the 1940s these new emotional rules were 'translating into actual socialization, in ways that would affect both the evolution and the experience of fear'.[33] The new rules of fear were most noticeable in schools, where modern pedagogy insisted that children should be relieved of the burden of too much pressure. With the passing of time, the medicalization of the fear response spread to the workplace and other sectors of society.

Though the psychologically informed and medicalized interpretation of personhood advanced steadily throughout the twentieth century, it often had to coexist with more old-fashioned and traditional views of what it meant to be human. From time to time the new rules of fear faced a backlash from the more traditionally minded section of society. The exigency of military conflict during the Second World War meant that people were mobilized to embrace the values of bravery and courage, and encouraged to stand up to their fears. It is likely that only a minority of parents and schools were prepared to fully adopt the new wisdom regarding childhood fears in the 1940s and 50s; Stearns suggests that it was only when the children who were socialized into the new rules of fear grew up that their influence came to dominate the outlook of the mainstream.[34]

During the 1970s, the triumph of the new rules of fear became increasingly evident. The rise of an ethos that legitimized fearfulness as the normal state was coterminous with the decline of the values associated with classical virtues, such as loyalty, heroism, commitment and sacrifice. In his superb study of this important cultural shift, Christopher Lasch attributes this development to the prominence that Western societies in general and America in particular came to give to the question of survival. One symptom of the obsession with survivalism was the normalization of crisis and a tendency to perceive every issue, no matter how 'fleeting or unimportant', as a 'matter of life or death'.[35] The tendency to inflate risk and danger was paralleled by the idealization of safety and survival as values in their own right. From this perspective, the exaltation of heroism and courage by previous generations was entirely incomprehensible. 'Survivalism leads to a devaluation of heroism', remarked Lasch. He noted that other values were also discarded, such as the 'entire stock of allegedly outworn ideals of honor, heroic defiance of circumstances, and self-transcendence'.[36] This fearful, survivalist outlook towards life would soon lead people to declare proudly, 'I Am a Survivor'. As Coker noted, 'in our post-heroic times survival is considered the act of real moral or emotional worth.'[37]

The new mood of survivalism identified by Lasch was symptomatic of a new cultural setting, in which the acknowledgement of people's fears and anxieties was validated and normalized. Gradually, the presumption that people should be protected from fear migrated from the nursery to the workplace. One of the most fascinating and yet unremarked illustrations of this trend was the redefinition of the meaning of bullying. Throughout most of the twentieth century, the problem of bullying tended to be interpreted as a distressing feature of childhood. But suddenly, from the 1990s onwards, a distressing feature of childhood was discovered also to be a menacing condition of adulthood. One survey after another reported that bullying had reached epidemic proportions in the workplace.[38] Teachers complained that parents frequently bullied them. Campaigners argued that bullying caused not only distress but also serious mental health problems. In Australia in 2012, the Productivity Commission estimated the total cost of workplace bullying in Australia at between $6 billion and $36 billion annually. At the time, the Workplace Relations Minister, Bill Shorten, described workplace bullying as a 'secret scourge that was far too common'.

Claims-makers drawing attention to the 'secret scourge' of bullying drew on the new rules of fear that presumed that individuals had to be protected from the consequences of the distress caused by interpersonal aggression and tension. The first step in the medicalization of interpersonal interaction was to elevate the perils of bullying; from the 1980s onwards, anxiety about bullying in schools grew steadily until it became defined as one of the central threats facing children. Fear of their child being bullied has become one of the main concerns cited by parents.[39] In line with the new rules of fear, children are no longer encouraged to stand up to bullies – instead they are instructed to rely on parents and teachers to sort out the problem.

As noted previously, during the 1990s the problem of bullying migrated into the adult world.[40] The swiftness with which a term that had for so long been confined to childhood became internalized as also a condition of adulthood was astonishing. No one seemed to ask the question of why a hitherto unpleasant but widespread experience of adult life came to be branded as 'bullying', nor were queries raised about the infantilized version of adulthood conveyed through the designation of 'being bullied'. The bullied adult personifies the sense of personhood communicated through our culture of fear.

Workplace bullying covers a multitude of sins. Virtually any negative or uncivil encounter can be, and often is, defined as bullying. The term encompasses sarcastic put-downs, vandalism, crude gestures, the withholding of information, even 'smiling the wrong way'. Unwanted eye contact, acts that belittle an individual, and flaunting one's status can also be described as bullying, as can acts of miscommunication. Nor does it matter whether a person intended to bully a colleague: widely accepted definitions of bullying insist that these acts are determined by the victim's feelings rather than the intention of the person accused of committing the offence. The Australian Medical Association defined bullying in the following terms: 'Sometimes bullying is deliberate, and intended to make a person upset. But it can sometimes still be bullying if someone repeatedly acts in ways to make a person upset or frightened, even if it is not deliberate.' According to this definition, what defines a bully is not the intention of the alleged bully, but the perception of the alleged victim. The argument that one did not intend to cause distress provides no defence against the charge: the pain caused by the unwitting bully is considered no less harmful than the harm inflicted on a victim by an intentional act.

The sudden discovery of bullying as a pervasive feature of workplace culture was rarely contested. The speed with which the bullying of adults was integrated into the vocabulary of the culture of fear showed that what used to be perceived as 'office politics' or as unpleasant workplace encounters were now depicted as menacing acts of victimization. This shift in the meaning of bullying was propelled by the transformation of social attitudes towards the meaning of personhood. The assumption that fragile adults – and adults were, by definition, fragile – needed to be protected from the harmful comments, gestures and behaviour of their colleagues had acquired the status of common sense.

The current narrative of bullying not only erases the distinction between adult and child – it turns this distressful experience into the condition of human existence. This climate of intimidation, where bullies flourish and millions live in a life of fear, has become yet more insidious with the appearance of 'cyber-bullying'. According to NOBullying.com, which claims to be 'The World's Authority on Bullying':

> America is suffering from a bullying epidemic. Bullies appear everywhere, from playgrounds to the hallway, in public restaurants and even online. The Internet has made it easy for bullies to harass and stalk their victims without suffering any repercussions. Once a bully gets into your head, it's extremely difficult to get him/her out. Bullying victims become constantly on edge, even if the bully is not physically present. They might suffer from paranoia, depression and panic attacks. Bullying happens not only to children, but to people of all ages and different social backgrounds. One of the most disturbing bullying statistics in 2013 by Safe Work Australia (SWA) found out that Australia has the highest workplace bullying rates all over the world. The report also stated that Australian employers lost $8 billion a year due to absenteeism and sickness, of which $693 million were caused by workplace bullying.[41]

The evocation of a world in which people are in constant fear of being bullied relies on a redefinition of the intensity and scope of all the negative experiences confronting people, and the impact of these experiences upon them. This new epidemic is constructed through the invention of a continuum of bullying that encompasses everything from an unpleasant remark online to an act of physical violence. Being bullied is the fate of the fearful subject socialized into the culture of fear.

THE DEVALUATION OF ADULT AUTHORITY

A number of accounts link the changing contours of socialization and the rise of new rules of fear to the authority that psychology achieved over the conduct of human relations. The new psychological explanations of human nature and personhood did indeed play a significant role in establishing fear as a major mental health problem, especially with regard to children.[42] Psychology, with its therapeutic values, rapidly succeeded in displacing many of the pre-existing norms.

However, simply focusing on the rapid expansion of psychology can detract attention from an equally significant development: the estrangement of adults from values that they themselves were socialized into. From the turn of the twentieth century onwards, a significant section of adult society became less and less able or willing to socialize children into the values upheld by the previous generations. This trend was particularly noticeable in the school, where pedagogy diverted its emphasis from character education towards a more psychologically informed teaching style.

The estrangement of many adults from the values upheld by their parents was paralleled by a discernible reaction against traditional education by 'modern' pedagogy. When, at the outbreak of the Great War in 1914, the *Times Educational Supplement* noted that 'every great war in the modern world has been followed by changes in education', it probably had little idea of the scale of the impending revolution in the classroom.

One of the most significant outcomes of the First World War on schooling was to strengthen the influence of so-called progressive education. The progressive critique of traditional values resonated with the mood of revulsion and demoralization that prevailed in the post-First World War era. At this conjuncture, calls to break with the past possessed significant cultural appeal, and many educators hoped that their progressive ethos could help create a brave new world through the influence they exerted on children. From their perspective, the older generations were beyond redemption. The ideal of child-centred education flourished alongside the growth of post-war disenchantment with the moral status of adulthood.

The arguments supporting child-centred education expressed the sensibility of demoralization and disorientation of a significant section of the cultural elites. As one important study of this period explains, 'among many of the progressives can be detected the feeling that modern Western civilization, and especially that part of it which was industrial and urban, had become corrupt'.[43] One significant manifestation of this sensibility was hostility to the prevailing forms of authority – including the authority of the adult over the lives of children.

The clearest expression of the waning of confidence in adult authority was a perceptible hesitancy and reluctance to take responsibility for the socialization of the younger generations. This reluctance to transmit the experience and legacy of the past to the young was particularly widespread among progressive educators in the interwar era. As R. J. W. Selleck noted in his study *English Primary Education and the Progressives: 1914–1939*, this group of educators were 'distressed and alienated' by the values that prevailed at the time and 'they shied away from imprinting the future generation with the marks of the present'. J. H. Nicholson, a Professor of Education at Newcastle University, forcefully articulated this sentiment. He lamented that 'we are an uneasy generation, most of us to some extent ill-adjusted to present conditions' and 'should therefore beware of passing on our own prejudices and maladjustments to those we educate'.[44]

At least for a significant section of the cultural elites and educators, the First World War called into question the norms and values that underpinned the exercise of adult authority. Scepticism about the moral status of the prevailing values had important implications for the conduct of intergenerational relations. It had a particularly direct impact on education, but similar trends were evident in the sphere of childrearing, where parents looked to new experts to instruct them in the science of parenting. In his 1953 sociological classic *The Lonely Crowd: A Study of the Changing American Character*, David Riesman noted that as adults felt less and less certain about 'how to bring up children', they opted to retain control through adopting techniques of psychological manipulation.[45]

At the time, it was the political philosopher Hannah Arendt who made the most important statement on the implication of the loss of adult authority. She informed a 1956 meeting of the American Society for Political and Legal Philosophy that 'authority has vanished from the modern world, and that if we raise the question what authority is, we can no longer fall back upon authentic and undisputable experiences common to all'.[46] To emphasize the dimension of the issues at stake, Arendt drew attention to an unprecedented development, which was the 'gradual breakdown of the one form of authority', which existed in 'all historically known societies, the authority of parents over children, of teachers over pupils and generally of the elders over the young'.[47] She observed that this form of authority 'required as much by natural needs, the helplessness of the child, as by political necessity' was always accepted by society. However, she added, 'ours is the first century in which this argument no longer carries an overwhelming weight of plausibility and it announced its anti-authoritarian spirit more radically when it promised the emancipation of youth as an oppressed class and called itself the "century of the child"'.[48] Although Arendt did not directly touch on the implications of the loss of adult authority on the process of socialization, she provided an important contribution for understanding the radical revision of the relationship between the older generation and the young.

The hesitant and defensive manner in which the task of socialization is pursued has created a demand for new ways of influencing children. A lack of clarity regarding the transmission of values has led to a search for alternatives, and the adoption of psychologically informed practices of behaviour management served as one influential approach.[49] From the standpoint of such expert-directed techniques, the role of parents is not so much to transmit values as to validate the feelings, attitudes and accomplishments of their children.

Though parents continue to do their best to transmit their beliefs and ideals to their children, there is a perceptible shift from instilling values to the provision of validation. Affirming children and raising their self-esteem is a project that is actively promoted by parents as well as schools. This emphasis on validation has run in tandem with the custom of a risk-averse regime of childrearing. The (unintended) consequence of this regime has been to limit opportunities for the cultivation of independence and to extend the phase of dependence of young people on adult society. Protecting the infantilized child from harm has become the main responsibility of the modern parent.

The socialization of young people has become increasingly reliant on therapeutic techniques that have the perverse effect of encouraging children and youth to interpret existential problems as psychological ones. Concern with children's emotions has fostered a climate where many young people are continually educated to understand the challenges they face through the language of mental health. Not surprisingly, they often find it difficult to acquire the habit of independence and make the transition to forms of behaviour associated with the exercise of moral autonomy.

The complex emotional tensions that are integral to the process of growing up are now discussed as stressful events with which children and young people cannot be expected to cope. Yet it is through dealing with such emotional upheavals that young people learn to manage risks and gain an understanding of their strengths and weaknesses. Instead of being encouraged to acquire an aspiration for independence, many youngsters are subject to influences that promote childish behaviour. This is the unintended outcome of parenting practices that rely on levels of support and supervision that are more suitable for much younger children, but are now encouraged even in higher education settings.

Neil Howe and William Strauss, authors of *Millennials Go to College*, note that the millennial generation is characterized as 'closely tied to their parents' and insistent of a 'secure and regulated environment'. Their book predicted that in the future, parental involvement in higher education would increase and would lead to an explicit partnership between students, parents and university authorities.[50] Their argument has as its premise the claim that, unlike previous generations, the current cohort of students finds it difficult to flourish in the less structured environment of the university.

Ensuring that they do not feel uncomfortable during the journey – or 'transition' – to adulthood is fast becoming one of the missions of higher education.

THE FEARFUL CHILD

Ideas about human fragility and vulnerability are most consistently developed through society's fears about the state of childhood. In modern times, the adult world has often found itself concerned and, at times, troubled by threats to children. But since the 1990s, fears about childhood have acquired an unprecedented power, and children are invariably portrayed as fundamentally fragile individuals who need to be protected from the threats posed by pressure, criticism, stress and fear. At times, concerns about the fragility of the child have become caricatures of themselves. In Australia, educators have been advised to cease marking children's homework in red pen because it 'can damage students'. Teachers were instructed to 'correct homework in less aggressive colours like green and blue, in an attempt to improve mental health in the classroom'.[51] A similar approach is used by teachers in Britain, where many teachers no longer put a cross next to a mistake, to avoid causing distress. The claim that a red pen poses a threat to children's wellbeing is based on the widely held view that children are defined by their weakness and are easily damaged by the distress caused by unpleasant experiences.

Anxieties about the precarious state of childhood mean that fear constantly lurks in the background, and discussion and debate on education is far more influenced by fear than by hope. Fear of fragile identities, fear of failure, fear of low self-esteem, fear of falling standards, fear of the pernicious effects of exams on students' mental health, fears about competition and competitive sports, and fear about discipline are recurring themes in debates on education. Often these fears are ratcheted up and anxieties about the fragile child acquire a life of their own. It is as if the adult world must attach a health warning to every new challenge facing children.

Take the trend towards depicting the transition from primary to secondary school as a frightening episode. Not so long ago it was assumed that children impatiently looked forward to going to the Big School. That was then. Today, according to one account:

> researchers, teachers and policy makers regard the transition from primary to secondary schools as so 'unsettling, daunting, stressful' that it can de-motivate up to 40 per cent of 11-year-olds badly enough 'never' to recover, thereby causing a marked dip in formal achievement.[52]

This catastrophic representation of an experience that was previously regarded as unproblematic is ceaselessly communicated through a language that emphasizes the unbearable psychological burdens borne by children. The primary–secondary transition is sometimes expressed through the processes associated with loss, mourning and grief. Some experts advise secondary schools to provide pupils with the means to experience 'closure'.

The emergence of vulnerability as the defining feature of childhood should be interpreted as a sublimated expression of adult concerns about human fragility. Until the 1980s, concerns about children's capacity to manage their fears coexisted with the belief that most young people possessed the resilience required to deal with adversity. But the tone of discussions about the state of childhood began to change, and increasingly the language adopted to deal with this issue acquired a febrile and dramatic character. The rhetoric of alarm directed at young people is most dramatically captured by the career of the term 'vulnerable children'. Today, this term is so widely used that it is easy to overlook the fact that it is a relatively recent invention.

Until the 1970s, the term 'vulnerable children' was used rarely, and mainly in social work literature. In the 1960s, a report published by the Michigan Youth Commission used the term 'to describe those children and youth who are particularly susceptible to anti-social behaviour'.[53] The authors of this report surrounded the word 'vulnerable' in quote marks and drew attention to the unusual use of this word. But with the rise of our culture of fear, 'vulnerable children' swiftly entered the vernacular. A search of the Nexis database found only nine references to this term during the 1970s. Its first recorded usage was on 16 November 1972 in the *New York Times*, where it was used to refer to children vulnerable to 'mental and emotional hazards'.[54] In the 1980s, references rose to 141; by the 1990s, to 3,266. But during the first decade of the twenty-first century, references to 'vulnerable children' had exploded, to 33,566; and in 2016 alone – the last year for which we have completed data – there were 17,781 references to this term.[55]

A study of the emergence of the concept of vulnerable children shows that in most published literature, it is treated 'as a relatively self-evident concomitant of childhood which requires little formal exposition'. It is a taken-for-granted idea that is rarely elaborated, and 'children are considered vulnerable as individuals by definition, through both their physical and other perceived immaturities'. Moreover, this state of vulnerability is presented as an intrinsic attribute: it is 'considered to be an *essential* property of individuals, as something which is intrinsic to children's identities and personhoods, and which is recognisable through their beliefs and actions, or indeed through just their appearance'.[56] As such, vulnerability represents both a statement about children's identity, and operates as a cultural metaphor used for endowing childhood with meaning.

But, of course, vulnerability does not end with childhood. As children pass through the different stages of the life cycle, they turn into adults who bear the stamp of vulnerability. The recent popularization of the term 'vulnerable students' on university campuses indicates how this pessimistic account of children's capacities is recycled and applied to older students, while the growing usage of the term 'vulnerable adults' indicates that this sentiment of fragility and powerlessness informs the current version of personhood and human nature.

As such, the defining feature of the current Western twenty-first-century version of personhood is its *vulnerability*.[57] Although society still upholds the ideals of self-determination and autonomy, the values associated with them are increasingly overridden by a message that stresses the quality of human weakness. And if vulnerability is, indeed, the defining feature of the human condition, it follows that being fearful is the normal state.

The changing pattern of socialization and its influence on fearing evolved over many decades. The new emotional landscape that highlighted the pre-eminence of fragility and vulnerability coincided with the climate of survivalism and risk aversion in the late 1970s. Stearns argues that 'it takes two generations, at the least, to integrate new emotional standards under normal circumstances'. It was only when the children who were socialized into the new emotional standards of validation grew up and began to influence their own offspring that the orientation towards a psychologically informed narrative of vulnerability and fear could acquire cultural hegemony.[58]

LITERALLY SCARED OF THE NEWBORN

Vulnerability reflects a loss of belief in humanity's potential to deal with adversity. Such pessimistic sentiments have often mutated into the belief that, rather than being problem solvers, people are often the problem. In the current era, a tangible sense of mistrust of human motivation often accompanies the mood of vulnerability. Calls to protect the vulnerable often direct their concerns at threat posed by other people. So, for example, claims about an epidemic of workplace bullying explicitly transmit the idea that human relationships are perilous. 'Humans are aggressive by nature,' argues NoBullying.Com, before asserting that bullying has 'probably been with us since the dawn of time'.[59] Thomas Hobbes, who described the state of nature as 'nasty, brutish and short', and elaborated a comprehensive politics of fear on the grounds that it was essential to restrain the destructive side of human nature, would have approved of this statement.

The representation of aggression as the natural feature of the human condition is ceaselessly dramatized through films, novels and other media. Interpersonal violence and various forms of domestic abuse are the staple theme of popular drama and films. We talk about 'toxic relationships', 'toxic parents' and 'toxic families'. Indeed, scare stories about the risks of human relationships are often very similar to discussions about the environment. The metaphor of toxicity is so frequently applied to childhood that one is entitled to wonder how children ever survive it.

The cultural dynamic of diseasing childhood has become so unrestrained that attempts to counter it are often denounced as irresponsible. One rare example of a politician attempting to respond to the constant promotion of fears towards childhood was the former UK Secretary of State for Children, Schools and Families, Ed Balls. In November 2007, he issued a statement arguing that childhood was 'not toxic' but 'better than it's ever been'.[60]

Fear directed at childhood should be interpreted as an indirect expression of a fear of ourselves. After all, it is adults, particularly parents, who are held responsible for the damaging injuries inflicted on children. If bullying is indeed an integral feature of human nature, than we are all entitled to fear one another. Not since the Dark Ages has there been so much concern about the malevolent passions that afflict humanity. Predatory monsters are seen everywhere, and people regard others with a suspicion that would have been rare just a few decades ago. Parents wonder whether the day-care centre workers looking after their children can be trusted; in schools, children with bruises arouse teachers' suspicion about their parents' behaviour, while parents wonder whether any physical contact between their child and his or her teacher is permissible. In the UK, any adult employee who might come into contact with children has to undergo a police check, and sections of the child protection industry believe this police vetting should be extended to the university sector, too.

As noted previously, numerous accounts of the time bomb scenario raise fundamental questions about threats to human survival. But the big question today is not whether humans will survive the twenty-first-century – it is whether our *faith in humanity* will survive it. As Ignatieff points out, the 'dread of human capacity for evil' offers an important resource for policy makers and campaigners.[61] The dread of the human capacity for evil is widely encouraged in virtually all contemporary threat narratives. Harari gave voice to a sensibility that verges on misanthropy, when he dismissed people's fears of 'massive volcanic eruptions or colliding asteroids' and stated that 'instead of fearing asteroids, we should fear ourselves'.[62]

King Herod's fear of the newborn was confined to one baby. Today's misanthropic fear entrepreneurs have cast their net wider. One Australian Professor of Obstetric Medicine believes that the survival of the planet demands stringent controls over the number of children parents can have. This is what Barry Walters has to say:

Anthropogenic greenhouse gases constitute the largest source of pollution, with by far the greatest contribution from humans in the developed world. Every newborn baby in Australia represents a potent source of greenhouse gas emissions for an average of 80 years, not simply by breathing, but by the profligate consumption of resources typical of our society. What then should we do as environmentally responsible medical practitioners? We should point out the consequences to all who fail to see them, including, if necessary, the ministers for health. Far from showering financial booty on new mothers and thereby rewarding greenhouse-unfriendly behaviour, a 'Baby Levy' in the form of a carbon tax should apply, in line with the 'polluter pays' principle.[63]

Throughout history, different cultures have celebrated birth as a unique moment signifying the joy of life. The reinterpretation of this event as 'greenhouse-unfriendly behaviour' speaks to an imagination in which carbon reduction trumps respect for the human life. Once every newborn baby becomes dehumanized as a professional polluter who is a 'potent source of greenhouse gas emissions', it becomes very difficult not to feel apprehensive about the threat posed by the growth of the human race.

A distinct feature of our culture of fear is its intense suspicion of the human species. Sooner or later, scaremongering becomes directed at ourselves. The systematic transmission of suspicion and fear inexorably leads to the promotion of mistrust of people's motives and, in the end, to the mistrust of people themselves. As potential polluters, babies cease to be those lovely cuddly things that bring so much joy to our lives. Robbing babies of what we perceive to be their endearing innocence makes it easier to scare people from having them, or 'too many' of them. Whereas babies used to be frequently depicted as a blessing, now the refusal to have them is depicted as a blessing for the planet.

This reversal in the regard for human life is explicitly advocated by the environmentalist writer Kelpie Wilson. Wilson presents abortion not so much as a necessary option to allow women to determine their lives, as a sacrifice well worth making in the interests of the environment. 'To understand that a tiny embryo must sometimes be sacrificed for the greater good of the family or the human species as a whole is the moral high ground that we stand on today,' she argues, because 'we have to consider how we will live tomorrow on a resource-depleted and climate compromised planet.' From Wilson's perspective, abortion is morally justified as a resource-saving strategy: she believes that 'most women who seek abortions do so in order to conserve resources for children they already have'. In this vein, scare stories about the 'physical limits of the planet' are presented as 'moral arguments about abortion'.[64]

The catastrophic imagination that underpins twenty-first-century Western culture has encouraged promoters of the idea that the growth of humanity is the mother of all time bombs to target the very aspiration for procreation. Controlling fertility is advocated as a matter of duty, not choice. 'Couples making decisions about family size do so in the belief that it is a matter for them and their personal preferences alone,' states a population control advocacy group with incredulity.[65] The idea that people ought to have the right to make choices about their family size is dismissed as an outrage.

But let us consider the meaning of this. Since the beginning of time, one of the clearest markers of an enlightened civilized society is the moral status it attaches to human life. Outwardly, twenty-first-century Western society expresses an unprecedented degree of affirmation for human life. This is an age where the principle of human rights is extolled by the dominant cultural and political institutions, and the phenomenal growth in health expenditure provides evidence of the importance that prosperous societies affix to human wellbeing. Western societies can go to extraordinary lengths to keep alive a premature baby or to prolong the life of the elderly and chronically ill.

And yet the ethos of human rights and heroic medicine exists in an ambiguous relationship with contemporary's society's estrangement from its own humanity. To put it bluntly: it is difficult to celebrate human life if society fears the growth of the number of people on earth. A message transmitted ceaselessly by our culture of fear is that people should fear themselves and their fellow human beings. This misanthropic outlook is one of the main drivers of society's obsessive preoccupation with safety: the subject of our next chapter.

6

The Quest for Safety in a Dangerous World

Safety is more highly valued than any other condition in the culture of fear, acquiring the status of a moral good that trumps all others. Reports indicate that Americans are prepared to exchange their privacy online for safety.[1] In the name of safety, parents are willing to give away the freedom of their children to explore the outside world without adult supervision. Numerous universities argue that policing speech is a small price to pay for ensuring that students' safety is protected from offensive words. Sections of the public will exchange existing freedoms for the security promised by the authors of a growing number of anti-terrorist laws.

Donald Trump has turned the dramatization of the rhetoric of safety into a veritable art form. His constant refrain that America was unsafe was matched by his boast that only he could keep the people safe. In accepting his nomination for US president at the 2016 Republican National Convention, Trump asserted: 'I have a message for all of you: the crime and violence that today afflicts our nation will soon — and I mean very soon — come to an end. Beginning on January 20th 2017, safety will be restored.'[2] The vision evoked by Trump's campaign rhetoric is of an America that is broken and unsafe. His promise that 'we will make American safe again' directly resonated with the premise of the culture of fear. His critics described this statement as a 'dark, dark convention speech'. Florida Congressman John Mica responded that this 'emphasis on safety and security' is 'a message that will resonate'.[3]

Critics of Trump's depiction of a toxic and unsafe America indict this man as a practitioner of the politics of fear who opportunistically manipulates people's anxiety. But beyond Trump, the rhetoric of safety has acquired the status of a commanding narrative in many parts of the world, to the point where it has a quasi-religious quality.

Thousands of company websites declare their adherence to this virtue, and swear that 'the safety of their customers' is their number one priority. Companies boast of their 'safety culture' and regularly produce documents that are titled, their 'philosophy of safety'. Safety has become a 'motherhood and apple-pie' value that is beyond challenge. A BBC webpage for children titled 'Stay Safe' offers the 'ultimate internet survival guide', with 'the tips and tricks you'll need to stay safe online, beat the cyber-bullies and become a super-surfer'.[4] Numerous institutions provide 'safe spaces'. These affectations are not simply rhetorical gestures – they are a response to the widening range of experiences that are deemed to be potentially unsafe. Banning children from participating in snowball fights for health and safety reasons illustrates that the authority of safety has acquired an expansive dynamic.[5]

The Manifesto Club, a UK-based campaigning group devoted to the promotion of freedom in everyday life, has published a collection of photographs of what it considers 'unnecessary, absurd and patronising safety warnings'. It includes a sign in front of a Sussex beach stating 'Caution, uneven surfaces' and a placard outside a Tooting cemetery warning that 'all memorials have the potential to harm'.[6] These signs symbolize a culture that insists on assessing anything that exists from the perspective of safety.

Most accounts on the culture of fear and its fixation on security and safety tend to illustrate their argument by pointing to the really big and spectacular threats that are regularly featured in the media. This rhetoric of catastrophism surrounds the threat posed by climate change, global terrorism, the nuclear arms race and a variety of different epidemics to the safety of the human species. Often commentators suggest that though these safety concerns may be overblown, their menacing presence explains why people appear to feel so threatened and so worried about their safety. In this vein, the Dutch criminologist Hans Boutelier notes that 'the observation that safety is now a universal motif in Western society is a bit of a platitude', and claims: 'My point of departure in this book is that the need for safety in contemporary society is a real need that cannot simply be explained away. It is based on real threats and on the moral discontent generated by risk society described by Ulrich Beck.'[7]

Though Boutelier is right to insist that the 'need for safety' is a 'real need', it does not necessarily follow that all or even most calls for more safety represent responses to 'real threats'. At any rate, the need for safety may well be fuelled by concerns that have very little to do with a so-called risk society. Research frequently indicates that what people fear most are often the very personal and everyday threats of unemployment, poverty, insecurity of old age and crime.[8] The need for safety is one that is culturally specific and experienced through the highly individuated way that people fear in contemporary society.

The compulsive manner with which safety is sought is characteristically an expression of personal insecurity, or the absence of ontological security. As we argue below, in the twenty-first century anxieties about security and safety are not so much about fears concerning spectacular global disasters, nor about the integrity of a community or a nation, but about the individual person. Safety is perceived in a personalized manner and the demand for it is often provoked by a suspicion of other people's motives. Pointing to America's reaction to the 9/11 tragedy, Stearns observed how the loss of confidence in government led people 'to view danger in personal terms'.[9] Mistrust, loss of confidence in institutions, and the sensibility of feeling disconnected create a demand for safety. In turn, the therapeutic language through which existential insecurity is communicated – being 'at risk', vulnerable, traumatized, stressed – turns the quest for safety into a highly personal journey.

THE SAFETY IMPERATIVE
In the first instance, society's obsession with safety should be understood as a sublimated expression of its magnification of harm,

which has meshed with its low level of tolerance for distress, injury and pain. The elevation of safety into a moral value is underpinned by precautionary ideals and a manifest intolerance towards uncertainty and risks. There are very few experiences, relationships, technologies or products that are unambiguously estimated to be safe. Patient leaflets and information directed at customers play it safe by drawing attention to any conceivable risks and side effects. Even cuddly soft toys that parents buy to comfort their children come with advice about possible dangers.

A leaflet on 'Soft Toy and Safety' attempts to reassure parents by informing them that 'soft toys are great playthings for small children, as they can stretch their imaginations with little risk of ending up hurting themselves'. However, the leaflet warns:

> Always choose cloth toys over fake fur or hair when you're buying for very little people, as they love to chew and suck things they shouldn't and this means that fur and hair are a choking hazard. Likewise it is important to avoid toys with hard buttons or eyes that could come off. Never leave soft toys near a sleeping baby.[10]

After issuing a warning with the use of the 'Never' word, the author of this leaflet hints that parents who take their child's safety really seriously might opt for buying handmade rather than mass-produced toys:

> There have been a number of stories in the press recently concerning toy safety and working conditions in the factories that make big brand toys. People are becoming more aware of safety issues like toxic chemicals in paints, and on a global level, climate change and the green movement is making more parents think about buying responsible, eco-friendly toys.

Through linking the challenge of purchasing a toy to high-profile global threats like climate change and toxic chemicals, the issue of safety acquires a boundless quality.

When even the purchase of a teddy bear becomes subjected to the imperative of risk assessment, very little in life can be deemed to be unambiguously safe. Consequently many activities that were seen as normal and unexceptional in my youth are now either banned or regulated out of existence. My mother, who used to leave me in my pram outside a shop while she bought a loaf of bread, would now be denounced as irresponsible. When I was ten years old I earned pocket money from my newspaper round. Today, the employment of a ten-year-old is deemed unsafe and no newsagent in the UK would risk employing such a 'young' child. Fears about strangers has led to the near elimination of hitchhiking. Many adults believe that it is not safe for children to walk to school unless they are supervised. Safety concerns extend into the conduct of human relationships: like other academics, I have been warned that it is unsafe to shut my office door when I talk to a student. Apparently the safety of both of us could be compromised if a closed door shields our interaction.

My own postgraduate students have far fewer opportunities to experiment, take risks and embark on an adventure than I did. One of my most significant character-forming experiences was the year I spent in Kenya, carrying out field research on Mau Mau rebels for my PhD. During this time, I visited and interviewed Mau Mau activists in their homes. My work often led me to remote villages in the Rift Valley of Kenya, where it was not possible to stay in touch with the outside world. No one asked me about potential risks regarding my personal safety – I was trusted by my supervisor to get on with my research. With the exception of three or four letters that I sent to my supervisor and my parents, I was out of contact with my university and my family. Today, most institutions of higher education in the Anglo-American world would not allow me or other postgraduate students to have the freedom to embark on such a journey of intellectual discovery. University Ethics Committees would conclude that such a venture was unsafe, risky and therefore probably unethical. Their attempt to turn safety into an ethical value compromises the freedom to explore, and in some case, the quality of research.

The regime of safety imposed on my postgraduates is a modified version of the approach that experts urge parents to adopt before purchasing a soft toy. Take the training leaflet titled 'How can I be safe while interviewing people?', available on the website of the Centre for Urban History of the University of Leicester. It is a question that neither I, nor any of my peers, ever asked before we embarked on our fieldwork. Insofar as we had anxieties about the conduct of interviews, it was about how to pose the right questions and how to gain the trust of our respondents, in order to provide us with useful information.

'How can I be safe while interviewing people?' echoes the dominant sentiment that it is better to be safe than sorry, stating:

> We're not suggesting that oral history interviewing is a particularly hazardous occupation! The vast majority of people who offer you an interview will be absolutely genuine and pose no risks at all. However, as interviewing often involves visiting people in their own homes, with limited prior contact with them, it is still worth thinking about possible hazards and how to minimise or avoid them.[11]

The leaflet more or less acknowledges that oral history interviewing is not 'particularly hazardous'. Nevertheless, it insists that it is still worth 'thinking about possible hazards'. The hazard in question turns out to be 'visiting people in their own homes'. The safety tips then offered by this leaflet adopt the tone that a parent sometimes directs towards a four-year-old. It asks, 'How will you be travelling to and from the interview?' before advising that 'it might be appropriate to travel by bus in daylight, but less advisable if you are returning in the evening'. Just in case the would-be interviewer is totally oblivious to demands of urban mobility, the leaflet advises:

> Make sure you know which train or bus to catch, at what time(s), and the stop closest to your destination. Check the timetable! Even in large cities, bus services can be few and far between in the evenings. Avoid waiting alone at a bus stop at night, particularly in poorly lit or deserted areas.

The leaflet evokes a vision of urban Britain where the perils of a bus journey and the dangers posed by visiting people in their homes demand 'that someone knows where you are going'.

On its own, banal safety advice directed at research students has little influence on people's attitudes and behaviour. But when university ethics committees and other risk-averse institutions pile in with a similar message, even routine activities may become an issue of personal safety.

Advice on safety assumes that people lack the moral or emotional resources to cope with life, and often treats adults as if they were confused children. Take, for example, Cardiff University's 'Personal Safety Guide': 'Let's be honest, your most important consideration before a night out is probably what you're going to wear. But alcohol can severely affect your decision-making skills, and so it is really important to put safety measures in place before heading out.'[12] A menacing entertainment landscape of perils and risks is evoked by the call to 'put safety measures in place before heading out' for a night on the town.

The University of Edinburgh's 'Personal Safety' webpage is generous with its offering of platitudinous advice. Before drawing up its long list of safety tips, it states, 'Edinburgh is generally considered to be a safe city, but as with any city environment, you are advised to be mindful of your safety and personal security at all times, especially at night.' Its message of 'it may be safe ... but' is followed by a stream of banal advice, such as, 'if studying late or by yourself, tell somebody'. The guidance concludes with a statement that directly speaks to people's existential insecurity: 'If you feel unsafe or something is not right, contact the Security Section.'[13] In other words, the mere feeling that 'something is not right', which has hitherto been seen as an uncomfortable feature of the human predicament, is here transformed into a safety issue.

Society's all-consuming fixation with personal safety either implicitly or explicitly conveys the message that mistrusting the people we encounter is a sensible approach. Institutions, both public and private, have adopted intricately worded codes of conduct that are designed to protect individuals from the harms that others might inflict on them. In some instances, anxiety about personal safety has led to the reintroduction of the old practice of using chaperones to police human relations. In bygone days, chaperones were relied on to ensure that people behaved properly and acted with a sense of propriety; today, the demand of personal safety has led to the reintroduction of what had been thought a quaint and outdated practice.

The placard advertising the availability of a chaperone in my local pharmacy is devoted to explaining how this person serves to assure our safety:

Our Chaperone Policy

Our pharmacy is committed to providing a safe comfortable environment so that both you and our staff can be confident that best practice is being conducted at all times. This is why it may sometimes be necessary to have a chaperone present within the consultation room.

A chaperone provides a safeguard for both patients and employees during a private consultation. Should you feel that it would make you more comfortable, you can ask to have a chaperone present at any time during your consultations ...

Your pharmacist may also request for a chaperone to be present, but they will always ask for your permission first.

The presumption that both patient and the pharmacist would benefit from accessing a chaperone to 'safeguard' them conveys the message that this encounter is potentially unsafe. By implication, it also calls into question the presumption of trust that underpins the professional relationship between a pharmacist and customer, a doctor and patient, or an academic and a student.

The assumption that the relationship between adults and children constitutes a serious safety issue has led to the micro-management and scrutiny of intergenerational interaction. The booklet *Help ... I want to work safely with young people and children*, published by

The Churches' Child Protection Advisory Service (CCPAS), depicts a world that refuses to trust adults who work with children. The booklet advises, 'Keep everything public. A hug in the context of a group is very different from a hug behind closed doors.'[14] Closed doors and private interaction are no longer acceptable to a society fed on a constant diet of suspicion. It is as if, by definition, the closed door constitutes a threat to the safety of a child.

In effect, one-to-one contact between adults and children has become stigmatized. A guideline published by the Salvation Army advises its members to ensure that 'an adult is not left alone with a child or a young person where there is little or no opportunity for the activity to be observed by others'. It adds that this 'may mean groups working within the same large room or working in an adjoining room with the door left open'. Salvation Army members were far from happy with this rule, since many of their activities involve musical practice. Since band members play different instruments at various levels of proficiency, a lot of the training took place one-to-one. Nevertheless, the new order dictates that doors should be left open – and, presumably, ears closed. In numerous accounts, the closed door – which symbolizes the private sphere – is depicted as a threat to human safety. An essay titled 'Fear of Crime and the Myth of the Safe Home' criticizes criminologists who associate the public space with danger and the private sphere with safety,[15] and communicates the message that even your most intimate relations must not be trusted. The idea that even the home is not a safe space raises questions about the precarious quality of the human condition. It indicates that within the context of the culture of fear, safety is conspicuous by its absence.

Anxiety about personal safety is continually fuelled by media headlines, and warnings issued by advocacy organizations and campaign groups. Take the misleading headline that informs readers that '80 per cent of children don't feel safe on social media'. The study on which this headline is based simply claimed that four out of five children surveyed indicated that websites should do more to protect them from harmful messages – that 87 per cent stated that they knew how to keep themselves safe online did not prevent the advocacy groups behind the study from promoting a claim that directly contradicted the findings of the report.[16]

However, though the media and fear merchants incessantly draw attention to the threats confronting personal safety, it is important to note that they merely amplify pre-existing anxieties. Many social and cultural psychologists believe that anxieties about personal safety are the outcome of the process of individuation. The erosion of community ties that parallel individuation 'threatened people with new insecurities,' argued the psychologist Erich Fromm.[17] Fromm claimed that the restoration of solidarity required conscious effort on the part of people otherwise distracted by their personal insecurities.

No doubt Fromm has a point when he draws attention to the link between the loss of the strong social bonds that existed in traditional communities and the sense of personal anxiety that prevails in modern societies. However, it is important to note that though the erosion of community ties has been going on for almost two centuries, it is only in the late twentieth century that society's obsession with safety acquired such a powerful momentum. Looking back on the modern era there are moments – during the Second World War or the post-war economic boom – when circumstances helped people to maintain and forge new ties with another. However, there was a perceptible shift towards the hardening of the process of individuation in the 1970s. So, when Christopher Lasch developed his argument about the rise of a mood of survivalism, his focus was on what he characterized as the 'psychic survival' of the individual.

Anxiety about psychic survival is closely linked to the changing perception of the self and its relation to the world. In this context, the meaning of personal identity has lost some of its sense of continuity and became more fluid. Significantly, the relation between identity and a durable public world is experienced as increasingly fragile. Lasch argued: 'Identity has become uncertain and problematical not because people no longer occupy fixed social stations ... but because they no longer inhabit a world that exists independently of themselves.'[18]

As people become estranged from their common world, their identity becomes increasingly entwined with their private life, which in turn personalizes the sense of insecurity. One symptom of this development is the tendency for private anxieties to become public issues. Personal insecurities expressed through self-harming, food disorders, concern about body image, and fears about relationships have become public safety issues.

The quest for personal safety is not simply a response to external threats, but a reaction to the internal turmoil associated with existential insecurity. The current sensibility of 'it's all about me' was anticipated by Lasch, when he remarked on the growth of a 'culture of narcissism': 'a disposition to see the world as a mirror, more particularly as a projection of one's own fears and desires'.[19] That is why advocates of identity politics express so much concern about the supposed threats to their persona. Though the rhetoric of identity politics often celebrates survival, it continually draws attention to its experience of victimization, its sense of vulnerability, and its entitlement to be validated and protected from hurt.

The heightened sense of personal insecurity, which translates the problems of daily life into a psychological language of harm, is most systematically captured by the relatively recently invented concept of *micro-aggression*. The term micro-aggression is associated with the publications of counselling psychologist Derald Wing Sue. Sue defines micro-aggression as 'the brief and commonplace daily verbal, behavioral, and environmental indignities, whether intentional or unintentional, that communicate hostile, derogatory, or negative racial, gender, and sexual orientation, and religious slights and insults to the target person or group'. What's important about this definition is that these indignities need not be the outcome of intentional behaviour: indeed, Sue argues that 'perpetrators of micro-aggressions are often unaware' of the indignities that they inflict on others.[20]

The attention directed on the unconscious or unwitting dimension of micro-aggression is crucially important. People accused of this misdemeanour are not indicted for what they have done, nor for what they said, and not even for what they think they think – but for their unconscious thoughts. Micro-aggression is represented as a form of non-intentional cultural harm whose recognition is monopolized by the victim. Unlike conventional acts of aggression, which are visible, there is little tangible evidence of micro-aggression, other than the subjective reaction to it.

One reason why the concept of micro-aggression has gained influence is because it provides a narrative that resonates with personal insecurity. Micro-aggression highlights the subjective experience of rejection, anxiety and isolation, and recasts it as an insidious threat to personal safety. The concept of micro-aggression helps reframe the experience of disappointment, rejection and pain through a language that diminishes the role of conscious intent. Like the concept of bullying, discussed in the previous chapter, micro-aggression serves to explain and validate the ontological insecurity confronting an individual. Through its emphasis on the harms of interpersonal communication, it highlights the close connection between fragile identities and the quest for personal security.

WHEN WE FEAR ON OUR OWN

Though it has acquired its most systematic expression within identity politics, the concern with psychic survival prevails throughout society. The growing preoccupation with identity has important implications for the way that fear works and safety is perceived. Fear has become increasingly privatized: far more than in previous times, people experience threats as isolated and lonely individuals. Consequently, instead of helping to forge a sense of solidarity, the act of fearing encourages fragmentation. Even in circumstances such as wars and conflicts that tend to encourage a display of solidarity, the public's response often adopts a personal tone. Frequently, it is not 'we' but 'I', as in 'I don't feel safe'. Such a response is often solicited by the media after a disaster or a terrorist outrage. Questions like 'how do you feel?', 'describe your emotions' or 'what did it mean for you?' personalize the response to what is in fact a blow to an entire community. Such questions inevitably focus attention on 'my story'. One newspaper headline cited a television presenter Vogue Williams stating, 'I don't feel safe living in the UK anymore'[21] – following the terrorist bombing in Manchester in May 2017. This story about an individual's anxiety about her personal safety pushed concern for a community's security to the background.

Despite a common culture of fear, the response to perceived threats often assumes an individuated character. The absence of a shared experience of fearing both exposes and reinforces the relative weakness of a common web of meaning through which society makes sense of the threats it faces. The therapeutic language of trauma and anxiety guides people to experience their fear in an individuated and atomized manner. In contrast to previous times when threats were often experienced as a danger to the community, they tend to be internalized as a private problem of personal safety. For example, the UK's National Police Chiefs' Council has issued a statement that advises the public that in case of a terrorist attack, people should 'Run, Hide, Tell'.[22] Some security experts have rightly criticized this guidance as being far too passive, claiming that the advice adopted by the FBI in America, 'Run, Hide, Fight', is a more effective way of securing a community's safety.[23]

Bereft of the reassurance offered by the sense of solidarity and community security, people who fear on their own can perceive a vast range of issues as a potential threat to their security. As Bauman wrote, 'with fears privatized' there is 'no hope left that human reason' will help us, 'to end up in a secure and agreeable shelter'.[24] One study, in which people were interviewed about the personal risks they faced, found that respondents tended to represent 'crisis, fears and anxieties as self-produced and individual problems, the products of "personal biography"'.[25] In the absence of a master-narrative that endows security with shared meaning, a concern with safety has become a permanent feature of life.

THE PROJECT OF TRANSFORMING SAFETY INTO A VALUE
Throughout history, people have reflected on the relationship between safety and fear. 'Fear is the foundation of safety,' noted

the Christian Church Father, Tertullian (*c.*AD 155-*c.*240). But the meaning attached to safety has undergone important modifications. Until modern times, the safety of an individual tended to be seen as far less significant than the safety of a community. As Cicero explained: 'For just as the laws set the safety of all before the safety of individuals, so a man who is good, wise, law-abiding and conscious of his civic duty will care for the advantage of all more than of a single individual – himself.'[26] No doubt Cicero's civic-minded account of safety served as an ideal that was violated by people who, in practice, regarded their personal security as more important than the welfare of their community. Nevertheless, the coupling of safety and civic duty lent a public dimension to the meaning of the term.

As noted previously, Thomas Hobbes is the philosopher most widely associated with the project of assigning safety a central role in political discourse. In the aftermath of the upheavals of the English Civil War, Hobbes attempted to harness people's basic impulse of self-preservation to justify a theory of sovereignty underpinned by fear. However, although Hobbes relied on people's instinct of self-preservation, his concept of safety was based on the outlawing of violence and through the action of the Sovereign, securing peace for the community. His was not an individualist concept of safety, but that of public safety.[27]

Safety has frequently featured as a subject of political discourse. But in many instances, it was not regarded as a moral norm. Moral norms are rules of morality that serve to guide people's behaviour and a community's conventions. Despite the pragmatic necessity for security, numerous sources questioned the ideal of safety as a value in itself. The concern with safety was sometimes portrayed as a distraction from tackling the challenges faced by a community. Tacitus declared that 'the desire for safety stands against every great and noble enterprise'.[28] This sentiment was widespread in ancient Athens, whose culture promoted taking risks and seizing opportunities. It avowed the ideals of fame and heroism and regarded safety not as a value, but as a matter of pragmatic necessity.

In his fascinating account of Athenian culture, the sociologist Alvin Gouldner explained that its people did not attach great value to safety. According to Gouldner, an illustration of Athens' risk-taking approach was its decision to evacuate the city in order to concentrate on defeating the overwhelming Persian forces in a sea battle.[29] The audacious Athenian culture was widely admired during the centuries following the demise of this city-state. The German philosopher Friedrich Nietzsche praised the Athenian leader, Pericles, who in his famous Funeral Speech celebrated his people's 'indifference and contempt for safety, body and life'.[30] Nietzsche characterized society's preference for safety and comfort over risk as a form of slave morality.

Many nineteenth-century philosophers and thinkers shared a modified version of his contempt for the valuation of safety. John Stuart Mill admonished those for whom safety trumped all other causes. It is worth citing his view at length:

> War is an ugly thing, but not the ugliest of things: the decayed and degraded state of moral and patriotic feeling which thinks that nothing is worth a war, is much worse. When a people are used as mere human instruments for firing cannon or thrusting bayonets, in the service and for the selfish purposes of a master, such war degrades a people. A war to protect other human beings against tyrannical injustice; a war to give victory to their own ideas of right and good, and which is their own war, carried on for an honest purpose by their free choice, — is often the means of their regeneration. *A man who has nothing which he is willing to fight for, nothing which he cares more about than he does about his personal safety, is a miserable creature who has no chance of being free, unless made and kept so by the exertions of better men than himself. As long as justice and injustice have not terminated their ever-renewing fight for ascendancy in the affairs of mankind, human beings must be willing, when need is, to do battle for the one against the other.* (My emphasis.)[31]

Mill, who was an admirer of the Athenian spirit of audacity, argued that 'a certain degree of insecurity, in some combinations of circumstances, has good as well as bad effects, by making energy and practical ability the conditions of safety'. From this 'perspective, safety was not the outcome of a 'passive prevention of harm' but, as Aaron Wildawsky argued, 'safety must be discovered, and cannot be merely chosen'.[32]

The sentiments expressed by Mill were informed by a moral outlook that regarded duty and responsibility for the welfare of others as essential to the conduct of a good life. In recent times, the displacement of a moral by a therapeutic code has altered the way that duty has come to be understood. From time to time, public rhetoric still refers to the importance of duty in its classical sense, as the assumption of responsibility for others and for the community. But this version of public duty is frequently contradicted by the claim that the duty that really matters is duty to oneself. 'Values are personal preferences, inclinations and choice,' observed the sociologist James Davison Hunter.[33] According to Ulrich Beck, one of the key components of this therapeutically influenced value system is the 'principle of "duty to oneself"'.[34]

The valorization of safety even influences institutions that are involved in violent conflicts and in the business of fighting wars. Timothy J. Edens, a Brigadier General in the American Army, has argued that 'safety can be one of the core elements to our Army's values', and that he hoped that soldiers will see 'safety as part of the Warrior Ethos'.[35] This point is reiterated by a company producing military armour, which states that 'our core value is safety; our core mission is to help bring you home safe!'[36]

The contemporary narrative of safety privileges the personal and deals with its public aspects in a technical and instrumental manner. Though it uses the rhetoric of values, it eschews a moral framework which provides values with their normative foundation. There are tens of thousands of webpages that are devoted to affirming safety as the 'core value' of their institutions. 'Change Safety from a program to a Core Value' announces the webpage of Contracting Business, explaining that: 'there's a big difference in how a company thinks and behaves when safety is a *value* as opposed to a program or a customer requirement. A company that has safety as a core value has a safety culture. This means that safety has become a way of life.'[37] Virtually every values-related statement insists that they take their core value of safety so seriously that it has 'become a way of life'. So the website of Enbridge echoes the usual refrain: 'Safety isn't just a priority. It's our way of life. It's a core value that makes us Enbridge.'[38]

Our inspection of 150 value statements selected randomly online, indicates that they use similar platitudes regarding safety as a 'core value'. They all evidently understand that safety dominates society's preoccupations, and that anxiety about its absence is integral to the spirit of our times. Institutions frequently use the term 'safety culture' to describe their way of life. Businesses and institutions often declare their commitment to their 'safety philosophy', describing this as people-oriented and personal – for example: 'People do safety, not systems and processes.'[39] One energy company explains that its philosophy of safety is directed at 'our employees', who are 'our most valuable resource', and that 'no phase of business is more important than their personal safety'.[40] The company points out that it really means business:

> To foster this [safety FF] philosophy Parman Energy has a full-time safety manager to develop and administer safety training for faculty and staff. The Safety and Compliance Manager's chief focus is not only to ensure this philosophy is followed, but to motivate employees to act safely in all aspects of their life (work and home) so that they can be there for their families.[41]

Narratives that promote a safety culture or philosophy attempt to convert technical and practical security measures into a language of values. Yet, the meaning of the value of safety is rarely explained through a moral language that pertains to ideals about right and wrong or good and evil. Instead, it is communicated in instrumental terms as a series of practical tips. In fact, the use of the term 'core value' has little to do with values that are moral. It is worth noting that decisions about embracing a particular core value are based on business and public relations concerns. Consultants and websites offer to provide institutions with advice about what core value to choose, with one offering a 'Core Values List with 500 examples' and devoting a page to the question of 'How to Create Your Own Core Values List'.[42] Other companies offer off-the-shelf mission statements, whose core values are tailored to meet the needs of their customers.

The instrumental imperative that motivates institutions to advertise their commitment to the value of safety is founded on the recognition that there is a real demand for security. The attempt to turn safety into a value is also prompted by the recognition that it is the absence of agreement on shared values that enhances the public's sense of anxiety and insecurity. Through the attempt to transform safety into a value, the very absence of a sense of security is transformed into a shared positive affirmation of a common code. Yet there is a world of difference between what we value – safety and security – and what is a moral value, such as autonomy or freedom. The valuation of safety represents a statement about harm. In practice, the real driver of the deification of safety is the aspiration to achieve a harm-free world. As one mission statement, titled 'Safety – Making it Happen', explains, 'the term "safety" means different things to different people, but essentially it captures an ideal of "absence of harm"'.[43]

THE DANGERS OF A HARM-FREE WORLD

The idealization of a harm-free world speaks to a culture that regards the consequences of harms as far more damaging and catastrophic than previously imagined, and attempts to negate it through an expansive regime of safety. It is the intolerance directed at potential harm that underpins the project of transforming safety into a value. The mission statement, 'Safety – Making it Happen', explicitly linked the translation of 'safety into a value' to the 'goal of "zero" (injuries, accidents, tolerance, etc.)'.[44]

The promoters of safety philosophy often advocate the goal of zero harm. As one advocate of 'Treating Safety as a Value' outlined:

The 'safety is a value' ethos is founded on the fundamental philosophy that all injuries are preventable and that the goal of zero injuries can be achieved. To introduce this concept to a workplace, company leaders must develop a vision and commit to it. This commitment must be cascaded down through the management structure.[45]

The author of this statement promises that the 'reward of zero injuries over the long term will make the effort worthwhile – in both financial and human terms'. From this perspective, the objective of a zero injury environment is not only realistic but also worthwhile. The importance that advocates of a zero harm society attach to safety means that all other concerns and principles have to be subordinated to this goal.

Back in 2012, General Peter Wall raised concerns about the influence of Britain's anti-risk culture on the army, noting: 'I sense there is an expectation in some circles in society that this sort of zero risk culture that is understandably sought in many other walks of life ought to be achievable in the battlefield.' Wall argued that society had to accept that the 'zero risk culture sought in other walks of life' should not in fact apply to the battlefield[46] – that he even needed to make this argument illustrates the widespread influence of zero harm attitudes over society.

Though the safety utopia outlined by the advocates of zero harm often comes across as a form of cultural fantasy, this objective is vigorously pursued by numerous institutions and campaign groups, which regard the word 'accident' as an expression of a secular blasphemy. Calls to ban the use of this word are motivated by the belief that the injuries that people suffer are avoidable. In 2007, 'accident' was expunged from the new edition of Britain's *Highway Code*, published by the UK Department of Transport – the words 'collision', 'crash' or 'incident' serve as substitutes for describing events that once were known as accidents.[47]

The mantra that states that 'all harm is preventable' encourages a mood of blame to be directed at people involved in accidents. Injuries suffered by children are constantly scrutinized for evidence of parental irresponsibility or abuse. That is why in 2014, the UK government took it upon itself to introduce a rule that ensures that all children who visit an Accident and Emergency unit in a hospital are logged on a national database set up to identify potential victims of abuse.

The introduction of a rigorous safety regime in workplaces, public institutions and throughout society has made a significant contribution to the reduction of physical injuries. As a result, most economically advanced societies are safer than in any previous stage of human history. But paradoxically, the achievement of unprecedented levels of physical safety coincides with a heightened sense of insecurity. As the previous chapter noted, this reaction is precipitated by the way that people have been socialized to respond to threats. In these circumstances, the constant pursuit of a utopian vision of a harm-free world does little to help people feel secure. Since it continually draws attention to safety as an absent condition, it reinforces the sense of insecurity.

Although mission statements celebrating safety tend to focus on preventing physical injuries and harms, in recent times the threats that preoccupy society are increasingly directed at damages caused to people's emotions. Emotional injury to the individual is frequently portrayed as more damaging than a physical injury; as something that can leave the person 'damaged for life'. Unlike physical harm, emotional harm is limited only by the imagination. Regardless of intent, a gesture or a comment can be perceived in a way that causes damage. According to child protection guidelines used in Britain, emotional abuse can refer to virtually every parental failing, from 'failure to meet a child's need for affection' to being so 'over protective and possessive' that they prevent their children from experiencing 'normal social contact or normal physical activity'.[48] The expansion of the diagnosis of emotional harm is not confined to children: as discussed above, contemporary cultural norms work to continually lower the threshold of acceptable distress and therefore encourage individuals to interpret unpleasant experiences as damaging to their health and emotions.

The omnipresence of emotional harms lends the deification of safety an expansive and intrusive dimension. The adverb 'safe', as in 'safe sex', 'safe drinking', 'safe eating', 'safe schools' and 'safe space' signals responsible behaviour; the exhortation to 'stay safe' is a secular version of the call 'may God be with you'. That is why the demand for safety and protection from harm is so readily recognized as a legitimate claim for an entitlement to be validated and recognized. The attribution of safety to an experience or to a product endows it with qualities that automatically earn our approval, while individuals and institutions are frequently attacked for not exercising enough caution.

INVERTED QUARANTINE

Inverted quarantine is a concept developed by the sociologist Andrew Szasz in his study *Shopping Our Way to Safety: How We Changed from Protecting the Environment to Protecting Ourselves*.[49] Unlike a traditional quarantine, which seeks to isolate a disease to keep it from spreading to the public, an inverted quarantine represents the opposite impulse of people isolating themselves from the harms that they perceive as threatening them. Inverted quarantine constitutes a response to the fear that the human condition is inherently unsafe.

Arguably the most striking example of a demand for an inverted quarantine is the emergence of the ideal of a safe space. Like a gated community set up to keep out undesirable outsiders, the purpose of a safe space is to protect its inhabitants from unwelcome criticism and thoughts.

It was in 2015 that media attention directed at the demand for safe spaces in Anglo-American universities led to the widespread recognition of this phenomenon. However, the demand for this form of inverted quarantine emerged a long time before that. The concern with psychic survival that surfaced in the late 1970s provided the initial impetus for the emergence of attitudes that eventually led to the formulation of the demand for safe space. This early relationship between psychic survival and safe space was captured in the title of psychiatrist Anthony Fry's 1987 book *Safe Space: How to Survive in a Threatening World.* For Fry, a safe space was necessitated by the perilous world that exists outside the self. He wrote: 'as I looked carefully at this rather threatening world, it seemed that safe space for many of us was becoming increasingly hard to find and that for a whole variety of reasons, material, social and personal conditions were becoming ever more unsuitable for human beings'.[50] Fry's ideal was what he described as the 'protected spaces of childhood', and in many respects his metaphor of safe space captures the security of the child still in the womb.[51]

The equation that Fry drew between the ethos of child protection and the aspiration for safe spaces underlines the infantilized version of personhood that is attracted to this form of inverted quarantine. More than any aspiration thrown up in our culture of fear, the concept of safe space highlights its two key features – the contention that the space inhabited by humanity is fundamentally unsafe, and the assertion that people are inherently 'at risk' and 'vulnerable', and therefore unlikely to cope with the challenges that life hurls at them. The survivalist outlook that corresponds to the consciousness of being vulnerable directs people to imagine their world as unsafe. 'Everyday life has begun to pattern itself on the survival strategies forced on those exposed to extreme adversity', observed Lasch.[52]

The absence of safety is the premise for the argument for safe spaces. But from what types of threats do safe spaces provide protection? Typically the demand for safe space is justified on the grounds that, since people are emotionally fragile, they need to be quarantined from the toxic effects of criticism and judgement. From this perspective the issue of personal safety is enmeshed with the provision of protection from words and ideas that are likely to damage an individual's identity further. The fears expressed by safe space advocates are not so much directed at physical injury but at threats to their psyche and identity.

A safe space aims to regulate social distance and psychic boundaries between people, and the language used to articulate safe space policies frequently deploys the metaphors of space, distance and boundaries. The protest campaign Occupy Bristol demanded respect for 'people's physical and emotional boundaries', and exhorted its supporters, '**Be responsible** for your own actions and safety and the safety of those around you.'[53] Occupy London's Safe Space Policy also focuses on the enforcement of maintaining a psychic space, advising: 'respect each other's physical and emotional boundaries' and 'Be aware of the space you take up and the positions and privileges you bring.'[54] This inverted quarantine is directed not simply at isolating people from external threats but at keeping them safe from those closest to them, in case they intrude on their personal space.

Campaigners and activists have raised the demand for safe spaces in a variety of settings. Social workers, school teachers, psychologists, educators, doctors, sex workers and probation officers are some of the interest groups who have raised support for safe spaces. Safe space is often portrayed as a human right for vulnerable groups such as refugees,[55] and it has also become integrated into the vocabulary of twenty-first-century political protest. As indicated above, the international Occupy Movement, which emerged in September 2011, is committed to the provision of safe spaces, often on the grounds that these are vital for helping the movement's supporters gain confidence. During the conference of the British Labour Party in Brighton, a safe space was established for female delegates fed up with listening to heated debates.[56] The demand for safe space is not confined to the left of the political divide: a leader of the University of California at Los Angeles' Bruin Republicans described her group as 'a space for conservative students to share opinion without facing criticism or attacks from faculty and students who disagree with them'.[57]

Anxiety about the absence of safety in general, and the demand for safe spaces in particular, are most systematically formulated and developed within institutions of higher education. It is within the university system that the arguments that support the different manifestations of the culture of fear have acquired a systematic and quasi-ideological underpinning. If the arguments advanced by academic fear entrepreneurs are valid then, by all accounts, the university has become one of the most dangerous places of work.

Claims that universities are enveloped by an epidemic of harassment are quickly followed by reports that campuses face an unprecedented epidemic of stress. In some instances the scale of the problem simply beggars belief. In April 2017, a report on an 'epidemic of stressed students' in Australia suggested that more than 70 per cent of students reported high or very high levels of psychological distress, and apparently more than a third of the respondents stated that they contemplated self-harm or suicide.[58] In Britain, a National Union of Students' survey in 2015 indicated that 78 per cent of students had experienced mental health problems, and a third of the respondents claimed to have had suicidal thoughts.

One would imagine that a university is a relatively benign and comfortable institution within which to work. But that's not how things function in the culture of fear. 'Academics "face higher mental health risk" than other professions' is the headline of an article that contends that the 'majority of people' working in British universities find their job stressful.[59] It appears that in comparison to other professions – surgeons, emergency workers, the police, the military – teaching in a university is an unusually stressful and dangerous experience.

The main impulse fuelling concern with campus safety is anxiety about people's psychic security and identity. A safe space should be interpreted as a metaphor of validation: for its supporters, the appeal lies in the immunity it promises from being made to feel uncomfortable. As the legal scholar and former head of the American Civil Liberties Union (ACLU) Nadine Strossen has stated, the meaning of this metaphor now implies protection from 'exposure to ideas that make one uncomfortable'.[60]

That many university students are emotionally drawn towards practices that promise to protect them from judgement is not surprising. From an early age, school children are socialized into the commanding pedagogic values of empathy, self-esteem and unconditionally respecting the view of others. With so much time and resources devoted to affirming the identity of young people it is not surprising that they believe that they have a right to be validated. So when they arrive at university they regard an ideal classroom environment as one where their selves and their views are accepted and affirmed. Many undergraduates may have never heard of a safe space, but their socialization has disposed them to expect their institutions to validate their identity. Conversely, many undergraduates regard serious criticism and debate as an unacceptable challenge to their persona.

In effect, a safe space provides a quarantine from the threat of judgement. That is why free speech and robust debate are often diagnosed as unsafe and a danger to mental health. Supporters of safe space regard the absence of judgement as one of the most cherished features of the university, and this point is explicitly recognized by many higher education institutions. The Student Services Value Statement of St Andrew's University promises to 'actively reflect' on its 'practice to ensure our environment is non-judgemental'.[61] Universities regularly portray their safe spaces as havens from judgement. 'Safe Zone provides an avenue for LGBTQ individuals to be able to identify places and people who are supportive, non-judgmental, and welcoming of open dialogues regarding these issues', declares Montana State University.[62]

Commentaries and studies dealing with the subject of fear tend to overlook the dread of judgement, which is often experienced as the most intimate of threats. This development is implicitly recognized by the changing language that surrounds judgement. Judgement has acquired ominous and threatening associations. The recently invented term *judgy* conveys the connotation of condescension to others,[63] and is attached to someone who is seen to be over-critical. The contrast between the negative connotation of 'judgy' and the positive association of 'non-judgy' is clearly expressed in Anne Regan's 2012 story *Animal Magnetism*, in which one of the characters 'lowered his eyebrows and crossed his arms and tried to look non-judgy even if he felt a little judgy'.[64]

Contemporary society's fear and dislike of criticism and judgement is manifested in its adoption of *shaming* as a cultural epithet. Shaming is promiscuously applied to condemn different types of criticism and judgement. Body shaming, Fat shaming, Slut shaming, Skinny shaming, Weight shaming, Snack shaming and Online shaming are just some of the dozens of ways that the unwelcome words are treated as a cultural crime. Asking a mother why she does not breastfeed her infant immediately leads to the charge of Formula shaming. Even the hint of an act of judgement is regarded as a direct threat to a person's identity.

The attempt to curb the exercise of judgement on campuses can be seen as a version of the zero harm utopia promoted by non-academic institutions. As discussed above, arguments for zero harm are often expressed through the idiom of 'zero tolerance for injury'.[65] Like the argument for safe spaces, the case for zero harm insists that there should be zero tolerance for practices that might cause physical or emotional injury. The metaphor of 'zero tolerance' conveys the notions of zero judgement and zero discretion. These are policies that are meant to be applied indiscriminately and punish without regard to circumstances. It spares judges and officials from having to think about the circumstances affecting a particular event and exempts them from exercising their capacity to discriminate and judge. In the case of zero tolerance towards offensive speech on campuses, it means sparing people the burden of having to draw their own conclusions about the merits of an argument.

The idea of zero tolerance is also informed by risk aversion. It represents an attempt to abolish, administratively, the risks associated with the expression of an unwelcome idea or belief. Of course, in one sense, tolerance is risky. Once conventional restraints on belief, opinion and speech are removed it becomes difficult to predict the future course of public life. The freedom to speak and to pursue knowledge has a habit of going off in unexpected directions.

Predictably, anxiety about safety and the demand for safe space feeds on itself. No sooner is one concession made to a safe space advocate than a demand for another one is raised. The meaning of safe space continually expands to embrace greater and greater claims for safety. At one time the term safe space referred to a specific physical area – usually a room – where students felt comfortable and safe to discuss their problems. In recent times, safe space has expanded to encompass the entire university. That's what members of the Goldsmith University's Islamic Society meant when they stated that the 'university should be a safe space for all'. This conceptual inflation of safe space is frequently advanced in policy documents on the subject. For example, the Union Council of Imperial College, London, has a Safe Space Policy, which 'encompasses all Union-run venues'. Similarly the Safe Space Policy of the Student Union of King's College London covers 'any KCLSU space, or event'.[66] Advocates of safe space often argue that it should encompass every classroom.[67]

The conceptual creep of safe space is grounded in the recognition that safety enjoys a unique status as an uncontested value. Yet precisely because support for an inverted quarantine is driven by the presumption that the world is unsafe, those devoted to the cause of safe spaces can never feel secure. Indeed, the very demand for safety contains an inner logic towards discovering more and more threats to fear. By definition, the intangible harms to the psyche are not bounded by space, and not even the most heavily policed safe space can reassure the fearful subject.

Many observers are bemused about the rapid escalation of the demand for safe space. Some of those who find the safe space idea melodramatic or incomprehensible dismiss it as a temporary fad that will soon give way to a different target of campus protest. That may well be the case. But so long as the powerful animosity directed at the act of judgement continues to dominate the cultural landscape, it will continue to demand protection from free speech and criticism and spontaneous interaction between people.[68]

THE FREEDOM–SAFETY TRADE-OFF

One of the most unattractive features of the deification of safety is the apparent tendency to subordinate the value of freedom to its dictates. Within the moral framework of the culture of fear, safety and security are first-order values, while freedom is reduced to a second-order value, at best. In numerous instances on American campuses, free speech has been equated with hate speech or denounced as a weapon of white privilege. A study published by the Brookings Institute in September 2017 indicated that 51 per cent of its American student respondents agreed with the statement that it was OK to shout down a speaker with whom they disagreed. Even more disturbing was its finding that 19 per cent of the respondents believed that it is all right to use violence to prevent a 'controversial' speaker from speaking.[69]

The relationship between freedom and safety has been a subject of debate throughout history. In numerous instances, the very human impulse to achieve safety was used as an excuse to limit the exercise of freedom. This point was recognized by Alexander Hamilton, one of the Founding Fathers of the United States. 'Safety from external danger is the most powerful director of national conduct,' he wrote in November 1787, warning that 'even the ardent love of liberty will, after a time, give way to its dictates' which will 'compel nations' to 'destroy their civil and political rights'. With a hint of fatalism, Hamilton suggested that 'to be more safe, they at length become willing to run the risk of being less free'.[70] Another Founding Father, Benjamin Franklin, was unequivocally against the practice of trading in freedom for safety. He famously remarked that, 'those who would give up essential Liberty, to purchase a little temporary Safety, deserve neither Liberty nor Safety'.

Calls for the freedom–safety trade-off claim that the liberties that people enjoy need to be balanced with a community's need for security. This argument has been raised and re-raised by authorities throughout history. Relieving people of the burden of freedom in order to make them feel safe is a recurring theme in the history of authoritarianism. A new version of this argument was elaborated in response to the post-9/11 War on Terror. On both sides of the Atlantic, the exigencies of safety and security are used to justify laws and procedures that limit civil liberty. One of the most troubling dimensions of this development is the relentless trend towards the colonization of people's private life. Advocates of expanding intrusive instruments of surveillance actively promote calls for a trading off of privacy for safety,[71] and in many instances citizens have been convinced to accept Big Brother watching them in order to keep them safe.

Many intelligent observers have criticized the ease with which political leaders have been able to win the public's acquiescence to the freedom–safety trade-off. Numerous academics have pointed to the threat that a range of new anti-terrorism laws such as the American Patriot Acts pose for civil liberties. But when a similar trade-off is proposed in relation to limiting tolerance towards offensive speech in order to protect the emotional state of members of the university community, such criticisms are conspicuous by their silence. In fact, trading off freedom for some alleged psychic benefit is not unlike the argument that authoritarian-minded politicians frequently employ for justifying policies that curb people's rights in order to 'preserve their freedom'. Take Donald Trump's campaign slogan: 'Build That Wall' on the American–Mexican border. A wall, designed to prevent Mexican migrants from entering the United States, was regarded as a symbol of existential security by many of Trump's supporters. Trump's ideal of a quarantine to 'keep America safe' appeals to an impulse that is not unlike the one fuelling demand for safe spaces.

Arguments for a trade-off deprive freedom – in any of its forms – of moral content. The culture of fear continually promotes the idea that our safety depends on giving up some of our freedoms, and its celebration of the Precautionary Principle has led to the loss of valuation for the freedom to take risks. The freedom to pursue scientific experiments and to innovate is often restrained by the imperative of safety and concern with side effects. The loss of independent mobility and freedom of the outdoors for children symbolizes the intimate coupling of an illiberal imagination and fear. In universities, academic freedom is frequently undermined by the rulings of ethics committees who claim that liberty must give way to 'ethical' considerations. On university campuses, arguments for censoring speech often state that such limits are necessary for ensuring that people are not hurt or offended. From this standpoint, censorship is justified as a form of public therapy that protects people from feeling hurt.

The demands of psychic survival and self-esteem are used as an argument for trading in freedom for the illusory goal of feeling safe. Yet as the arguments in this book have indicated, the culture of fear continually feeds itself. The act of trading in freedom does not make people feel safe. It heightens people's awareness of their lack of control over their lives and thereby enhances their sense of insecurity. The loss of any of our freedoms simply undermines people's capacity to deal with the threats they face. As we suggest in the next chapter, taking freedom more seriously is the first step towards negating the corrosive influence that the culture of fear exercises over society.

Conclusion: Towards a Less Fearful Future

Once we grasp how the culture of fear works, we can begin to free ourselves from its fatalistic influence. Understanding how fear works is the first step towards limiting its damaging impact on people's lives. History shows that there are different ways of fearing. As the sociologist Norbert Elias argued in *The Civilising Process*, a study of history helps us realize 'the degree to which fears and anxieties that move people are human-made'.[1] Human-created conventions, cultural attitudes and practices are not unalterable facts of life. They can be challenged, altered and transformed.

The culture of fear presents itself as an eternal condition, as an inalterable fact of life. Advocates of precautionary values, who dogmatically assert that there is no alternative but to act with caution, use every opportunity to transmit this defeatist sentiment. They proclaim that 'there is no alternative' to their worldview. But there is always an alternative. Human societies have often proved able to overcome obstacles and move forward. If we understand how fear works in the twenty-first century then we can actually do something effective to neutralize its toxic effects. This chapter outlines an approach that provides an alternative to the values and attitudes that sustain the culture of fear and its pessimistic view of humanity and its future.

CHALLENGING THE LOSS OF HISTORICAL MEMORY

The teleology of doom that our present-day culture of fear projects towards the future is nurtured and supported by its gloomy and often cynical representation of the past. Today's version of Freud's notion of expectant fear directs society's anxieties towards the perilous world of a future unknown. As our discussion of the metaphor of the ticking time bomb indicated, it is as if humanity stands helpless, unable to alter its future fate. However, the culture of fear also encourages society to interpret the past through the prism of fear. The mentality it cultivates is one that regards the past as a scary and ignoble succession of events, where humanity lacks not only direction but also any redeemable qualities. Reading history backwards, the ethos of precaution projects back into the past its present-day concerns. In this way, it strives to legitimate its version of fear by representing vulnerability as the eternal condition of life. It also conveys cynicism towards readings of the past that celebrate episodes of heroism and courageous behaviour.

The claim that the fearful person of the twenty-first century is the natural successor to their ancestors in bygone days is frequently recycled through contemporary versions of history. There is a discernible tendency towards 'debunking' historical narratives that allude to heroic deeds and acts of altruistic sacrifice, and towards deconstructing the meaning of long-cherished values, such as courage, heroism and loyalty. As Christopher Coker has noted: 'Henry V's decisive defeat of the French at Agincourt in 1415, as well as Shakespeare's account of it with the infamous "band of brothers", can now be portrayed as being about people suffering from "a centuries-old 'deception' about the glory of war."'[2]

Heroism is often mocked or dismissed as implausible. A new genre of popular culture and historical narratives is devoted to exposing the sordid 'secret lives' of past heroes. Claims of heroism are countered with disparagement and scorn. At best they are depicted as flawed characters, at worst they are condemned as power-hungry frauds. As Michiko Kakutani, the former literary critic of the *New York Times*, remarked, 'formerly we used to canonise our heroes' but the 'modern method is to vulgarise them'. Kakutani argues that biography has turned into a blood sport, committed mercilessly to debunking its subject.[3] Bringing heroes down to earth comes instinctively to a culture that finds duty, sacrifice or risk taking alien to its nature. In numerous accounts, heroism is dismissed as an old-fashioned and even offensive trait. As Christopher Coker remarks in his book, *The Warrior Ethos*, 'we tend to deprive' heroes 'of the fullness of their lives in order to support and sustain the smallness of our own'.[4]

The influence of the culture of fear on history is also illustrated by the practice of projecting the contemporary survivalist mentality on to the landscape of the past. In numerous accounts, the 'survivor' has displaced the hero as the object of acclaim. 'In our post-heroic times survival is considered the act of real moral or emotional worth', remarks Coker.[5]

This anti-heroic historiography is particularly drawn towards using psychological explanations to expose and denounce what it imagines as a past of ceaseless victimization. The shift of focus from the historical hero to the survivor of history mirrors the trend towards the emergence of the fragile and vulnerable subject as the central character in the culture of fear.

During the past two centuries, the key motif in the rewriting of history was the desire to promote the unique greatness of a particular people, nation or culture. National myths were about heroic deeds and glorious events. Such myths were not simply used as sentimental celebrations of the past: they were mobilized to construct a positive vision of the future. The myth of the American frontier promised a great destiny for that society. British, French and German national myths were mobilized to provide an optimistic representation of future possibilities. Today, the rewriting of history is driven by a very different impulse. The previous tendency towards mythologizing the 'good old days' has been displaced by the project of rebranding the past as the 'bad old days'.

One feature of the anti-heroic turn of history is the negative representation of the past as an unending story of human misdeeds and suffering. Its other notable feature is to read history backwards and rediscover the present-day conception of vulnerability as an eternal condition of human life. Advocates of this therapeutic turn of history argue that people in the past felt just as emotionally fragile and vulnerable as they do today but that they lacked our sophisticated psychological awareness to understand and diagnose their mental health problems. To use the fashionable expression of our time, 'they were not aware' or in some cases 'they were in denial'. There is a veritable industry devoted to the project of retrospectively diagnosing people who faced adversity in the past, as individuals with mental health issues.

Many twenty-first-century historians find it difficult to acknowledge that people in the past actually experienced adversity guided by a different set of moral norms and values. The anachronistic disparagement directed at historical claims that people responded to hardship and misfortune with bravery and fortitude says more about twenty-first-century attitudes towards distress than about the experience of people struggling with life in the past. Such critics cannot grasp the possibility that because previous systems of value endowed people's suffering with meaning they could cope with their distress without becoming traumatized.

The argument that, until recently, historians have ignored or underestimated the hidden epidemic of mental health problems is frequently used to justify rewriting accounts of the past. Take one example: the catastrophic disaster in Aberfan in 1966. This was one of the most devastating industrial tragedies in post-war Britain, in which a coal-slide engulfed the local school in the Welsh village of Aberfan, killing 116 children and 28 adults. At the time, many, including officials and health professionals, expected that this tragedy would overwhelm this small Welsh community. Yet observers were struck by the speed with which the community attempted a return to normalcy. For example, the surviving children resumed their education a fortnight after disaster struck and villagers tended to look to their own coping resources, keeping mental health professionals at bay.

A year after this disaster, Mary Essex, a family and child psychologist from the University of Wales, noted that the surviving children seemed normal and adjusted.[6] A report in *The Times* concluded that 'the villagers had done admirably in rehabilitating themselves with very little help'. That was then. A quarter of a century later, commentators adopted a sceptical view towards the 1966 version of events. In their 2000 book, *Aberfan: Government and Disasters*, Ian McLean and Martin Johnes explicitly questioned the depiction of the post-disaster Welsh community as one that had successfully managed to rehabilitate itself. They speculated that 'at the time, there was perhaps not a full awareness of the long-term consequences of personal tragedies', and expressed certainty that 'subsequent research does suggest that long-term effects would be likely at Aberfan'.[7]

The power of the contemporary narrative of human fragility dominates historical memory. Those who have internalized its assumptions find it difficult to comprehend the resilient post-disaster behaviour of this Welsh mining community. Instead of exploring their sources of resilience, commentators are far more likely to treat the survivors as hidden victims whose emotional needs could find no outlet back in the 1960s.[8]

Retrospective studies of past events can provide some useful insights into what actually happened but they provide a poor guide for explaining how at the time people felt about their experience of adversity. They are certainly not appropriate instruments for understanding what motivated an individual to react to adversity in a particular way, or for providing insights into the internal life of people in bygone days. Plundering history for scraps of evidence that prove that survivors in the past suffered from the same mental health conditions that are so widely diagnosed today serves to legitimate the attitudes that characterize our culture of fear. Through depicting the history of humanity in such a gloomy, anti-heroic manner, this approach validates the *zeitgeist* of the present day. The teleology of doom is sustained by a historical memory that overlooks the legacy of human achievement and is fixated on people's failures and misdeeds. A fatalistic sensibility towards life is projected both back into the past and forwards into the future, by a cultural imagination dominated by a sense of limits and passivity.

For thousands of years, humanity's capacity to influence its destiny has been a subject of philosophical and scientific debate. When the Romans coined the phrase 'Fortune favours the brave', they expressed a powerful belief in people's potential to exercise their will and shape their future. With the ascendancy of the Enlightenment and the commanding influence of science and knowledge, belief in humanity's creative and transformative potential flourished. Today, such ideas have lost much of their authority. Though society relies on science and knowledge far more than in previous times, these are less celebrated and affirmed than in the nineteenth or twentieth centuries.

Contemporary society attaches little significance to its intellectual and cultural legacy. Some historians claim that the people of Europe have become psychically distanced from the past to such an extent that they no longer need history to cultivate their identity or to make sense of who they are. 'Clearly Europeans have a sense of themselves as survivors of a history they have left far behind them; they do not see history as their origin or the foundation on which they stand,' argued the historian Christian Meier. He added:

> History is not something they desire to carry on (in a better way if possible). Hence they feel no gratitude to their forebears for what they achieved with so much labor; on the contrary, they are fixated on all the things they don't understand (and are making an effort to understand), such as wars, injustice, discrimination against women, slavery, and the like. They feel uncoupled from their history, the seriousness of which they are, generally speaking, less and less able to imagine.[9]

As evidence of this trend, Meier cites the attempt of the EU to distance itself from Europe's historical past. 'Thus, as far as I can see, the European Union is emerging as the first political entity of the modern era that has no need for its own history and for a historical orientation,' he states.[10]

The distancing of society from its history and cultural legacy has important implications for the way that communities understand and view their future. Through history, communities have drawn on their experience of the past to provide themselves with guidance to face what lies ahead: their interpretation of the past and the web of meaning it provided has played a central role in helping people manage their fears. The legacy of the past also consists of values such as duty, courage and freedom, which are essential for the development of a more sensible orientation towards threats. Rethinking those values and adopting them as our own can help us develop a more confident view of the future.

Historical accounts that belittle people's capacity to assume a measure of responsibility for their affairs clearly favour the risk averse. Such an attitude is integral to a culture of fear, which instructs people to bow to their fate. In such circumstances, humanity is indeed powerless to prevent the explosion of a ticking time bomb. That is why the restoration of historical memory is essential for providing an antidote to the one-dimensional tendency to perceive the future through the perspective of fear.

Taking our past seriously does not require that society uncritically romanticizes the 'good old days'. What society needs is not the glorification of the past, but the perspective of historical consciousness. As our reflections on the history of fear indicate, the way that society has engaged with fear and uncertainty has altered and changed through time. A consciousness of history helps sensitize us to the fact that human beings were responsible for these changes. They were able to deal with the threats they faced by developing practices that are today deemed as superstitious; later on, they came to understand that the religions they created were indirectly linked to their demand to endow fear with meaning. From the eighteenth century onwards many people drew the conclusion that reason and science were the most effective instruments for mastering fear. Since that time humanity has adopted and rejected numerous strategies for dealing with uncertainty and fear.

A consciousness of history demonstrates the transience of any culture of fear and can help society find a more creative and more robust way of managing uncertainty. An enlightened society will take a critical look at its past and examine how it can develop the best features of its legacy to help it face the future with confidence.

Most important of all, challenging the history of gloom is essential for confronting the prevailing mood of fatalism.

Humanity's history is not something to be ashamed of. Ancient Greece was responsible for acquainting humanity with the spirit of philosophy and opening us to the promise of science. From Judaism and Christianity, the Western world gained a series of moral principles that are upheld as ideals to this day. From the Romans we inherited an appreciation of the law and a legal system that provides security and order. Time and again people have rediscovered the idea of liberty and freedom as fundamental principles that bear upon their existence. The combined contribution of the Ancients – Greeks and Romans – Christian philosophy, the Renaissance and the Enlightenment helped to consolidate an openness to experimentation leading to the growing influence of reasoning and science. As a result, despite many setbacks, humanity learned to deal with many of the challenges it faced.

History provides an important intellectual resource for illustrating how people managed to tame their fears and move forward. The Renaissance and the Enlightenment were genuinely history-making episodes: they drew on the experiences of Ancients to call into question prevailing assumptions and prejudices. Learning the lessons of the past can help inspire new generations to adopt a positive – in some cases, even a fearless – approach towards the future.

CONFRONTING THE MOOD OF FATALISM

The cultural, social and political ideals that have flourished in our culture of fear are all enveloped by a palpable mood of fatalism. This fatalistic sensibility is most vividly expressed in relation to how society views the future. What underpins a loss of belief in humanity's capacity to influence the future is a pessimistic account of human agency. Such pessimistic accounts of human impotence towards the future are often reinforced by influential views that query the capacity of people to make rational decisions about important matters that affect their lives.

People's capacity to possess the wisdom to understand and shape their circumstances is widely questioned by influential commentators and cultural and political figures. This attitude was systematically elaborated by the philosopher Hans Jonas, whose lack of confidence in human rationality led him to consider opting for a platonic tyrant. In his case, a lack of respect for human rationality was intertwined with a sceptical orientation towards the benefits of democratic debate and popular sovereignty. That is why fear has come to be perceived as a positive asset for gaining moral consensus.

A loss of faith in public life and in people's decision-making capacity is one source of the current practices of the politics of fear. And the one fear that is central for understanding political life today is that which is directed at the behaviour of the masses. Leading figures frequently question the ability of the *demos* to behave responsibly, as demonstrated by numerous commentators in recent elections. 'If there are issues on which the populace at large should be trusted to vote, something as complicated and economically sophisticated as EU membership is definitely not one of them,' argued the biologist Richard Dawkins.[11] As far as he was concerned, complicated issues are way beyond the intellectual capacities of ordinary people, and allowing a vote on these matters therefore violates the natural order of things. Current critiques of populism employ a strident language to dehumanize their targets, illustrated by Hillary Clinton's reference to Trump supporters as a 'basket of deplorables' during the 2016 American Presidential Elections. In this case people were not regarded as simply misguided political opponents, but as a lower form of human life. This sentiment was vividly captured by the title of an article by Dean Obeidallah in the *Daily Beast*: 'Donald Trump Can't Merely Be Defeated – He and His Deplorables Must Be Crushed'.[12]

The hysterical tone adopted by public figures of all shades of political opinion expresses a disdain and in some cases contempt for the public. This development is often associated with what some commentators characterize as the 'coarsening' or 'debasement' of politics and of public life. Arguably, an even more troubling trend is the loss of valuation for democracy and public debate. One of the most important insights of the Enlightenment was its understanding that the exercise of public opinion and debate was essential for clarifying issues and solving the problems confronting society. Writing in this vein, the political theorist, Stephen Holmes, argued: 'That public disagreement is a creative force may have been the most novel and radical principle of liberal politics.'[13]

Until the second decade of this century, even those who were suspicious of the ideal of public debate were reluctant to voice their reservations about it. It is only in recent years that such suspicions have been raised publicly. The fact that criticism of the value of public debate has become increasingly explicit on university campuses indicates that rather than being viewed as a 'creative force', it is often condemned as a source of harm. Attacks on free speech and the rationality of the masses mirror the traditional reactionary attitude of contempt for the *demos*. Free-speech sceptics perceive open debate as risky and because risk is equated with danger they are less than enthusiastic about the process of democratic decision-making.

At least in one respect, critics of popular democracy are absolutely right.

The electorate can, and in some instances does, make wrong choices. It is true that an election or a referendum provides opportunities for demagogues and unscrupulous politicians to simplify issues and seek to manipulate public opinion. But the possibility that the wrong side wins an election or a debate is not a serious argument against democracy.

It is not surprising that precautionary culture is more comfortable with the opinion of an expert than with the unpredictable verdict of the electorate. Genuine democratic debate is inherently risky because there are no guarantees about the outcome. But it is a risk well worth taking, because it is only through participation in democratic debate that citizens can acquire meaningful moral and political responsibility. It is only through being open to the uncertainty of the democratic process that we can test out our ideas, experiment, gain insights and learn from our experience. Embracing this risk, democratic debate opens the way to new ideas. It means a willingness to embark on a journey, which may lead society in unexpected directions. That, of course, is a risk, but through the public's involvement in such an adventure we can develop a common understanding of the problems that confront us and develop a consensus on how to deal with the threats we face. Taking democracy and freedom more seriously is the precondition for gaining the confidence necessary for influencing our future.

It is worth reminding ourselves that throughout history the valuation of freedom, democracy and debate went hand in hand with the positive idealization of risk taking and the refusal to defer to Fate. It is widely believed that the term risk has its origins in the seventeenth-century Italian term, *riscare*, which means 'to dare'.[14] For its time, the culture of the Italian Renaissance possessed an unusually positive attitude to risk taking and daring. Unlike today, when society regards risk as something 'one is exposed to against one's will', the word *riscare* was connected to the idea of a risk 'one chooses to take'.[15] This active orientation towards uncertainty was in many cases linked to a positive endorsement of the value of public life. An affirmation of the making of choices represented a radical departure from the fatalistic sensibility of the medieval era.

The early humanists of the Renaissance emphasized the importance of activating public life through living democracy and freedom. Even at this early point in enlightened human history, they realized that on major questions in particular, the people played an important role in the conduct of public life. It is in the writings of the Renaissance humanist and philosopher Niccolò Machiavelli that we find one of the earliest arguments for taking seriously the views of the public. Machiavelli is popularly known for advising his prince to use fear to control a fickle, greedy public. But what is often overlooked is that Machiavelli also believed in the freedom of people to express their views. In his chapter 'The Multitude is Wiser and More Constant than a Prince', which appears in his *Discourses on Livy*, he drew on the experience of Rome and concluded that the multitude is no less wise than the ruler. He dismissed those who claimed that the multitude is likely to get things wrong, and stated that such a defect 'can be attributed to all men individually and most of all to princes, for each person who is not regulated by the laws will commit the very same errors as an uncontrolled crowd of people.[16]

For Machiavelli, what mattered was that people were governed by the rule of law. In these circumstances, he argued, the public could develop considerable truth-finding potential: 'As for making judgments, when the people hear two opposing speakers of equal skill taking different sides, it is only on the rarest occasion that it does not select the best opinion and that it is not capable of understanding the truth it hears.'[17] Machiavelli suggested that, on the big questions, the multitude was far more likely to get things right than an individual prince or expert. For this philosopher, what was really important was people's potential for developing an ability to consider and decide upon what was in the best interests of the community.

Although the relationship between adopting a positive attitude towards risk taking and cultivating a robust public sphere was not spelled out explicitly by Renaissance thinkers, it constitutes a central element of a modern humanist approach towards engaging with the future. As Jaap Hanekamp reminds us, 'the mastery of risk' is a 'revolutionary idea that defines the boundary between the past and modern times'.[18] As he explains:

> It is the notion that the future is more than a whim of the gods and that men and women are not passive before nature, as if they are merely pawns on the chessboard of life and its gods. Human beings discovered a way across that boundary via the tool of probability calculus. The future was not a mere reflection of the past or the murky domain of oracles and soothsayers who held a monopoly over 'knowledge' of anticipated or feared events.[19]

The link drawn by Hanekamp between the mastery of risk through probabilistic thinking and developing a confident outlook towards uncertainty is integral to the development of a less fearful approach to the future. Refusing to regard people as helpless pawns, and remembering that they are the potential authors of their destiny, is essential for confronting the current mood of fatalism: and the experience of genuine public deliberation would provide communities with a legacy they could draw on in the future.

RETHINKING SOCIALIZATION

The challenge of how to socialize young people is of great import for the future of society. It also has a direct bearing on the question of how to manage uncertainty and fear. More than any other historical development, it was the adoption of new therapeutic methods of socializing young people that served as a catalyst for the ascendancy of the culture of fear. New so-called modern attitudes towards childrearing and education played a major role in the elevation of the significance of fearing in our life. The exhortation to insulate childhood from fear was coupled to the marginalization of ideals such as courage – which possessed great significance in previous regimes of socialization. As Stearns pointed out: 'Convincing the child that his or her environment was risk free was essential; teaching him or her to overcome risk with courage dropped away – a truly fundamental change.'[20]

The new emotional culture did not set out to make people more fearful. However, once the project of tending to the emotions acquired commanding influence it became increasingly difficult to manage and restrain the corrosive influence of fear on public life. This became painfully evident in the aftermath of 9/11. As Stearns recalled: 'Faced with genuine threat and a legitimate need for fear, Americans have been unwittingly but thoroughly socialized to overreact, from a combination of inexperience, learned resentment, and a quest for reassurance.'[21]

Arguably, Stearns could have added 'learned helplessness' to the list of behavioural deficits that dispose the public towards adopting fatalistic and risk-averse responses to the uncertainty it faces. Advice discouraging people to manage challenges on their own was reinforced by influential trends advocating help-seeking behaviour. In a world of 'help-lines', dialling a number is promoted as the first step to be taken when dealing with a problem.

Whatever view one takes on the question of how young people should be brought up it is generally agreed that something has gone awry in the way that they are socialized. It is widely acknowledged that the current model of socialization has failed to cultivate the habit of independence in the young. The phenomenon of extended adolescence can be interpreted as both a loss of aspiration for independence and as a fear of growing up. This development has profound implications for intergenerational relations. Steven Mintz, in his study of adulthood *The Prime of Life*, claims that 'separation from parents is critical for maturation, and for a growing number of the young, psychological independence is achieved more slowly than in previous generations.'[22]

At least in the Anglo-American setting, the commitment to socializing children is conspicuously weak. As David Walsh noted in his study, *The Growth of the Liberal Soul*, 'the inability of liberal societies to develop any institutional means of transmitting its own virtues' has precipitated a cultural crisis.[23] The main weakness of the current regime of socialization is its failure to transmit enlightened moral values to young people. Hannah Arendt wrote at length about the difficulties of socializing the young without transmitting the values of the past. 'Since the world is old,' she observed, 'always older than they themselves, learning inevitably turns towards the past, no matter how much living will spend itself in the present.'[24] The call to 'learn from the past' often comes across as a platitude, yet it is impossible to engage with the future unless people draw on the insights and knowledge gained through centuries of human experience. Individuals gain an understanding of themselves through familiarity with the prior unfolding of the human world. That understanding also gives them the confidence and strength to engage with the uncertain future that lies ahead of them.

That something really serious has gone wrong in the way that young people are socialized is shown by the numerous initiatives launched to provide children and youth with more self-esteem, confidence, resilience or grit. Arguments proposing that children should be taught resilience or grit in schools implicitly recognize that they are missing out on something important in the way they are brought up. Unfortunately the introduction of a new education fad is unlikely to improve matters since it relies on a technical solution to solve the problem of socialization.

Advocates of teaching resilience and grit mistakenly assume that these techniques can assist the project of educating children's character. This approach tends to perceive character as a technical accomplishment that can be achieved through training. Anyone who has invested time and effort in attempting to cultivate children's character in the classroom knows that what they are engaged in is encouraging the development of their moral qualities. Character is a moral concept and implies the possession of virtues, the most important of which is the virtue of judgement.

Throughout history the question of whether character or virtue can be taught has been a subject of debate. Although disagreement about the formation of character and the possession of virtues continues to this day, it is generally recognized that what is at issue are moral and not technical accomplishments. Virtues such as that of the capacity to judge and courage are not technical skills but achievements acquired through reflection and the gaining of wisdom. Education can play an important role in acquainting children with the meaning of classical virtues such as courage and prudence. But classroom interventions cannot serve as an effective substitute for the failure of adult society to socialize the young into an agreed normative outlook.

In recent years, policy makers of education in the UK and the US have often exhorted schools to promote grit in their classrooms. Some of them hope that grit provides children with greater moral clarity, others that it will make them more determined.[25] Proponents of grit recognize the importance of helping the younger generation to be more self-sufficient, less fearful and anxious, and more determined. However, to realize that objective, society must rethink the way it socializes young people. In particular the adult world needs to give up its one-dimensional reliance on therapeutic validation as its prime instrument of socialization. It needs to take more seriously the moral education of young people, and in particular to attend to the challenge of developing an orientation towards acquainting the youth with moral values; particularly of courage, duty and judgement.

Most parents realize that much more can be done to help their children gain greater independence. The cultivation of independence of thought and of behaviour is essential for helping young people to acquire the confidence necessary for dealing with their fears. Aristotle explained that confidence 'is the opposite of fear' and that 'what causes it is the opposite of what causes fear'.[26] In our world 'what causes' confidence and fear are manifold but they are fundamentally linked to the account that society offers regarding the meaning of personhood. The representation of personhood today normalizes the status of human vulnerability, and through elevating the sense of powerlessness offers little help to managing the emotion of fear. Through its fixation on emotional fragility, the contemporary version of personhood intensifies our sense of dread and calls into question our capacity to deal with the threats we face.

Society needs to re-examine what it expects of its citizens and reflect on the question of what it means to be a human. Arguments that support the current version of a personhood of low expectation are often justified through reference to a spurious discovery of a hitherto unacknowledged psychological deficit, particularly in childhood or adulthood. The constant raising of the threat level through arguments that contend that many of the threats faced by society are far more dangerous than previously imagined, reinforce such claims. Though some of these claims may be valid, it does not follow that society needs to adopt a passive, risk-averse and fearful response to it. Whether we adopt the philosophy of precaution or embrace a more courageous risk-taking approach depends on how society perceives what it means to be a human.

RETHINKING PERSONHOOD

The raising of expectation of our children and of young people is essential for ensuring that humanity becomes less fearful about the future. In the first instance we need to question the dominant fearful view of childhood. Labelling children as 'vulnerable' or 'at risk' does them no favours. Parents, teachers and other adults naturally want to protect children from harm. But the current regime of child protection does not so much keep young people safe as pressure everyone to become slaves to their safety. This ethos of child protection enforces an unprecedented and unnecessary length of dependency on parents and adults. This extension of childhood or adolescence deprives young people of many opportunities that could enable them to learn about their strengths and weaknesses, and develop their capacity for independent reasoning and decision-making and moral autonomy.

Children must not be treated as emotionally fragile, vulnerable creatures who are unable to deal with the pressures of life. Given the right direction, in interaction with their peers and family members, they can learn to manage risks and cope with the unanticipated challenges of life. Instead of being insulated from the distressing and fearful aspects of life, children should be educated to understand them and to develop their capacity to deal with disappointment and painful experiences. The creation of a more risk-taking and challenging environment for young people requires a fundamental reorientation in the way that the adult world engages with them. It also demands rethinking our ideal of personhood in line with a more optimistic view of the capacity of people to respond to the problems and threats thrown up in the course of their lives.

It is important not to confuse the call to reconsider the meaning of personhood with the attempt to artificially boost the way people think about themselves. It is not about opting for techniques of positive psychology that claim to make people happy, or about demanding greater effort and resilience. The development of a more robust ideal of personhood rests on providing people with greater opportunity to experiment, and to take risks, in order to acquire the experiences that will give them greater confidence to deal with uncertainty. Such confidence will enable them to appreciate many of the virtues – courage, duty, reasoning – that have allowed humanity to move forwards in difficult circumstances.

Back in the eighteenth century, the German philosopher Immanuel Kant posed the question, 'What is Enlightenment?' Kant argued that Enlightenment comes about when people overcome their fear of reasoning for themselves. What stood in the way of Enlightenment, he claimed, was 'lack of resolution or the courage' to use one's understanding of the world. That is why he asserted that the motto of the Enlightenment was *Sapere Aude*, which means: 'Have the courage to use your understanding'.²⁷ Possessing the courage to know has always required an act of will. For Kant, courage and the development of human reasoning went hand in hand. The act of daring to know requires the 'freedom to make public use of one's reason in all matters', noted Kant. This German philosopher often used the metaphor of 'throwing off the yoke of immaturity' to signify the importance of growing up. His conception of personhood is one that uses 'one's own understanding' without relying on the 'guidance of another'. The spirit of daring that he counsels is essential if people are to gain the habit of moral independence.

Kant's exploration of the human condition led him to conclude that the obstacles that stood in the way of Enlightenment were ones that were 'self-incurred' by people. His project of creating a climate that would assist humanity to emerge from its 'self-incurred immaturity' was motivated by the belief that individuals possessed the potential to rise to the occasion. The motto of *Sapere Aude* has special relevance for those who seek to diminish the influence of the culture of fear. Today's 'self-incurred' and immature version of personhood is also in need of a radical fix. Through focusing on the potential of people to assume a degree of control over their life, the limitations that the culture of fear has imposed on human development can be contested. Having the courage of our understandings helps assist society to embark on the road to Enlightenment. It also allows society to interpret its experience through the perspective of knowledge and reason rather than of fear.

To go beyond the current psychologically framed conception of personhood, society will have to re-engage with the language of morality. Society needs to find a way of reappropriating classical virtues and recasting them in a manner that can address the needs of today. The state of feeling vulnerable and fearful comes far too naturally when people are not expected to take responsibility for the security of their community and for their personal life. When, in the face of a threat, people are expected to remain passive and to leave dealing with it to others, values like duty, courage and risk taking become irrelevant. However, such values become crucial to the project of building a less fearful future.

AN ALTERNATIVE TO THE PERSPECTIVE OF FEAR

The fatalistic sensibility of our era echoes the anti-humanist themes that periodically plague modern society. These themes are expressed through a mutually reinforcing anti-humanist triad that promotes misanthropy, the dethronement of authority of knowledge and an impoverished sense of human subjectivity. The narrative of misanthropy instructs people to distrust both themselves and other people, and to be particularly wary of strangers. It also holds humanity responsible for the threats facing the planet and goes so far as to identify people as the problem. The dethronement of the authority of knowledge conveys the idea that human reasoning is over-rated and is unlikely to be able to solve the problems caused by people. This downbeat version of the status of human reasoning and knowledge continually highlights a sense of limits. Finally, the pessimistic account of humanity and its capacity to reason reinforces a loss of faith in the power of human agency. This impoverished sense of subjectivity is constantly refracted through the present-day version of personhood and its characterization of vulnerability as the defining feature of the human condition. Confronting this anti-humanist depiction of the world and the fatalistic attitudes it promotes is the precondition for undermining the commanding influence of the perspective of fear.

The culture of fear does not simply make us unnecessarily apprehensive and scared; it also restrains people from exercising their agency and realizing their potential, as well as encroaching on and curbing our freedom. The antithesis of fear and freedom has been widely recognized by thinkers from the Enlightenment onwards. Back in January 1941, President Franklin D. Roosevelt described Freedom from Fear as one of the fundamental freedoms in his famous 'Four Freedoms Speech'.[28] In that statement, Roosevelt used the term freedom from fear to refer to a world where people did not worry about the threat of war and physical aggression. Roosevelt was not a utopian and he grasped that fear as such was a fact of life that could not be abolished through passing a law.

Today the challenge of achieving freedom from fear requires that the cultural norms and values that underpin the perspective of fear should be contested and their influence overcome. Decades of misguided socialization of people means that the anti-humanist values that underwrite the culture of fear will not be undermined overnight. But their authority can be restrained and in some instances their toxic influence can be neutralized. It is not easy for individuals to transcend the fatalistic *zeitgeist* of our time, but through refusing to play the passive role assigned to them they can find their personal quest for freedom to be a rewarding experience.

As we noted previously, the virtue of courage has played an important role in the management of fear. Courage, along with other virtues, such as reasoning, judgement, prudence and fortitude, offers an effective and flexible antidote to the fear perspective. Educating young people to embrace these values can ensure that new generations of people can develop their self-confidence and adopt a more balanced and optimistic attitude towards the future. Courage is an ideal that can be cultivated through social practices that encourage people to take the initiative and develop the habit of taking responsibility for the world. Through the taking of initiative and the assumption of responsibility for oneself and others, people gain the experiences necessary for the development of confidence and courage. Aristotle noted that confidence can emerge from the experience of confronting the threats we face. He asserted that 'we feel confidence' if we 'have often met danger and escaped it safely'.[29]

Those who possess courage still feel fear but are not overcome by it. A courageous individual will draw on the power of reasoning and of judgement. The use of judgement is historically expressed through the virtue of Prudence, which refers to the ability to govern and discipline oneself through the use of reason. As a virtue, Prudence derives, in part, from the ancient Greek concept of *phronesis*, which translates into the term practical wisdom. Prudence conveys an ability to 'recognise and follow the most suitable or sensible course of action'.[30] On occasions, Prudence is misunderstood as a form of behaviour associated with the exercise of caution. However, Prudence is a multi-dimensional form of behaviour and possesses an ability to exercise sound judgement through a willingness to engage with uncertainty and take risks. So, unlike the risk-averse value of safety, Prudence is open to engaging with uncertainty and, when it judges it to be suitable, to take risks.

Though often portrayed as one of the four Cardinal Virtues, the ideal of Prudence can be understood as a quality of the mind that gains an understanding of the world through the use of reasoning and judgement. It is these characteristics that ensure that those with courage do not simply react but also reflect on the nature of the threat they face. In this way courage helps to provide a response that offers a realistic balance between opportunity and threat. Most important of all, courage provides society with hope and offers an antidote to the cultural power of fear. It recognizes that uncertainty can give rise to hope as well as to fear.

Hannah Arendt has gone so far as to argue that courage does not only provide society with hope but also underwrites society's capacity to exercise freedom. Arendt noted that 'courage liberates men from their worry about life for the freedom of the world'. She cited approvingly Winston Churchill's claim that courage is 'the first of human qualities, because it is the quality which guarantees all the others.' Courage helps individuals and society not to be overwhelmed by their fears.[31]

In our discussion of the ascendancy of the value of safety we pointed to the institutional advocacy of non-judgementalism as one of the most destructive features of twenty-first-century morality. The loss of judgement is closely linked to the downsizing of the status of reasoning and of tolerance. Intolerance of uncertainty is invariably associated with a paternalistic sensibility to control, regulate and micro-manage people's lives. The restoration of the value of judgement is the precondition for the reconstitution of a form of public life that is genuinely open to criticism, questioning and experimentation. Tolerance of such attributes helps create an environment where people can regard the challenges they face as an opportunity to influence their future. It is through the exercise of judgement that society learns to tame its fears and create a space for humanity to acquire a degree of control over its destiny. The exercise of judgement and reasoning helps to demystify the culture of fear and redirect society towards refusing to defer to Fate.

As a result of the therapeutic turn of socialization, the values that have helped to guide humanity to manage the threats it faced have lost their commanding influence. It is the relatively weak authority of these values that has led to the emergence of the perspective of fear as the key motivational force of our time. Virtually every value that is integral to an open-minded, tolerant, experimentative and human-centred society runs counter to the norms upheld by the culture of fear. Reappropriating these values is essential for neutralizing the corrosive effects of our fear culture. Reacquainting ourselves and particularly the young with these values is the point of departure for displacing the perspective of fear with that of hope.

The contrast between the values that help direct society towards a confident future and the culture of fear is highlighted in the table below.

Confidence towards the Future	Culture of Fear
Valuation of experimentation	Valuation of safe space
Trust in human potential	Misanthropy
Courage to judge	Non-judgementalism
Prudence	Safety
Uncertainty as opportunity	Uncertainty as a problem
Openness to risk taking	Risk aversion
Probabilistic thinking	Worst-case thinking
Human agency	Deference to Fate
Moral autonomy	Vulnerability
Openness towards the future	Policing of uncertainty

Though humanity can never be free of the emotion of fear and will always face some type of threat, it is both necessary and possible to create the condition where society can liberate itself from our culture of fear. It is necessary because, as we noted, prevailing attitudes towards safety reduce freedom to a second-order value. It holds back human development. It restrains the freedom to explore, experiment, take risks and make choices. Our aim is not to counter fear appeals with a counter-appeal not to fear. It is naïve to believe – as some modernist thinkers have hoped – that science, reason and knowledge can abolish some of the corrosive features and outcomes of fearing. Nonetheless, it is entirely possible to envisage a world where fear ceases to be regarded as the principal motivating force in public life. Challenging and marginalizing the use of fear as the foundation for policies and public appeals can provide a compelling alternative to the present state of political stasis and exhaustion. Developing a future-oriented alternative to the perspective of fear is a key challenge facing society.

The most effective way of countering the perspective of fear is through acquainting society with values that offer people the meaning and hope they need to effectively engage with uncertainty. The problem raised in the previous chapters is not fear as such but society's difficulty in cultivating values that can guide it to manage uncertainty and the threats it faces. Those concerned with the corrosive effects of the politicization of fear need to dig deeper. The political use of fear is sustained in a cultural terrain, where avoiding risk and acting with caution is equated with responsible behaviour. The ascendancy of safety as a stand-alone value that trumps all others is rarely contested. Critics of the politics of fear are often unaware of or ignore the foundation that sustains the object of their hostility.

Precautionary culture, which thrives on people's anxiety and weakness, has acquired a commanding authority in society. However, its authority is not beyond challenge. Its constant recourse to negative arguments for sustaining its outlook cannot inspire society. It can provoke fear, anxiety, outrage and suspicion but it cannot gain people's trust and commitment. Most important of all, it lacks the ability to engage with people's idealism or their aspiration for hope. Which is why the current state of the culture of fear cannot indefinitely endure.

One final point. That we are expected to fear the future is bad enough. What's even worse is that the prevailing teleology of gloom reduces people to the passive role of helpless observers in a world beyond human control. The most disturbing feature of our era is not its cultivation of the habit of fearing but the cultivation of our sense of vulnerability. Must we be defined by our vulnerability? Must we be fearful? The moment we ask these questions, we are well on the way to intuiting that there is always an alternative.

ACKNOWLEDGEMENTS

I have benefited from the insights and criticisms of numerous colleagues during the course of carrying out research for this book. I am particularly grateful to Professor Bill Durodié of Bath University for directing my attention towards numerous valuable sources on the subject of safety. Dr Jennie Bristow of Canterbury Christ Church University read through the chapters and her insightful comments helped me to rethink and develop some of my arguments. My son, Jacob Furedi, provided valuable criticism of the first draft of the book.

NOTES

INTRODUCTION

1 For an interesting reflection on this trend, see Alex Williams 'How Anxiety Became Society's Prevailing Condition', *Independent*, 17 June 2017, http://www.independent.co.uk/news/long_reads/anxiety-prozac-nation-depression-mental-health-disorder-america-panic-usa-memoirs-self-help-book-a7785351.html (accessed 3 July 2017).

2 Neil Strauss, 'Why We're Living in the Age of Fear', *The Rolling Stone*, 6 October 2016.

3 N. R. Kleinfield, 'An Intense New Chief: Robert R. Frederick; Running RCA From Behind the Scenes', 17 March 1985, *New York Times*. My search of the Nexis database for the term 'culture of fear' took place on 14 April 2017.

4 Andy Rooney, 'Andy Rooney on Bad News', 6 May 1990, *60 Minutes*.

5 'The tyrant, his sons and a culture of fear', *Evening Standard*, 19 January 1996.

6 Chris Thomson, 'Ofsted is responsible for a culture of fear in schools that too often results in job losses', *TES*: 5 October 2016, https://www.tes.com/news/school-news/breaking-views/ofsted-responsible-a-culture-fear-schools-too-often-results-job (accessed 4 April 2017).

7 https://www.amazon.co.uk/Bullies-Culture-Intimidation-Silences-Americans-x/dp/1476710007.

8 For a discussion of the concept of a rhetorical idiom see Ibarra and Kitsuse (2003), pp. 25 and 26.

9 Glassner is cited in Strauss (2016).

10 Lily Rothman, 'Why Americans Are More Afraid Than They Used to Be', *Time*, 6 January 2016, http://time.com/4158007/american-fear-history/ (accessed 25 January 2017).

11 Elias (2005), p. 327.

12 See http://www.spiked-online.com/newsite/article/3053#.We35sRNSyi4.

13 Schoenfield and Ioannidis (2013).

14 See, for example, A. Trevor Thrall, 'Introducing the American Fear Index', 14 September 2017, CATO Institute, https://www.cato.org/blog/introducing-american-fear-index (accessed 4 October 2017).

15 Stearns (2006), pp. 4–5.

16 Ibid., p. 13.

17 Ibid.

18 Cited in 'A scared bunny and his appetite for ants', the *Independent*, 10 June 1995, http://www.independent.co.uk/news/a-scared-bunny-and-his-appetite-for-ants-downed-us-pilot-in-tears-as-he-tells-his-story-of-survival-1585833.html (accessed 3 April 2016).

19 See Tim Dickinson 'How Roger Ailes Built the Fox News Fear Factory', *Rolling Stone*, 9 June 2011, http://www.rollingstone.com/politics/news/how-roger-ailes-built-the-fox-news-fear-factory-20110525.

20 Cited in Strauss (2016).

21 Kerr is cited in Strauss (2016).

22 Cited in Jackson (1932), p. xliii.

23 Furedi (2016).

24 See Selena E. Harper and Professor Bruce Lusignan, 'Fear Factor: Terrorism, Bush, The Media Post 9/11', 6 June 2003, https://web.stanford.edu/class/e297a/FEAR%20FACTOR.htm (accessed 7 July 2012).

25 Ibid.

26 See Altheide (2002).

27 See O'Neill and Nicholson-Cole (2009).

28 See Hayley Watson and Frank Furedi, 'Review of Existing Surveys on Public Opinion of Security', Changing Perceptions of Security and Interventions, Seventh Framework Programme, EU, http://www.cl.cam.ac.uk/~rja14/shb10/watson.pdf (accessed 2 January 2016).

29 Altheide (2017), p. 63.

30 Ibid.

31 Grupp (2003), p. 43.

32 Guzelian (2004), pp. 712 and 767.

33 Cutler (2015), p. 7.

34 See 'A Third of US Public Believe 9/11 Conspiracy Theory', Scripps Howard News Service, 2 August 2006.

35 Hammond (2017), pp. 8–10.

36 Furedi (2013a).

37 See Altheide (2002).

38 See Frank Furedi, 'Good, Bad Or None of Our Business', *The Australian*, 9 April 2011.

39 Ian Sample, 'Global meltdown: scientists isolate areas most at risk of climate change', *Guardian*, 5 February 2008.

40 Hammond (2017), p. 1.

41 'dread, n.', *OED Online*, Oxford University Press, June 2017, http://www.oed.com.chain.kent.ac.uk/view/Entry/57581?rskey=wJ4kMN&result=1&isAdvanced=false (accessed 7 July 2017).

42 For example, in the late nineteenth century the media was complicit in promoting a panic in the UK and US about the so-called white slave trade. It succeeded in turning rumours of white women sold into prostitution in foreign lands into a cultural myth that exercised the public imagination for decades.

43 See Mueller (2006), pp. 2, 3 and 13.

44 Thucydides (1900), p. 138.

45 Alcabes (2009), p. 36.

46 See Maxine Frith, 'Are you one of the rising numbers of the "worried well"?', *Daily Telegraph*, 20 July 2014.

47 Svendsen (2008), p. 7.

48 See, for example, Stearn (2006), p. 76.

49 For a discussion of this paradox see Johnston (2003).

50 Freud (1920), www.bartleby.com/283/ (accessed 3 January 2017).

51 Svendsen (2008), p. 24.

52 Bauman (2006), p. 3.

53 Freud (1920), www.bartleby.com/283/ (accessed 3 January 2017).

54 Kierkegaard (1986).

55 Freud (1920), www.bartleby.com/283/ (accessed 3 January 2017).

56 See Furedi (2009a).

57 Aristotle, *Rhetoric*, Book II, Chapter 5, available online – http://rhetoric.eserver.org/aristotle/index.html (accessed 3 March 2017).

58 Svendsen (2008), p. 46.

59 Ibid., p. 36.

60 Bauman (2006), p. 2.

61 See Furedi (2012).

62 See *Essays of Montaigne*, http://oll.libertyfund.org/titles/montaigne-essays-of-montaigne-vol-1 (accessed 5 June 2017).

63 Gray and Ropeik (2002), p. 106.

64 Garland (2001), p. 10.
65 Bannister and Fyfe (2001), p. 808.
66 Bauman (2006), pp. 21 and 72.
67 Ibid., p. 28.
68 Ibid.
69 Beck (2003), p. 257.
70 Cited in Nancy Schafer (2004), 'Y2K as an Endtime Sign: Apocalypticism in America at the *fin-de-millenium*', *The Journal of Popular Culture* 38(1): 87.
71 Mills (1959), p. 11.

CHAPTER 1 CHANGING STORIES OF FEAR

1 Cited in Laura Hill ' "We were beyond scared" – War heroes recall D-Day horrors as they receive France's highest honours', *Chronicle Live*, 3 February 2017, http://www.chroniclelive.co.uk/news/north-east-news/we-were-beyond-scared-war-12552747 (accessed 3 March 2017).
2 2 Chronicles 32:7.
3 See the discussion in http://ww1centenary.oucs.ox.ac.uk/religion/gott-mit-uns/ (accessed 14 December 2017).
4 See Hochschild (2003).
5 Plato, II, 386a, p. 1022.
6 Plato, III, 386b, p. 1022.
7 Ibid.
8 Ibid., p. 1024, and III, 388a, p. 1025.
9 See Emily Austin's study Fear *and Death in Plato* on this subject in Austin (2009).
10 Plamper (2009), p. 268.
11 Ibid., p. 266.
12 Ibid., p. 281.
13 Ibid., p. 270.
14 Stearns (2006).
15 See Furedi (2014), p. 13.
16 See 'The Emotional Cycle of Deployment: A Military Family Perspective', http://www.hooah4health.com/deployment/familymatters/emotional cycle.htm.

17 Mueller (2000), p. 12.

18 Weber (1915), p. 335.

19 Bauman (2006), p. 52.

20 Becker (1973).

21 See Epicurus' *Letter to Menoeceus* (124–7), available online, http://classics.mit.edu/Epicurus/menoec.html (accessed 21 April 2017).

22 Beye (1963), p. 163.

23 Cited by Jack Sherefkin, 'Immortality and the Fear of Death', 4 February 2016, New York Public Library, https://www.nypl.org/blog/2016/02/04/immortality-fear-death (accessed 2 February 2017).

24 Wilkins (1996), p. 14.

25 Segal (2014), p. 9.

26 Freud (1918), pp. 41 and 68.

27 Ibid., p. 61.

28 Ibid., p. 62.

29 Ibid., p. 69.

30 Pearson (2014), pp. 112 and 116.

31 See Aristotle (2000), p. 41.

32 Harrison (2002), p. 15.

33 William James, 'Lecture 3 – The Reality of the Unseen', http://thepdi.com/William%20James-The%20Reality%20of%20the%20Unseen.pdf (accessed 25 January 2017).

34 Harrison (2002), p. 15.

35 See the discussion in Bowden (2008), p. 60.

36 Cited in Wilson (1998), p. 298.

37 Kempe (2003), pp. 151–2.

38 Behringer (1999), p. 335.

39 See Epicurus' *Letter to Menoeceus*, http://classics.mit.edu/Epicurus/menoec.html (accessed 21 April 2017).

40 Cited in Wootton (1983), p. 58.

41 Ibid., p. 64.

42 Ibid., p. 70.

43 See Vico (2002).

44 Wooton (1983), p. 76.

45 David Hume, 'Of Suicide', 1744, *Essays, Moral, Political, and Literary*, available online, http://www.econlib.org/library/LFBooks/Hume/hmMPL48.html (accessed 12 June 2017).

46 Hume (1889), no pagination, also available on https://ebooks.adelaide. edu.au/h/hume/david/h92n/index.html (accessed 12 February 2017).

47 This lecture is available online on https://users.drew.edu/~jlenz/ whynot.html (accessed 8 April 2017).

48 See Albert Einstein, 'Religion and Science', *New York Times*, 9 November 1930.

49 Pfeiffer (1955), p. 41.

50 Penelope Nelson, 'Fear of God' (online), *Southerly* 40(3) (September 1980): 285–91. Availability: <http://search.informit.com.au/document SummaryDn=918731208786292;res=IELLCC>_ISSN: 0038-3732 (cited 10 April 2017).

51 See Deuteronomy 10:20–21.

52 Deuteronomy 3:22.

53 Exodus 14:13.

54 Job 28:28.

55 Robin (2004), p. xx.

56 See 'Question 125, Fear' in the *Summa Theologia*, http://www.new advent.org/summa/3125.htm.

57 Bader-Saye (2005), p. 97.

58 Ibid., p. 99.

59 Ibid.

60 Bertrand Russell, 'Why I am Not a Christian', on https://users.drew. edu/~jlenz/whynot.html (accessed 8 April 2017).

61 Cited in Kelly and Kelly (1998), p. 259.

62 See Rowell (1976).

63 Jalland (2000), p. 59.

64 Cited in Bourke (2005), p. 46.

65 Small (1898), p. 133.

66 Bourke (2005), p. 47.

67 See Phillip Jenkins' study of the role of religion during the Great War: Jenkins (2014).

68 For example, see Nisbet (1932).

69 E. F. Little, 'Priest or Prophet', *Methodist Review* (July 1919): 557 and 567.

70 John Alfred Faulkner, 'Are There Evil Spirits', *Methodist Review*, September 1919, p. 627.

71 Andrew Gillies Rochester, 'Shall the Severity of God Be Preached?', *Methodist Review* (January 1919): 46.

72 Ibid., p. 53.

73 'Devil and Hell are Mere Superstitions: Pastor Declares Age-Old Idea has Outlived Usefulness', *Los Angeles Times*, 13 October 1919.

74 Herbst (1938), p. 486.

75 Nederman and John of Salisbury (1991), p. 28.

76 R. Allendy, 'A Case of Obsession: Fear of Hell', in *The Psychoanalytic Review* 1 (January 1934): p. 93.

77 A. Parsons, 'The Defeat of Fear', *Britannia and Eve* (26 April 1929): p. 716.

78 'Control of Fear is Urged', *New York Times*, 6 July 1931, p. 6.

79 See 'Answers Our Medical Specialist', *Answers London*, 15 September 1923.

80 Overy (2009), p. 169.

81 'Workers Fight Cut in French Lace Tax', *New York Times*, 28 June 1935, p. 39.

82 'Rise in Our markets Impresses Europe', *New York Times*, 1 August 1932, p. 23.

83 See John Steele, 'Finds Chicago's "I Will" Spirit Boosting Trade', *Chicago Daily Tribune*, 19 November 1930, p. 7, and 'Predicts Steady Rise in Reality Activity', *New York Times*, 29 January 1939.

84 'Unemployment in the USA', *The Times*, 19 September 1931, p. 11.

85 'Labour Party and Sir Strafford Cripps', *The Times*, 29 November 1934.

86 'Psychology of Fear', *Manchester Guardian*, 22 December 1937, p. 37.

87 Mary Chadwick is cited in Overy (2009), p. 169.

88 H. Warner Allen, 'The Worship of Fear: Safety First', *The Saturday Review*, 21 October 1933.

89 Anonymous, in *Answers*, London, 10 August 1940, p. 6.

90 Stearns (2006), p. 93.

91 Ibid., p. 94.

92 Rosita Forbes, 'Fear of Living', *Nash's Pall Mall Magazine*, April 1933, p. 28.

93 Valéry (1927), p. 1.

94 Hughes (1969), p. 15.

95 See Kesselring (2003), pp. 30–3 for a discussion of Roosevelt's confident approach to fear.

96 *Harper's Bazaar*, 1918, Vol. 53, p. 39.

97 See, for example, H. Warner Allen, 'The Worship of Fear: Safety First, *The Saturday Review*, 21 October 1933.

98 'Susan Sage's Page', *Answers*, 28 September 1929.

CHAPTER 2   WAITING FOR THE TIME BOMB TO EXPLODE

1   See 'Warm Weather "to boost food bugs"', *BBC News*, 4 January 2006.

2   See http://www.sciencedirect.com/science/article/pii/S0195925509000420 (accessed 4 October 2017).

3   See (https://www.cancer.gov/about-cancer/causes-prevention/risk/diet/ cooked-meats-fact-sheet (accessed 2 September 2017).

4   For example, see 'Britons "pretty gloomy" about the future, global poll finds', *Daily Telegraph*, 2 May 2017, http://www.telegraph.co.uk/news/ 2017/05/02/britons-pretty-gloomy-future-global-poll-finds/ (accessed 9 July 2017).

5   'Soaring obesity could see millennials die at younger age than their parents', *Daily Telegraph*, 25 June 2017.

6   See Laura Gray, 'Will today's children die earlier than their parents?', *BBC News*, 8 July 2014, http://www.bbc.co.uk/news/magazine-28191865 (accessed 5 September 2016).

7   'Soaring obesity could see millennials die at younger age than their parents', *Daily Telegraph*, 25 June 2017.

8   Bruce Y. Lee, 'Smallpox Could Return Years After Eradication', *Forbes*, 18 August 2016, https://www.forbes.com/sites/brucelee/2016/08/28/ smallpox-could-return-years-after-eradication/2/#5d1045d4680d (accessed 3 December 2016).

9   See http://news.bbc.co.uk/1/hi/health/456831.stm, and 'Strain of bubonic plague as deadly as the Black Death "could return to Earth"', *Daily Mirror*, 28 January 2014.

10   Bruckner (2013), p. 75.

11   David Cox, *Quartz*, 12 April 2016, https://qz.com/657514/superbugs- could-kill-10-million-people-by-2050-if-a-lot-of-things-dont-change- fast/ (accessed 7 September 2016).

12   Philip Bump, 'Explaining the "100 million to die from climate change" claim', *Grist*, 26 December 2012, http://grist.org/climate-energy/ explaining-the-100-million-to-die-from-climate-change-claim/ (accessed 21 January 2016).

13   Ian Johnstone, '600 million children "face death, diseases and malnutrition by 2040 as water resources evaporate"', *Independent*, 21 March 2017 (accessed 27 July 2017).

14   'Fast food timebomb: Obesity fears grow as burger, fried chicken and pizza joints flood Britain's high streets', *Daily Mirror*, 25 July 2017 (accessed 27 July 2017).

15   http://www.dailyprogress.com/newsvirginian/opinion/guest_columnists/opinion-in-venezuela-washington-s-ignoring-a-ticking-time-bomb/article_1647a158-71a3-11e7-abbb-275061cb0cb3.html (accessed 27 July 2017).

16   'The Climate Bomb Lurking Under Arctic Permafrost', *Arctic Deeply*, 25 July 2017, https://www.newsdeeply.com/arctic/articles/2017/07/25/the-climate-bomb-lurking-under-arctic-permafrost (accessed 27 July 2017).

17   'Advice', in *Business Matters*, 25 July 2017, http://www.bmmagazine.co.uk/in-business/businesses-can-defuse-workforce-timebomb/ (accessed 27 July 2017).

18   http://www.express.co.uk/finance/personalfinance/832825/Bank-of-England-Alex-Brazier-recession-debt-credit-news (accessed 27 July 2017).

19   https://www.metro.news/men-in-west-face-fertility-time-bomb/686986/ (accessed 27 July 2017).

20   http://www.bristolpost.co.uk/news/bristol-news/cocaine-laced-de-worming-chemical-236930 (accessed 27 July 2017).

21   'Police: "Iheanacho was to some degree a ticking timebomb"', *Daily Mail*, 27 July 2017.

22   See Bruckner (2013).

23   Terry Eartwind Nichols, 'Are You a Social Time Bomb', 17 August 2017, The Good Men Project, https://goodmenproject.com/featured-content/what-is-a-social-time-bomb-and-do-you-hear-something-ticking-tncl/ (accessed 18 August 2017).

24   See 'time bomb, n.', *OED Online*, Oxford University Press, June 2017, http://www.oed.com.chain.kent.ac.uk/view/Entry/292031?redirectedFrom=time+bomb& (accessed 27 July 2017).

25   http://www.yourdictionary.com/time-bomb (accessed 27 July 2017).

26   See 'An Asteroid With Explosive Power Of 3 Billion Atomic Bombs Barely Misses Earth!, 18 September 2016, http://www.indiatimes.com/lifestyle/self/as-an-asteroid-with-explosive-power-of-3-billion-atomic-bombs-barely-misses-earth-261917.html (accessed 8 June 2017).

27 David Scrieberg, 'Asteroids Are Coming: Do You Know Where Your Children Are?', Forbes: 28 June 2017, https://www.forbes.com/sites/davidschrieberg1/2017/06/28/asteroids-are-coming-do-you-know-where-your-children-are/#5e765dc51c3f (accessed 4 July 2017).

28 See http://www.southbossierbaptist.org/blog/timebomb (accessed 1 August 2017).

29 https://www.mydentist.co.uk/about-us/news/2017/05/24/kids-teeth-time-bomb-as-third-of-parents-wrongly-think-trips-to-dentist-hit-them-in-pocket (accessed 5 August 2017).

30 See advertising blurb for Burke (2015)

31 See Macvarish (2016).

32 David Cameron, 'Life Chances Speech', 11 January 2016, https://www.gov.uk/government/speeches/prime-ministers-speech-on-life-chances (accessed 5 June 2017).

33 Svendsen (2008), p. 71.

34 See 'future-proof, adj.', OED Online, Oxford University Press, June 2017 (accessed 8 August 2017).

35 Bush and Codrington (2008).

36 Walker is cited in 'Can you "future proof" your child', Mail Online, 19 June 2015, Read more: http://www.dailymail.co.uk/femail/article-3129326/Can-future-proof-child-parenting-expert-shares-tips-helping-child-develop-emotional-maturity-says-starting-teens-late.html#ixzz4polyNkfd (accessed 3 May 2017).

37 For example, see '15 ways to future-proof your relationship', Irish Independent, 2 February 2017, http://www.independent.ie/style/sex-relationships/15-ways-to-futureproof-your-relationship-35421372.html (accessed 5 June 2017).

38 'apocalypse, n.', OED Online, Oxford University Press, June 2017, Web. 9 August 2017.

39 Wilkinson (1841), p. 438.

40 See Aristotle, Rhetoric, Book II, Chapter 5, http://rhetoric.eserver.org/aristotle/index.html (accessed 4 March 2016).

41 See, for example, 'Baby Boomers who may outlive their kids', http://www.webmd.com/children/news/20100409/baby-boomers-may-outlive-their-kids (accessed 9 January 2017).

42 http://www.penguinrandomhouse.co.za/book/future-proof-your-child-parenting-wired-generation/9780143025801 (accessed 12 April 2017).

43 See Chrystia Freeland, 'Al Gore and the age of hyper-change', *Washington Post*, 27 February 2013.

44 Mason (1835), p. 116.

45 Edmund Burke (1729–97), *On the Sublime and Beautiful*. The Harvard Classics. 1909–14, http://www.bartleby.com/24/2/219.html (accessed 9 February 2017).

46 Laidi (1998), p. 1.

47 Wrenn (2013), p. 394.

48 Toffler (1970).

49 Unesco (1972), pp. 90–1.

50 See his comments in http://blog.basisindependent.com/mclean/pisa-asia-society-panel-0-0-0 (accessed 24 June 2017).

51 Barber (1997), p. 160.

52 Bill Law, 'A new focus for the curriculum', http://www.nesta.org.uk/a-new-focus-for-the-curriculum/.

53 Peter Marsh, 'The world struggles to keep up with the pace of change in science and technology', *Financial Times*, 17 June 2014.

54 Ibid.

55 See Furedi (1997), pp. 55–60.

56 Cited in Bruckner (2013), p. 118.

57 In Beck, Giddens and Lash (1994), p. 185.

58 Giddens (1992), p. 85 and Beck (1992), p. 183.

59 Harari (2016), p. 58.

60 US Department of Defense, Department of Defense News Briefing, 'Secretary Rumsfeld and Gen. Myers, www.defenselink.mil/transcripts/2002/t02122002_t212sdv2.html (accessed 7 June 2007).

61 Meyer, Folker, Jorgensen, Kyare von Krauss, Sandoe and Tveit (2005), p. 237.

62 Bauman (2006), p. 11.

63 Ibid., p. 54.

64 Anonymous author, *The Public: A Journal of Democracy*, Vol. 1, p. 20, available online at https://books.google.it/books?id=PDHmAAAAMAAJ.

65 The radicalism of anti-change is discussed in Furedi (2005), Chapter 1.

66 See Ben Webster, 'Prince "wrong" on climate link to Syria war', *The Times*, 8 September 2017.

67 See Rees (2003).

68 Ibid., p. 74.

69 Cited in Nerlich and Halliday (2007), p. 57. One betting website suggests that the bet may have been for only $400; see http://longbets.org/9/.

70 Geldof is cited in http://www.bbc.co.uk/news/blogs-magazine-monitor-24432491 (accessed 1 March 2017).

71 See Reddy (2001), p. 105.

72 Marcus (2002), pp. 103–4.

73 Walton (1996), p. 304.

74 Bourke (2005), pp. 389–90.

75 Cited in Dick Taverne, 'Careless science costs lives', *Guardian*, 18 February 2005.

76 'It's a hell of a town', *Guardian*, 19 May 2005.

77 See Lawson, Yeo, Yu and Greene (2016), p. 65.

78 See http://journals.sagepub.com/doi/abs/10.1177/109019810002700506?journalCode=hebc (accessed 4 October 2017).

79 See *The Weekly Underwriter*, 1949, no. 161, p. 982.

80 See http://www.telegraph.co.uk/news/health/news/8639569/Latest-generation-of-children-will-live-20-years-longer-than-their-grandparents.html (accessed 9 July 2016).

81 Cited by Rob Lyons, 'Stop Smoking or your Children Will Die', Spiked online, 10 August 2010, http://www.spiked online.com/newsite/article/9403#.WZb_gHd96i5 (accessed 4 March 2017).

82 Adam Withnall, 'Unhealthy lifestyles will see British children die before their parents', *Independent*, 12 August 2013.

83 Cited in ibid.

84 Faye (2012), p. 198.

85 See http://money.cnn.com/2016/01/28/news/economy/donald-trump-bernie-sanders-us-economy/index.html (5 July 2017).

86 'Most Millennials Think They'll Be Worse Off Than Their Parents' *Fortune*: 1 March 2016, http://fortune.com/2016/03/01/millennials-worse-parents-retirement/ (accessed 1 April 2016).

87 Pope (1804), 'Epistle IV: "Of the Nature and State of Man with respect to Happiness"', p. 62.

CHAPTER 3   MORAL CONFUSION – THE MAIN DRIVER
OF THE CULTURE OF FEAR

1 This point is made by Rowe (2009), p. 23.

2 Dill and Hunter (2010), p. 288.

3 Anonymous, 'Review of Cox's Sermon on Regeneration', *The Quarterly Christian Spectator* (1830), Vol. 2, New Haven: A. H. Maltby, p. 350. My chronology of historical references is based on searching the Google Ngram data base for the term moral panic. Where possible the original texts were consulted.

4 *The Biblical Repertory and Theological Review*, published by Russell and Martien, Philadelphia, p. 519.

5 Creighton (1905), pp. 149–51.

6 Ibid., p. 154.

7 See *Royal Commission on the Liquor Traffic: Minutes of Evidence* iv, part II, 1895, Queen's Printer: Ottawa, paragraphs 1734 5a, 1741 5a, 1741 6a, https://archive.org/stream/reportroyalcommo1mclegoog/ reportroyalcommo1mclegoog_djvu.txt (accessed 21 April 2014).

8 Riezler (1944), p. 495.

9 Beck (1992), p. 73.

10 See my essay on twenty-first-century heresy, http://www.spiked-online. com/newsite/article/2792#.WhahIbSFii4 (accessed 4 September 2017).

11 http://www.bbc.co.uk/news/education-33380155 (accessed 5 July 2017).

12 https://www.nspcc.org.uk/globalassets/documents/annual-reports/ childline-annual-review-2015–16.pdf (accessed 4 January 2017).

13 Morgan Reardon, 'The crisis in our classrooms', *Sun*, 15 April 2017.

14 Helen Ward, 'Imposing synthetic phonics "is almost abuse" says academic', *The Times Educational Supplement*, 28 January 2014.

15 See https://www.tes.com/news/school-news/breaking-views/phonics- v-whole-word-battle-has-always-been-about-politics-not (accessed 4 August 2017).

16 See https://www.cnbc.com/2014/09/26/president-carter-slavery-is-worse- now-than-in-1700s.html# (accessed 5 June 2016).

17 https://www.unseenuk.org/ (accessed 23 June 2017).

18 Jeff Nesbit, 'Slavery Did Not End in the 19th Century', 28 July 2015, https://www.usnews.com/news/blogs/at-the-edge/2015/07/28/ modern-slavery-no-one-knows-the-extent (accessed 4 February 2016).

19 Ibid.

20 "'We're not slaves", more than 100 migrant workers say as they launch protest at arrest of farm bosses'. http:// www.telegraph.co.uk/ news/2018/02/09/not-slaves-100-migrant-workers-say-launch- protest-arrest-farm/ (accessed February 2018).

21 Richard Ford and Phil Miller, 'Immigration centres accused of slavery over £1-an-hour pay', *The Times*, 8 January 2018.

22 O'Brien was subsequently discredited and forced to resign as archbishop for engaging in sexual activity with young clergy.

23 http://www.theecologist.org/blogs_and_comments/commentators/other_comments/701072/climate_change_we_are_like_slaveowners.html (accessed 8 July 2013).

24 See Kazanjian (2015), p. 418.

25 Thucydides (1900), 2.53.3.

26 Cited by Jeff Nesbit, 'Slavery Did Not End in the 19th Century', 28 July 2015, https://www.usnews.com/news/blogs/at-the-edge/2015/07/28/modern-slavery-no-one-knows-the-extent (accessed 4 February 2016).

27 See 'Superstition: A Lecture Delivered at the Royal Institution, April 24, 1866' by Rev. Charles Kingsley, *Fraser's Magazine* 73, p. 705.

28 Clark (2005), p. 212.

29 See Pearl (1983), p. 467.

30 See Prior (1932).

31 Ibid., p. 170.

32 Behringer (1999), p. 339.

33 Ibid., p. 335.

34 Clark (1980), p. 120.

35 Hulme (2008), p. 5.

36 Cited in Currie (1968), p. 11.

37 Locke (1663–4), p. 120.

38 Einstein is cited in Madalyn Murray O'Hair's *All the Questions You Ever Wanted to Ask American Atheists*, see https://www.thoughtco.com/einstein-quotes-on-ethics-and-morality-249859 (accessed 12 May 2017).

39 Cited in Kate Devlin, 'Obese children to die before their parents', *Daily Telegraph*, 6 March 2008.

40 Ian Roberts, 'How the obesity epidemic is aggravating global warming', *The New Scientist*, 27 June 2007.

41 Higgins (2005), p. 201.

42 See http://www.who.int/reproductivehealth/topics/sexual_health/sh_definitions/en/ (accessed 12 December 2017).

43 https://www.netmums.com/coffeehouse/children-parenting-190/general-parenting-192/945363-do-you-like-your-child-have-tan-all.html (accessed 7 March 2017).

44 Cited in https://www.theguardian.com/society/2004/jul/18/cancercare. observermagazine (accessed 2 May 2017).

45 Cited in Shoveller, Savoy and Roberts (2002), p. 146.

46 http://www.bbc.co.uk/blogs/ethicalman/2009/12/in_praise_of_ scepticism.html (accessed 29 June 2014).

47 Peter Christoff, 'The ABC has to explain why it has bought a documentary that is bokum', *The Age*, 9 July 2007.

48 Alcabes (2009), p. 10.

49 Dillinger (2004), p. 180.

50 James Lovelock, 'The earth is about to catch a morbid fever that may last as long as 1000 years', *Independent*, 16 January 2006.

51 David Roach, 'Gore cites political will, claims scriptural mandate on environmental issues', *Baptist Press*, 31 January 2008.

52 Cited in Strengers and Van Neck (2001), p. 78.

53 Stolberg (2000), p. 6.

54 Ibid., p. 8.

55 Spitz (1952).

56 Fitzpatrick (2001), p. 201.

57 Cited in Kukla (2006), p. 159.

58 See Pat Thomas, 'Suck on this' *Ecologist online*, 1 April 2006, http:// www.theecologist.org/archive_detail.asp?content_id=586.

59 http://www.babymilkaction.org/.

60 See http://www.4women.gov/breastfeeding/index.cfm?page=ladiesnight.

61 Personal communication, 4 January 2014.

62 Svendsen (2008), p. 13.

63 Altschuler (2003), p. 169.

CHAPTER 4   THE PERSPECTIVE OF FEAR – HOW IT WORKS

1 Even accounting for the increase in academic publications, this increase illustrates a growing interest in this topic.

2 'Americans now drink more bottled water than soda', *The Wall Street Journal*, 10 March 2017, available online at http://www.marketwatch. com/story/americans-now-drink-more-bottled-water-than-soda- 2017-03-09 (accessed 4 September 2017).

3 See 'Bottled water "not as safe as tap variety"', *Daily Telegraph*, 2 January 2013.

4   Shehnaz Toorawa, '6 scary facts about bottled water', 5 September 2017, https://www.soundvision.com/article/6-scary-facts-about-bottled-water (accessed 5 September 2017).

5   See National Hydration Council, 'Myths about bottled water still confusing consumers', 18 May 2016, http://www.naturalhydrationcouncil.org.uk/press/myths-about-bottled-water-still-confusing-consumers/ (accessed 24 May 2017).

6   Cited in Bogardus (1940), p. 332.

7   Ibid.

8   Habermas (1975), pp. 73, 75.

9   Furedi (2013b), p. 407.

10 Laura Donnelcy, 'Low-fat diet could kill you, major study shows', *Daily Telegraph*, 29 August 2017.

11 Ibid.

12 David Benjmain 'The Risk of High-Fat Diets', 11 May 2015, Livestrong. com, http://www.livestrong.com/article/249377-the-risks-of-high-fat-diets/ (accessed 25 June 2016).

13 'What is a Gamble?', *Northwestern Mining Journal*, Vols 5–7, p. 96.

14 See our discussion of zero-risk in Chapter 6.

15 See 'risky, adj.', *OED Online*, Oxford University Press, June 2017 (accessed 30 August 2017).

16 See 'Netmums survey: Many mums given risky parenting advice', *BBC News*, 29 March 2011.

17 Professor Terje Traavik, 'GMO risks and hazards: Absence of evidence is not evidence of absence of risk', Third World Network, www.twnside. org.sg/title/terje-cn.htm.

18 Beck (2003), p. 260.

19 Cited in https://www.theguardian.com/science/2015/aug/21/study-of-holocaust-survivors-finds-trauma-passed-on-to-childrens-genes?CMP=share_btn_tw.

20 Stern and Wiener (2006), p. 2.

21 European Environment Agency (2002), 'Late Lessons From Early Warnings', http://reports.eea.europa.eu/environmental_issue_report_2001_22/en.

22 Mack (2004), p. v.

23 Ibid, p. vi.

24 Kateb (2004), pp. 891 and 896.

25 Hollander (2004), p. 15.

26 Wodak (2015).

27 Johnson's speech is available on http://www.presidency.ucsb.edu/ws/ index.php?pid=26225&st=&st1 (accessed 24 June 2016).

28 Jonas (1984), p.x.

29 Ibid., p. 27.

30 Ibid.

31 Ibid., p. 149.

32 Ibid., p. 151.

33 See, for example, Dinneen (2014).

34 See the discussion in Panchev (2013).

35 This development is discussed in Chapter 7 of my study, *The Politics of Fear*, Furedi (2005).

36 Ignatieff (1997), p. 18.

37 Shklar (1989), p. 33.

38 Ibid., pp. 23, 29, 30.

39 Beck (2002), p. 46.

40 Beck (1992), p. 49.

41 See 'A third of US public believe 9/11 conspiracy theory', Scripps Howard News Service, 2 August 2006.

42 Graeme Wilson, 'Shocking scale of abuse', *Sun*, 13 June 2012.

43 This point is explored and elaborated in Furedi (2013a).

CHAPTER 5   CREATION OF THE FEARFUL SUBJECT

1 Loseke (1999), p. 120.

2 'personhood, n.', *OED Online*, Oxford University Press, June 2017 (accessed 14 September 2017).

3 MacIntyre (1984), p. 192.

4 See Risk Assessment – College of Policing APP, https://www. app.college.police.uk/app-content/civil-emergencies/civil./risk-assessment/ (accessed 4 July 2017).

5 See https://www.app.college.police.uk/app-content/risk-2/?s= (accessed 4 July 2017).

6 Lacquement (2004), p. 46.

7 https://www.westmercia.police.uk/media/5804/FOI-6602-Health--Safety-Policy-water-rescue---Risk Assessments/pdf/FOI_6602_Health_ _Safety_Policy_water_rescue_-_Risk_Assessments.pdf.

8   D. Kennedy, 'Failure to save dying boy prompts call to scrap "community" police', *The Times*, 22 September 2007.

9   See 'Trigger warnings', Chapter 8 in Furedi (2017a).

10 Claire Colebrook, 'End-times for humanity', *Aeon*, https://aeon.co/essays/the-human-world-is-not-more-fragile-now-it-always-has-been (accessed 8 September 2017).

11 http://internationalpsychoanalysis.net/2009/06/11/the-courage-to-survive/ (accessed 2 July 2017).

12 Hasson (2015), pp. 68–9.

13 Zavaliy and Aristidou (2014), p. 180.

14 Ibid., p. 179.

15 Ibid., p. 174.

16 Rob Fajardo, 'How to Have the Courage to be Yourself', https://journal.thriveglobal.com/how-to-have-the-courage-to-be-yourself-9e8dd4705980 (accessed 18 September 2017).

17 Wolfe (1998), p. 54.

18 See Furedi (2017a), Chapter 4.

19 See 'Toxic Words – Verbal Abuse Can Hurt You', http://ezinearticles.com/?Toxic-Words---Verbal-Abuse-Can-Hurt-You&id=1350602.

20 Michelle Roberts, 'Cancer fight "hampered in UK by stiff upper lip"', *BBC News*, 30 January 2013.

21 See Stearns (2006), p. 93.

22 'Fear in Children – Harriet Martineau's Early Experience', *Christian Register*, 15 January 1848.

23 Nicholson (2003), p. 100.

24 Stearns (2006), p. 99.

25 Ibid., p. 95.

26 'The Conquest of Fear: Modern Methods in the Nursery', *Answers*, 24 February 1934.

27 'Nerves in the Nursery', *Answers*, 9 February 1924.

28 Watson is cited in Stearns (2006), p. 96.

29 *Indiana Framer's Guide*, 9 December 1922.

30 Ruth Danehower Wilson, *McClure's Magazine*, December 1922, p. 40.

31 George Draper, 'Paralyzing The Child', *Forum*, July 1926, p. 83.

32 He added, 'the motive for discipline must always be the development of character or intelligence. For the intellect, also, requires discipline, without it accuracy will never be achieved.' See Bertrand Russell, 'Your Child and the Fear of Death', *Forum*, March 1929.

33   Stearns (2006), p. 106

34   Ibid., p. 112.

35   Lasch (1984), p. 60.

36   Ibid., pp. 72–3.

37   Coker (2007), p. 2.

38   See Furedi (2001).

39   Interviews carried out in September 2001.

40   Previously the term was only applied to adults in the context of describing a character trait, such as domineering. See 'bullying, adj.', *OED Online*, Oxford University Press, June 2017, http://www.oed.com. chain.kent.ac.uk/view/Entry/24615 (accessed 26 October 2017).

41   'Bullying Statistics: The Ultimate Guide', NOBullying.com, 10 April 2017, https://nobullying.com/bullying-statistics (accessed 4 October 2017).

42   Stearns (2006), pp. 99–100.

43   Selleck (1972), p. 87.

44   See ibid., pp. 94, 118–19.

45   Rieseman (1953), pp. 49, 51, 57.

46   Arendt (2006), p. 81.

47   Arendt (1956), p. 403.

48   Ibid., p. 404.

49   These problems are discussed in chapter 4 of Furedi (2009b).

50   See Howe and Strauss (2003).

51   'Marking in red pen "can damage students"', *Daily Telegraph*, 11 December 2008.

52   Ecclestone and Hayes (2008), p. 34.

53   'Services and programs for "vulnerable" children and youth: an interim report', Youth Commission: Michigan, 1964, https://books.google. co.uk/books?id=7F5YAAAAMAAJ&q=%22vulnerable+children%22& dq=%22vulnerable+children%22&hl=en&sa=X&ved=0ahUKEwjJrIu qiaXWAhVGJ1AKHaIUDekQ6AEIKDAA (accessed 3 March 2017).

54   *New York Times*, 16 November 1972.

55   Nexis database search was carried out on 4 September 2017.

56   Frankenberg, Robinson and Delahooke (2000), pp. 588–9.

57   See Furedi (2004), Chapter 5.

58   See Stearns (2006), pp. 112–15.

59 Bullying Statistics: The Ultimate Guide', NOBullying.com, 10 April 2017, https://nobullying.com/bullying-statistics (accessed 4 October 2017).

60 See http://news.bbc.co.uk/1/hi/education/7101976.stm (accessed 5 May 2016).

61 Ignatieff (1997), p. 18.

62 Harari (2016), p. 73.

63 Walters and Egger (2007), p. 668.

64 See Kelpie Wilson, 'Abortion and the Earth', *Truthout*, 29 January 2008, www.truthout.org.

65 'A Population-Based Climate Strategy – An Optimum Population Trust Briefing', by David Nicholson-Lord, May 2007, www.optimum population.org.

CHAPTER 6   THE QUEST FOR SAFETY IN A DANGEROUS WORLD

1 http://www.thefiscaltimes.com/Articles/2013/06/12/Americans-Choose-Safety-over-Privacy-in-New-Poll (accessed 12 February 2017).

2 For a transcript of speech, see https://www.vox.com/2016/7/21/12253426/donald-trump-acceptance-speech-transcript-republican-nomination-transcript (accessed 8 May 2017).

3 See John Cassidy, 'Donald Trump's Dark, Dark Convention Speech', *New Yorker*, 22 July 2016, https://www.newyorker.com/news/john-cassidy/donald-trumps-dark-dark-convention-speech (accessed 5 September 2017).

4 https://www.bbc.co.uk/cbbc/shows/stay-safe (accessed 5 October 2017).

5 https://www.standard.co.uk/news/parents-anger-after-pupils-sent-home-for-breaking-snowball-ban-7275502.html (accessed 4 June 2017).

6 See http://manifestoclub.info/attention-please-manifesto-club-photobook/ (accessed 21 April 2016).

7 Boutelier (2007), p. 4.

8 Myself and a group of collaborators on The EU Seventh Framework Programme 'Changing Perceptions of Security and Interventions' came to this conclusion, 31 July 2009.

9 Stearns (2006), p. 42.

10   Sarah Clark, 'Soft Toy Manufacture and Safety', 16 March 2017, Toys Advice, http://www.toysadvice.co.uk/soft-toy-manufacture-safety. html.

11   'How can I be safe while interviewing people?', East Midlands Oral History Archive, https://www.le.ac.uk/emoha/training/no6.pdf (accessed 9 July 2017).

12   http://www.cardiff.ac.uk/secty/resources/Personal%20Safety%20 Guide.pdf.

13   See http://www.ed.ac.uk/history-classics-archaeology/information-current-undergraduates/new-undergraduates/personal-safety (accessed 5 October 2017).

14   See http://services.ccpas.co.uk/information/media/press-release-archive.

15   Stanko (1988).

16   See Mary Bulman, '80% of children don't feel safe on social media', *Independent*, 26 April 2017, http://www.independent.co.uk/news/uk/home-news/children-social-media-nspcc-harmful-content-online-a7704201.html.

17   Fromm (1965), p. 35.

18   Lasch (1984), p. 32.

19   Ibid., p. 33.

20   Sue et al. (2007), p. 271.

21   Vogue Williams, 'I don't feel safe living in the UK anymore', 28 May 2017, *Independent* (Ireland), http://www.independent.ie/style/celebrity/celebrity-news/vogue-williams-i-dont-feel-safe-living-in-the-uk-anymore-35763921.html (accessed 7 July 2017).

22   http://www.npcc.police.uk/NPCCBusinessAreas/WeaponAttacks StaySafe.aspx (accessed 12 October 2017).

23   For example, see https://www.thetimes.co.uk/article/official-advice-to-run-hide-tell-not-remotely-helpful-say-experts-5klrfkh3hgn (accessed 2 October 2017).

24   Bauman (1992), p. xviii.

25   Tulloch and Lupton (2003), p. 38.

26   'On the ends of good and evil', *De Finibus* 3.64 in Cicero (2006).

27   See Sorell (2010).

28   Tacitus, *Annals*, Book XV, 50.

29   Gouldner (1965), p. 65.

30 See Nietzsche, 'On the Genealogy of Morality', Chapter 2.11, available online, https://lyricswatch.com/artist/15692/lyrics/151512 (accessed 2 July 2017).

31 Cited in Smith (1998), p. 245.

32 Wildawsky (2017), p. 2.

33 Hunter (2000), pp. xiii and 76.

34 Beck and Beck-Gernsheim (2002), p. 38.

35 http:/safety.army.mil/Portals/o/Documents/MEDIA/DASAFMESSAGES/Standard/2014/DASAF_AUG14_FINAL.pdf.

36 http://www.dupont.com/industries/safety-protection/military-protection.html.

37 See http://www.contractingbusiness.com/archive/change-safety-program-core-value (accessed 12 October 2017).

38 https://www.enbridge.com/About-Us/Our-Values/Environment-Health-and-Safety.aspx (accessed 12 October 2017).

39 See https://www.bainessimmons.com/about-baines-simmons/philosophy/ (accessed 4 October 2017).

40 https://www.parmanenergy.com/about/safety-first-always-and-without-hesitation (accessed 7 September 2017).

41 https://www.parmanenergy.com/about/safety-first-always-and-without-hesitation (accessed 7 September 2017).

42 http://www.threadsculture.com/blog/company-culture/core-values-list-threads/ (accessed 4 October 2017).

43 See http://www.jacobs.com/about (accessed 7 May 2017).

44 Ibid.

45 Dominic Cooper, 'Treating Safety as a Value', *Professional Safety*, February 2001, p. 21.

46 See http://www.telegraph.co.uk/news/uknews/defence/9052473/Army-chief-soldiers-will-face-new-and-greater-risks.html (accessed 6 April 2013).

47 See F. Furedi 'The Crusade Against the A-word', Spiked online, 15 May 2007, http://www.spiked-online.com/newsite/article/3356#.WdznxxN Syi4.

48 Cited in Furedi (2004).

49 Szasz (2009).

50 Fry (1987), p. xiv.

51 See ibid., Chapter 7.

52 Lasch (1984), p. 57.

53 See http://www.occupybristoluk.org/about/safe-space-policy/ (accessed 2 February 2016).

54 http://occupylondon.org.uk/about/statements/safer-space-policy/ (accessed 4 March 2016).

55 https://www.newtactics.org/conversation/creating-safe-spaces-tactics-communities-risk.

56 http://www.dailymail.co.uk/news/article-4915050/Labour-sets-safe-space-delegates.html (accessed 25 September 2017).

57 https://dailybruin.com/2016/11/17/bruin-republicans-members-encourage-students-to-accept-election-results/ (accessed 6 January 2017).

58 See Julie Hare, 'Epidemic of stressed university students', *The Australian*, 6 April 2017.

59 'Academics "face higher mental health risk" than other professions', *THE*, 22 August 2017, https://www.timeshighereducation.com/news/academics-face-higher-mental-health-risk-than-other-professions (accessed 6 September 2017).

60 Strossen is cited in http://www.telegraph.co.uk/news/worldnews/northamerica/usa/12022041/How-political-correctness-rules-in-Americas-student-safe-spaces.html (accessed 14 January 2016).

61 https://www.st-andrews.ac.uk/media/student-services/documents/Student-Services-values-and-beliefs-2014–2017.pdf (accessed 23 March 2016).

62 See http://www.montana.edu/counseling/safezone.html (accessed 25 March 2016).

63 It is worth noting that the word judgy has not yet made it into the *OED*.

64 Regan (2012), p. 126.

65 See, for example, Aubry, Dvořák, McCrory et al. (2013).

66 https://www.imperialcollegeunion.org/your-union/policies/safe-space-policy (accessed 30 March 2016).

67 For example, see Chloe Lew, 'Campus safe spaces need expansion into classrooms', *Daily Bruin*, 25 May 2015.

68 See my chapter on 'Verbal Purification' in Furedi (2017a).

69 https://www.brookings.edu/blog/fixgov/2017/09/18/views-among-college-students-regarding-the-first-amendment-results-from-a-new-survey/ (accessed 3 October 2017).

70 Alexander Hamilton, 'The Consequences of Hostilities Between the States', *Federalist* 8, available online at http://avalon.law.yale.edu/18th_century/fed08.asp (accessed 3 September 2017).

71 See Altheide (2017), p. 42.

CONCLUSION: TOWARDS A LESS FEARFUL FUTURE

1 Elias (2005), p. 442.

2 Christopher Coker, (2007), *The Warrior Ethos: Military Culture and the War on Terror*, London: Routledge, cited in Bill Durodié, 'Death of the Warrior Ethos', http://www.durodie.net/index.php/site/printable/94/ (accessed 4 August 2017).

3 M. Kakutani, 'Critic's notebook: biography becomes blood sport', *New York Times*, 20 May 1994.

4 Coker (2007), p. 3.

5 Ibid., p. 2.

6 See *The Times*, 5 November 1966.

7 McLean and Johnes (2000), p. 115.

8 See Morgan et al. (2003).

9 Meier (2005), p. 17.

10 For a discussion of the EU's estrangement from European history see Furedi (2017b), Chapter 4.

11 See http://www.independent.co.uk/news/people/richard-dawkins-eu-referendum-brexit-david-cameron-a7059201.html.

12 http://www.thedailybeast.com/articles/2016/11/02/donald-trump-can-t-merely-be-defeated-he-and-his-deplorables-must-be-crushed.html.

13 Holmes (1993), p. 3.

14 Svendsen (2008), p. 52.

15 Ibid.

16 See Chapter LVIII, *Discourses on the First Ten Books of Titus Livius*, https://www.marxists.org/reference/archive/machiavelli/works/discourses/ch01.htm#s05 (accessed 18 January 2017).

17 Ibid.

18 Hanekamp (2005), p. 44.

19 Ibid.

20 Stearns (2006), p. 102.

21 Ibid., p. 114.

22 Mintz (2015), p. 21.
23 Walsh (1997), p. 89.
24 Arendt (2006), p. 192.
25 See, for example, https://www.tes.com/news/school-news/breaking-news/tristram-hunt-children-should-be-taught-grit-and-determination-school (accessed 21 October 2017).
26 *Rhetoric*, Book II, Chapter 5, http://rhetoric.eserver.org/aristotle/index.html.
27 See http://library.standrews-de.org/lists/CourseGuides/religion/rs-vi/oppressed/kant_what_is_enlightenment.pdf (accessed 24 May 2017).
28 http://www.americanrhetoric.com/speeches/fdrthefourfreedoms.htm.
29 See *Rhetoric*, Book II, Chapter 5, http://rhetoric.eserver.org/aristotle/index.html.
30 'prudence, n.', *OED Online*, Oxford University Press, June 2017, http://www.oed.com.chain.kent.ac.uk/view/Entry/153584?redirectedFrom=prudence (accessed 19 December 2017).
31 Arendt (1960), p. 154.

BIBLIOGRAPHY

Alcabes, P. (2009), *Dread: How Fear and Fantasy Have Fuelled Epidemics from the Black Death to Avian Flu*, New York: Public Affairs.

Altheide, D. (2002), *Creating Fear: News and the Construction of Crisis*, New York: Aldine De Gruyter.

Altheide, D. (2017), *Terrorism and the Politics of Fear*, 2nd edn, London: Rowman and Littlefield.

Altschuler, G. C. (2003), 'Apathy, Apocalypse, and the American Jeremiad', *American Literary History* 15(1): 162–71.

Arendt, H. (1956), 'Authority in the Twentieth Century', *The Review of Politics* 18(4).

Arendt, H. (1960), 'What is Freedom?' in Arendt, H. (2006), *Between Past and Future*, London: Penguin Books.

Arendt, H. (1960), 'What is Authority?', in Arendt, H. (2006), *Between Past and Future*, London: Penguin Books.

Aristotle (2000), *The Nicomachean Ethics*, Hackett Publishing Company: Indianapolis (ed. T. Irwin).

Armstrong, A. (2017), 'Germ Wars: The Politics of Microbes and America's Landscape of Fear', in M. Armstrong (2017), *Germ Wars: The Politics of Microbes and America's Landscape of Fear*, Vol. 2, Los Angeles: University of California Press.

Aubry M., J. Dvořák, P. McCrory et al. (2013), 'Zero Tolerance: The Future of Head Injury in Sports' *British Journal of Sports Medicine* 47, p. 249.

Austin, E. A. (2009), *Fear and Death in Plato*, Washington University in St Louis, PhD thesis.

Bader-Saye, S. (2005), 'Thomas Aquinas and the Culture of Fear', *Journal of the Society of Christian Ethics* 25(2): 95–108.

Bannister, J. and N. Fyfe (2001), 'Introduction: Fear and the City', *Urban Studies* 38(5–6).

Barber, M. (1997), *The Learning Game: Arguments for an Education Revolution*, London: Indigo.

Bauman, Z. (1992), *Intimations of Post-Modernity*, London: Routledge.

Bauman, Z. (2006), *Liquid Fear*, Cambridge: Polity Press.

Beck, U. (1992), *Risk Society: Towards a New Modernity*, London: Sage Publications.

Beck, U. (2002), 'The Terrorist Threat: World Risk Society Revisited', *Theory, Culture & Society* 19(4).

Beck, U. (2003), 'The Silence of Words: On Terror and War', *Security Dialogue* 34(3).

Beck, U. and E. Beck-Gernsheim (2002), *Individualization*, London: Sage Publications.

Beck, U., A. Giddens and S. Lash (1994), *Reflexive Modernization*, Cambridge: Polity Press.

Becker, E. (1973), *The Denial of Death*, New York: Free Press.

Behringer, W. (1999), 'Climatic Change and Witch-Hunting: The Impact of the Little Ice Age', *Climatic Change*, 43.

Beye, C. R. (1963), 'Lucretius and Progress', *The Classic Journal* 48(4): 160–9.

Bogardus, E. S. (1940), *The Development of Social Thought*, New York: David McKay Company.

Bourke, J. (2005), *Fear: A Cultural History*, London: Virago Press.

Boutelier, H. (2007), *The Safety Utopia: Contemporary Discontent and Desire as to Crime and Punishment*, Dordrecht: Springer.

Bowden, H. (2008), 'Before Superstition and After: Theophrastus and Plutarch on Deisidaimonia', *Past & Present* 199 (supplement 3): 56–71.

Bruckner, P. (2013), *Fanaticism of the Apocalypse*, Cambridge: Polity Press.

Burke, J. S. (2015), *The Nanny Time Bomb: Navigating the Crisis in Child Care*, Santa Barbara, Cal.: ABC-CLIO.

Bush, N. and G. Codrington (2008), *Future Proof Your Child: Parenting the Wired Generation*, London: Random House.

Cicero, M. T. (2006), *The Academic Questions, Treatise de Finibus & Tusculan Disputations of M.T. Cicero, with a Sketch of the Greek Philosophers Mentioned*, online publication (publisher unknown).

Clark, S. (1980), 'Inversion, Misrule and the Meaning of Witchcraft', *Past and Present* 87, pp. 96–127.

Clark, S. (2005), *Thinking With Demons: The Idea of Witchcraft in Early Modern Europe*, Oxford: Oxford University Press.

Coker, C. (2007), *The Warrior Ethos*, London: Routledge.

Creighton, M. (1905), *The Heritage of the Spirit & Other Sermons*, London: S.C.Brown and Lanham & Company Limited: 149–151, available online at https://archive.org/stream/heritagespiritooocreigoog/ heritagespiritooocreigoog_djvu.txt (accessed 19 April 2014).

Currie, E. (1968), 'Crimes Without Criminals: Witchcraft and its Control in Renaissance Europe', *Law & Society Review* 7: 7–32.

Cutler, M. J. (2015), Seeing and Believing: The Emergent Nature of Extreme Weather Perceptions, *Environmental Sociology* 1(4): 293–303.

Delumeau, J. (1990), *Sin and Fear: The Emergence of a Western Guilt Culture, 13th–18th Centuries*, New York: St Martin's Press.

Desmond, W. (2006), Lessons of Fear: A Reading of Thucydides, *Classical Philology* 101(4): 359–79.

Dill, J. and J. D. Hunter (2010), 'Education and the Culture Wars', in S. Hitlin and S. Vaisey (eds), *Handbook of the Sociology of Morality*, New York: Springer.

Dillinger, J. (2004), 'Terrorists and Witches: Popular Ideas of Evil in the Early Modern Period', *History of European Ideas* 30(4): 167–82.

Dinneen, N. (2014), 'Hans Jonas's Noble "Heuristics of Fear": Neither the Good Lie Nor the Terrible Truth', *Cosmos and History: The Journal of Natural and Social Philosophy* 10(2): 1–21.

Ecclestone, K. and D. Hayes (2008), *The Dangerous Rise of Therapeutic Education*, London: Routledge.

Elias, N. (2005), *The Civilizing Process – Volume 2: State Formation and Civilization*, Oxford: Basil Blackwell.

Faye, G. (2012), *Convergence of Catastrophism*, Berwick-Upon-Tweed: Artkos Media Ltd.

Fitzpatrick, M. (2001), *The Tyranny of Health*, London: Routledge.

Frankenberg, R., I. Robinson and A. Delahooke (2000), 'Countering Essentialism in Behavioural Social Science: The Example of the "Vulnerable Child" Ethnographically Examined', *The Sociological Review* 48(4): 586–611.

Freud, S. (1918), *Reflections on War and Death*, New York: Moffat Yard and Company.

Freud, S. (1920), *A General Introduction to Psychoanalysis*, New York: Boni and Liveright, 1920; Bartleby.com, 2010. www.bartleby.com/283/.

Fromm, E. (1965), *Escape From Freedom*, New York: Holt Books.

Fry, A. (1987), *Safe Space: How to Survive in a Threatening World*, New York: Dent.

Furedi, F. (1997), *The Culture of Fear: Risk Taking and the Morality of Low Expectations*, London: Cassell.

Furedi, F. (2001), 'Bullying: The British Contribution to the Construction of a Social Problem', in J. Best (ed.), *How Claims Spread: Cross-National Diffusion of Social Problems*, New Jersey: Transaction Publishers.

Furedi, F. (2004), *Therapy Culture: Cultivating Vulnerability in an Anxious Age*, London: Routledge.

Furedi, F. (2005), *The Politics of Fear*, London: Continuum Press.

Furedi, F. (2007), 'The Only Thing We Have to Fear is the "Culture of Fear" Itself', Spiked-online, 4 April 2007.

Furedi, F. (2009a), 'Precautionary Culture and the Rise of Possibilistic Risk Assessment', *Erasmus Law Review* 2(2).

Furedi, F. (2009b), *Wasted: Why Education Isn't Educating*, London: Continuum Press.

Furedi, F. (2012), 'The Objectification of Fear and the Grammar of Morality', in S. Hier (ed.), *Moral Panic and the Politics of Anxiety*, London: Routledge.

Furedi, F. (2013a), *Authority: A Sociological History*, Cambridge: Cambridge University Press.

Furedi, F. (2013b), *Moral Crusades In An Age of Mistrust: The Jimmy Savile Scandal*, London: Palgrave.

Furedi, F. (2014), *First World War: Still No End in Sight*, London: Bloomsbury.

Furedi, F. (2016), Moral Panic and Reading: Early Elite Anxieties about the Media Effect, *Cultural Sociology*, 10(4): 523–37.

Furedi, F. (2017a), *What's Happened to the University: A Sociological Exploration of its Infantilisation*, London: Routledge Press.

Furedi, F. (2017b), *Populism and the European Culture Wars: The Conflict of Values between Hungary and the EU*, London: Routledge.

Garland, D. (2001), *The Culture of Control: Crime and Social Order in Contemporary Society*, Oxford: Oxford University Press.

Giddens, A. (1991), *Modernity and Self-Identity: Self and Society in the Late Modern Age*, Cambridge: Polity.

Giddens, A. (1992), 'Risk, Trust, Reflexivity', in U. Beck, *Risk Society: Towards a New Modernity*, London: Sage.

Gouldner, A. (1965), *Enter Plato: Classical Greece and the Origins of Social Theory*, New York: Basic Books.

Gray, M. G. and D. P. Ropeik (2002), 'Dealing With the Dangers of Fear: The Role of Risk Communication', *Health Affairs* 21(6).

Grupp, S. (2003), Political Implications of a Discourse of Fear: The Mass Mediated Discourse of Fear in the Aftermath of 9/11' (unpublished paper: Berlin).

Guzelian, C. P. (2004), *Liability and Fear*, Stanford Public Law and Legal Theory Working Paper Series: Stanford, CA: Stanford Law School.

Hale, C. (1996), 'Fear of Crime: A Review of the Literature', *International Review of Victimology* 4: 79–150.

Habermas, J. (1975), *Legitimation Crisis*, Boston: Beacon Press.

Hammond, P. (2017), *Climate Change and Post-Political Communication: Media, Emotion and Environmental Advocacy*, London: Routledge.

Hanekamp, J. (2005), *Utopia and Gospel: Unearthing the Good News in Precautionary Culture*, Holland: Zoetemeer, https://pure.uvt.nl/ws/files/5129814/Hanekamp_utopia_11_02_2015.pdf.

Harari, Y. N. (2016), *Homo Deus: A Brief History of Tomorrow*, London: Harvill Secker.

Harrison, P. (2002), *'Religion' and the Religions in the English Enlightenment*, Cambridge: Cambridge University Press.

Hasson, G. (2015), *Mindfulness Pocketbook: Little Exercises for a Calmer Life*. Chichester: Capstone Publishing.

Herbst, W. (1938), *Questions of Catholics Answered*, St Nazlanz, Wisconsin: The Society of the Divine Savior.

Higgins, P. (2005), 'Exercise-based Transportation Reduces Oil-Dependence, Carbon Emission and Obesity', *Environmental Conservation* 32(3).

Hochschild, A. R. (2003), *Managed Heart: Commercialization of Human Feeling*, Los Angeles: University of California Press.

Hollander, J. (2004), 'Fear Itself', *Social Research* 71, winter 2004.

Holmes, S. (1993), *The Anatomy of Antiliberalism*, Cambridge, MA: Harvard University Press.

Howe, N. and W. Strauss (2003), *Millennials Go to College*, Washington, DC: American Association of Collegiate Registrars and Admissions Officers.

Hubbard, P. (2003), Fear and Loathing at the Multiplex: Everyday Anxiety in the Post-Industrial City, *Capital & Class*, 27(2): 51–75.

Hughes, H. S. (1969), *The Obstructed Path: French Social Thought in the Years of Desperation*, New York: Harper and Row.

Hulme, M. (2008), 'The Conquering of Climate: Discourses of Fear and their Dissolution', *The Geographical Journal* 174(1): 5–16.

Hume, D. (1889), *The Natural History of Religion*, London: A. and H. Bradlaugh Bonner, available online, https://ebooks.adelaide.edu.au/h/hume/david/h92n/index.html.

Hunt, A. (2003), 'Risk and Moralization in Everyday Life', in R. V. Ericson and A. Doyle (eds), *Risk and Morality*, Toronto: University of Toronto Press.

Hunter, J. D. (2000), *The Death of Character: Moral Education in an Age Without Good or Evil*, Boston: Basic Books, 2000.

Ibarra, P. R. and J. I. Kitsuse (2003), 'Claims-making Discourse and Vernacular Resources', in J. A. Holstein and G. Miller (eds), *Challenges & Choices: Constructionist Perspectives on Social Problems*, New York: Aldine de Gruyter.

Ignatieff, M. (1997), *The Warrior's Honor*, New York: Robert Holt.

Jackson, H. (1932), *The Fear of Books*, London: The Soncino Press.

Jalland, P. (2000), *Death in the Victorian Family*, Oxford: Oxford University Press.

Jenkins, P. (2014), *The Great Holy War*, Oxford: Lion Books.

Johnston, J. S. (2003), Paradoxes of the Safe Society: A Rational Actor Approach to the Reconceptualization of Risk and the Reformation of Risk Regulation, *University of Pennsylvania Law Review*, 151(3): 747–86.

Jonas, H. (1984), *Imperative of Responsibility: In Search of an Ethics for the Technological Age*, Chicago: The University of Chicago Press.

Kateb, G. (2004), 'A Life of Fear', *Social Research* 71, winter 2004.

Kazanjian, P. (2015), 'Ebola in Antiquity?', *Clinical Infection Disease* 61(6): 963–8.

Kelly, T. and J. Kelly (1998), 'American Catholics and the Discourse of Fear', in P. N. Stearns and J. Lewis (1998), *An Emotional History of the United States*, New York: New York University Press.

Kempe, M. (2003), 'Noah's Flood: The Genesis Story and Natural Disasters in Early Modern Times', *Environment and History* 9.

Kesselring, M. (2003), *How to Analyze the Works of Franklin D. Roosevelt*, Minneapolis: ABDO Publishing Company.

Kierkegaard, S. (1986), *Fear and Trembling*, London: Penguin.

Kukla, R. (2006), 'Ethics and Ideology in Breastfeeding Advocacy Campaigns', *Hypatia* 21(1): 157–80.

Lacquement, R. (2004), 'The Casual-Aversion Myth', *Naval War College Review* 57(1).

Laidi, Z. (1998), *A World Without Meaning: The Crisis of Meaning in International Politics*, London: Routledge.

Lasch, C. (1984), *The Minimal Self: Psychic Survival in Troubled Times*, New York: W. W. Norton.

Lawson, S. T., S. K. Yeo, H. Yu and E. Greene (2016), 'The Cyber-Doom Effect: The Impact of Fear Appeals in the US Cyber Security Debate', 8th International Conference on Cyber Conflict, Tallinn, 2016, pp. 65–80.

Lincoln, C. E. (1960), 'Anxiety, Fear and Integration', *Phylon* 21(3).

Locke, J. (1663–4), *Essays on the Law of Nature*, in M. Goldie (ed.) (1997), *Political Essays*, Cambridge: Cambridge University Press.

Loimer, H. and M. Guarnieri (1996), Accidents and Acts of God: A History of the Terms, *American Journal of Public Health* 86(1): 101–7.

Loseke, D. (1999), *Thinking about Social Problems: Introduction to Constructionist Perspectives*, New York: Aldine de Gruyter.

MacIntyre, A. (1984), *After Virtue: A Study in Moral Theory*, Notre Dame, IL: University of Notre Dame Press.

Mack, A. (2004), 'Editorial', *Social Research* 71, winter 2004.

Macvarish, J. (2016), *Neuroparenting: The Expert Invasion of Family Life*, London: Palgrave.

McLean, I. and M. Johnes (2000), *Aberfan: Government and Disasters*, Welsh Academic Press: Cardiff.

Marcus, G. (2002), *The Sentimental Citizen: Emotion in Democratic Politics*, University Park, PA: The Pennsylvania State University Press.

Mason, J. (1835), *A Treatise on Self-Knowledge*, Boston: John Loring.

May, R. (1950), *The Meaning of Anxiety*, New York: The Ronald Press Company.

Meier, C. (2005), *The Uses of History: From Athens to Auschwitz*, Cambridge, MA: Harvard University Press.

Meyer, G., A. P. Folker, R. Jorgensen, M. Kyare von Krauss, P. Sandoe and G. Tveit (2005), 'The Factualization of Uncertainty: Risk, Politics and Genetically Modified Crops – a Case of Rape', *Agriculture and Human Values* 22: 235–42.

Mills, C. W. (1959), *The Sociological Imagination*, New York: Oxford University Press.

Mintz, S. (2015), *The Prime of Life*, Cambridge, MA: Harvard University Press.

Morgan, L., J. Scourfield, D. Williams, A. Jasper and G. Lewis (2003), 'The Aberfan Disaster: 33-Year Follow-up of Survivors', *British Journal of Psychiatry* 182: 532–6.

Mueller, J. (2006), *Overblown: How Politicians and the Terrorism Industry Inflate National Security Threat, and Why We Believe Them*, New York: Free Press.

Mueller, K. (2000), 'Politics, Death, and Morality in US Foreign Policy', *Aerospace Power Journal*, summer.

Nederman, C. J. and John of Salisbury (1991), *John of Salisbury: Policratus*, Cambridge: Cambridge University Press.

Nerlich, B. and C. Halliday (2007), 'Avian Flu: The Creation of Expectations in the Interplay between Science and the Media', *Sociology of Health & Illness* 29(1): 46–65.

Nicholson, I. (2003), *Inventing Personality*, Washington, DC: APA Books.

Nisbet, P. (1932), *The Legend of Hell: An Examination of the Doctrine of Everlasting Punishment in the Light of Modern Scholarship*, London: Nisbet and Co.

O'Neill, S. and S. Nicholson-Cole (2009), ' "Fear Won't Do It": Promoting Positive Engagement With Climate Change Through Visual and Iconic Representations', *Science Communication* 30(3): 355–79.

Overy, R. (2009), *The Morbid Age: Britain Between the Wars*, London: Allen Lane.

Pain, R. (2009), 'Globalized Fear? Towards an Emotional Geopolitics', *Progress in Human Geography* 33(4): 466–86.

Panchev, D. (2013), ' "Good Moral Panics" and the Late Modern Condition', London: LASALA Foundation.

Pearl, J. (1983), 'French Catholic Demonologists and Their Enemies in the Late Sixteenth and Early Seventeenth Centuries', *Church History* 52(4).

Pearson, G. (2014), 'Courage and Temperance', in R. Polansky (ed.), *The Cambridge Companion to Aristotle's Nichomachean Ethics*, Cambridge: Cambridge University Press.

Pfeiffer, R. H. (1955), 'The Fear of God', *Israel Exploration Journal* 5(1) (1955): 41–8.

Pieper, J. (1966), *The Four Cardinal Virtues: Prudence, Justice, Fortitude, Temperance*, Notre Dame, IN: University of Notre Dame Press.

Plamper, J. (2009), 'Fear: Soldiers and Emotions in Early Twentieth-Century Russian Military Psychology', *Slavic Review* 68(2): 259–83.

Plato, *The Republic*, in J. M. Cooper (ed.) (1997), *Plato Complete Works*, Indianapolis: Hackett Publishing Company.

Pope, A. (1804), *The Poetical Works of Alexander Pope: With His Last Corrections, Additions and Improvements*, Vol. 3, Philadelphia: T. & G. Palmer.

Prior, M. E. (1932), 'Joseph Glanvill, Witchcraft, and Seventeenth-Century Science', *Modern Philology* 30(2).

Reddy, W. (2001), *The Navigation of Feeling: A Framework for the History of Emotions*, Cambridge: Cambridge University Press.

Rees, M. J. (2003), *Our Final Hour*, New York: Basic.

Regan, A. (2012), *Animal Magnetism*, Tallahassee: Dreamspinner Press.

Rieseman, D. (1953), *The Lonely Crowd: A Study of the Changing American Character*, New York: Doubleday.

Riezler, K. (1944), 'The Social Psychology of Fear', *The American Journal of Sociology* 49(6).

Robin, C. (2000), 'Fear: A Genealogy of Morals – Feelings of Vulnerability', *Social Research* 67(4) 1085–115.

Rodgers, D. T. (2012), *Age of Fracture*, Cambridge, MA: Harvard University Press.

Rowe, D. (2009), 'The Concept of the Moral Panic: An Historico-Sociological Positioning', in D. Lemmings and C. Walker (2009), *Moral Panics, the Media and the Law in Early Modern England*, Houndmills, Basingstoke: Palgrave Macmillan.

Rowell, G. (1976), *Hell and the Victorians*, Oxford: Oxford University Press.

Schlatter, R. (1945), Thomas Hobbes and Thucydides, *Journal of the History of Ideas* 6(3): 350–62.

Schoenfeld, J. D. and J. P. Ioannidis (2013), 'Is Everything We Eat Associated with Cancer? A Systematic Cookbook Review', *The American Journal of Clinical Nutrition* 97(1): 127–34.

Segal, S. (2014), *Lucretius on Death and Anxiety*, Princeton: Princeton University Press.

Selleck, R. J. W. (1972), *English Primary Education and the Progressives: 1914–1939*, London: Routledge & Kegan Paul.

Shklar, J. N. (1989), 'The Liberalism of Fear', in N. L. Rosenblum (ed.), *Liberalism and the Moral Life*, Cambridge, MA: Harvard University Press.

Shoveller, J. A., D. M. Savoy and R. E. Roberts (2002), 'Sun Protection Among Parents and Children at Freshwater Beaches', *Canadian Journal of Public Health*, 93(2): 146–8.

Skoll, G. (2010), *Social Theory of Fear: Terror, Torture, and Death in a Post-Capitalist World*, New York: Palgrave Macmillan.

Small, J. B. (1898), *The Human Heart Illustrated by Nine Figures of the Heart: Representing the Different Stages of Life, and Two Death-bed Scenes: The Wicked and the Righteous*, Salisbury, NY: York Dispatch.

Smith, G. (1998), *John Stuart Mill's Social and Political Thought: Critical Assessments*, London: Routledge.

Sorell, T. (2010), 'Hobbes, Public Safety and Political Economy', in R. Prokhovnik and G. Slomp (eds), *International Political Theory after Hobbes*, International Political Theory Series, London: Palgrave Macmillan.

Spitz, R. (1952), 'Authority and Masturbation: Some Remarks on a Bibliographical Investigation', *Yearbook of Psychoanalysis* 21(4): 490–527.

Stanko, E. (1988), 'Fear of Crime and the Myth of the Safe Home: A Feminist Critique of Criminology', in K. Yello and M. Bograd (eds), *Feminist Perspectives on Wife Abuse*, Newbury Park, California: Sage.

Stearns, P. N. (2006), *American Fear: The Causes and Consequences of High Anxiety*, New York: Routledge.

Stern, J. and B. Wiener (2006), 'Precaution Against Terrorism', in P. Bracken, D. Gordon and I. Bremmer (eds), *Managing Strategic Surprise: Lessons from Risk Management & Risk Assessment*, Cambridge: Cambridge University Press.

Stolberg, M. (2000), 'An Unmanly Vice: Self-Pollution, Anxiety, and the Body in the Eighteenth Century', *The Society for the Social History of Medicine* 13(1): 1–22.

Strauss, N. (2016), 'Why We're Living in the Age of Fear', *The Rolling Stone*, 6 October 2016.

Strengers, J. and A. Van Neck (2001), *Masturbation: The History of a Great Terror*, New York: Palgrave/St Martins.

Sue, D. W., C. M. Capodilupo, G. C. Torino, J. M. Bucceri, A. Holder, K. L. Nadal and M. Esquilin (2007), 'Racial Microaggressions in Everyday Life: Implications for Clinical Practice', *American Psychologist* 62(4): 271–86.

Svendsen, L. (2008), *A Philosophy of Fear*, London: Reaktion Books.

Szasz, T. (2009), *Shopping Our Way to Safety: How We Changed from Protecting the Environment to Protecting Ourselves*, Minnesota: University of Minnesota Press.

Thucydides (1900), *History of the Peloponnesian War*, Oxford: Clarendon Press.

Toffler, A. (1970), *Future Shock*, New York: Amereon Ltd.

Tomes, Nancy (2000), 'Public Health Then and Now', *American Journal of Public Health* 90(2).

Tulloch, J. and D. Lupton (2003), *Risk and Everyday Life*, London: Sage Publications.

UNESCO (1972) *The World of Education Today and Tomorrow: Learning to Be*, Paris: UNESCO.

Valéry, P. (1927), *Variety*, New York: Harcourt Brace.

Vico, G. (2002), *The First New Science*, ed. and transl. Leon Pompa, Cambridge: Cambridge University Press.

Walsh, D. (1997), *The Growth of the Liberal Soul*, Columbia: University of Missouri Press.

Walters, B. N. J. and G. Egger (2007), 'Personal Carbon Trading: A Potential "Stealth Intervention" for Obesity Reduction?', *Medical Journal of Australia* 187(11): 668.

Walton, D. N. (1996), 'Practical Reasoning and the Structure of Fear Appeal Arguments', *Philosophy & Rhetoric* 29 (4): 301–13.

Weber, M. (1915), 'Religious Rejections of the World and their Directions', in H. Gerth and C. Wright Mills (1958) (eds), *From Max Weber: Essays in Sociology*, New York: Galaxy Books.

Wildawsky, A. (2017), *Searching For Safety*, New Brunswick, NJ: Transaction Books.

Wilkins, R. (1996), *Death: A History of Man's Obsessions and Fears*, New York: Barnes & Noble Books.

Wilkinson, G. (1841), *Manner and Customs of the Ancient Egyptians*, Volume 1, London: John Murray.

Wilkinson, I. (1999), 'Where is the Novelty in our Current Age of Anxiety?', *European Journal of Social Theory* 2(4): 445–67.

Wilkinson, I. (2002), *Anxiety in a 'Risk' Society*, London: Routledge.

Wilson, E. O. (1998), *Consilience: The Unity of Knowledge*, London: Little, Brown and Company.

Wodak, R. (2015), 'The Politics of Fear': What Right-Wing Populist Discourses Mean, London: Sage.

Wolfe, A. (1998), One Nation After All: What Middle-Class Americans Really Think About, New York: Viking.

Wootton, David (1983), 'The Fear of God in Early Modern Political Theory', Historical Papers 181: 56–80.

Wrenn, M. (2013), 'Fear and Institutions', Journal of Economic Issues 47(2) 383–90.

Zavaliy, A. G. and M. Aristidou (2014), 'Courage: A Modern Look at an Ancient Virtue', Journal of Military Ethics 13(2): 174–89.

INDEX

A Portrait of the Artist as a Young Man (J. Joyce) 55–6
Aberfan disaster (1966) 240–1
abortion 205
accidents and blame 225–6
adult authority, devaluation of 195–9
afterlife, belief in the 37–8, 54–6, 83–4
Age of Anxiety 60
AIDS 133
alarmist predictions 71–7
Alcabes, Philip 22, 133
Allendry, René 60
Altheide, David 13
Altschuler, Glen C. 142
American Civil Liberties Union (ACLU) 230
American military 40–1, 180
Ancient Greece 23, 31–2, 37, 45–6, 119, 130, 220–1, 244, 256–7
Animal Magnetism (A. Regan) 231
anxiety and fear distinction 24, 25, 26
Apocalypse 80
Aquinas, Thomas 52
Arendt, Hannah 197, 250, 257
Aristidou, Michael 183
Aristotle 23, 25, 45–6, 80–1, 87, 183, 252, 256
armed forces 9–10, 35–6, 37, 38–42, 180, 222, 225
Ashton, John 103
Athenian culture 23, 221–2
Auden, W. H. 60
Aurelius, Marcus 185
authority of knowledge 87–90, 93, 255
autonomization of fear 26–7

Baby Milk Action 140
Bacon, Sir Francis 124
Bader-Saye, Scott 52
Balls, Ed 203
Barber, Michael 86
Bauman, Zygmunt 24, 26, 28–9, 42, 92, 219
Baxter, Richard 124
BBC (British Broadcasting Corporation) 132, 208
Beck, Ulrich 29–30, 88, 109–10, 158, 172, 222
Becker, Ernest 42
Berelowitz, Sue 175
the Bible 51–2, 164
Biblical Repertory and Theological Review 108
Biological Psychiatry 160
Black Death 73–4, 133
Bodin, Jean 122, 123
bottled water 147–9
Boutelier, Hans 209
Boyle, Robert 124
breastfeeding 139–41
Brexit 168–9
British Heart Foundation 102–3
Browne, Sir Thomas 124
Bruckner, Pascal 74
bullying 192–4, 202
Burke, Edmund 84
Bush, George W. 162, 173

Calvin, John 48
Cameron, David 78–9
cancer 7, 127, 130, 186

Carter, Jimmy 115
Casaubon, Meric 124
catastrophism 71–7
Cerullo, Morris 30
Chadwick, Mary 63
change and fear 25–6, 81–96, 157
Chanel, Coco 130
chaperones, pharmacy 214
Charles, HRH Prince 96
Chicago Daily Tribune 62
Childline 113
children, threats to 15–16, 21, 37, 73, 74,
    78–9, 82–3, 102–3, 113–15, 127,
    129–30, 131, 133, 139–41, 158–9,
    174–5, 186–91, 192, 195, 199–201,
    203, 208, 210–11, 214–16, 226
    see also socialization of children
Christian Register 187
Christianity 51–2, 54–9, 108, 124–5,
    138, 244
Churches' Child Protection Advisory
    Service (CCPAS) 215
Churchill, Winston 257
Cicero 48, 220
climate change 13, 72, 74, 90, 96,
    99–100, 118, 125–6, 132, 134, 210
Clinton, Hillary 2, 245
Cohen, Stanley 167–8
Coker, Christopher 238, 239
Cold War 163
Colebrook, Claire 181–2
College of Policing, UK 179–80
community, loss of 216, 219
companies/institutions and safety
    values 222–4
competitive scaremongering 5, 20, 22
confidence and fear 81, 87, 252, 256
confidence in humanity, lack of
    244–9, 255
    see also vulnerability, assumption
    of human
Contracting Business webpage 222–3

Copperfield, Dr 97–8
core values 223–4
courage 179, 182–7, 190, 191, 254,
    256, 257
Creighton, Bishop Mandell 108
crime, fear of 27, 146
criticism, fear of 184–5, 231–2
cultural scripts and fear 15–16, 23, 32, 51,
    59, 60, 68, 81, 90, 91, 97, 101, 141,
    158, 175
Culture of Fear (B. Glassner) 4, 20, 142
Culture of Fear (F. Furedi) 1, 4, 88
'culture of fear' idiom 1–6
'culture of fear' thesis 6–10
Curie, Marie 1
cyber-bullying 194
cyber-doom scenarios 100

D-Day 36
Daily Beast 245
Daily Express 75
Daily Mirror 75
Davis, Andrew 114
Dawkins, Richard 245
The Day After Tomorrow film 100
de Montaigne, Michel 27
de-moralization of fear 64–9
death, fear of 31, 36–46, 63, 83–4, 152–3
debate and opinion, public 245–8
Democritus 46
demonology 122–6, 143
disease 21–2, 73–4, 97–8, 102–3, 119, 127,
    133, 135–8
Draper, George 189
drone-strikes 41
duty, importance of 220, 222

ecological threats 164–5, 204
    see also climate change
The Ecologist 140
Edens, Timothy J. 222
education and understanding 85–6

education/school system 113–16, 195, 199–200, 250–1
    see also safe spaces; student welfare
Egypt, Ancient 80
Einstein, Albert 50, 126
Elias, Norbert 237
Elliot, Walter 54
emotional harm 226–7
Enbridge 223
Enlightenment 66, 94–5, 96, 136, 242, 244, 245–6, 253–4
Epicurus 42–3, 47–8
epistemophobia 88
Essex, Mary 240–1
Ethical Man blog 132
European Environment Agency 161
European Union 2, 168–9, 242–3, 245
evil, fear of 170–2
evil, human capacity for 174, 203–4
exam stress 113–14
expectant fear 24–5
extinction, human 97–8

Fake News 20
fatalism, flourishing of 244, 255
Fate 95
Faye, Guillaume 103
FBI (Federal Bureau of Investigation) 219
fear, increase of expressing 9–10
fear levels over time, measuring 8–9
'fear of fear' 26–7, 60–1, 63–4, 67–8
fear of the 'wrong things' 21–2, 121
feeling rules 36–7
Field, Dr Steve 102
financial fears 103–4
Financial Times 87, 88
First World War 36, 39, 41–2, 56, 65–6, 195
Fitzpatrick, Michael 138
food and fear 7, 127–8, 133, 153–4
Forbes magazine 77

Forbes, Rosita 66
Fortuna 95
Fortune magazine 104
Founding Fathers 234
'Fox News Fear Factory' 10
Franklin, Benjamin 234
free speech 232, 233–4, 235, 246
freedom from fear 255–6
freedom-safety trade-off 233–6, 259
Freud, Sigmund 23, 24–5, 44–5
Fromm, Erich 216
Fry, Anthony 227–8
future, fear of the 81–96, 100–5, 109–10, 157, 237–8, 248–9, 260
Future-Proof Your Child: Parenting for the Wired Generation (N. Bush and G. Codrington) 82–3
Future-proofing Your Child: Help your children grow into sensible, safe, happy, resilient, self-motivated teens and beyond (K. Walker) 79
future-proofing 79–80, 82–3
future shock 85

Geldof, Bob 98
gender and fears 14
Giddens, Anthony 83, 88–9
Glanvill, Joseph 123–4
Glassner, Barry 4, 5, 20, 142
global warming see climate change
God/the divine, fear of 38–9, 41, 46–59, 80, 119
The Good Men Project blog 76
Google Alerts 75
Gore, Al 83, 134, 144
Gouldner, Alvin 221
Greece, Ancient see Ancient Greece
Grupp, Stefanie 14
Guardian 17–18
Guzelian, Christopher 14

Habermas, Jürgen 151–2
Hades 37
Hamilton, Alexander 234
Hammond, Phil 16
Hanekamp, Jaap 248
Harari, Yuval Noah 89, 203–4
harm, expansive definition of 159–60,
   177, 226–7
harm-free culture 224–7
Harper, Selena 12
Harrison, Peter 46
health risks and fears 21–2, 73–4,
   97–8, 100, 102–3, 127–32, 133,
   134–8, 140–1
Hell, fear of 54–9, 60
heroism 220–2, 238–9
Hiom, Sara 131
historical consciousness 243
history, negative interpretations of
   human 237–44
Hitler, Adolf 63
Hobbes, Thomas 119, 124, 152–3, 170,
   202, 220
Hochschild, Arlie 36
Hollander, John 162
Holmes, Stephen 246
Holocaust survivors 160
Homo Deus: A Brief History of
   Tomorrow (Y. N. Harari) 89
Hossain, Toufique 117
Howe, Neil 198–9
Huckabee, Mike 117
Hughes, Henry Stuart 66
Hume, David 49
Hunter, James Davison 222
Hunter, Paul 72
Hussein, Saddam 120
hyper-change, global 83, 94

identity and anxiety, personal
   216–17, 218–19
Ignatieff, Michael 169

Imperative of Responsibility (H. Jonas)
   164–7
individuation and personal
   anxiety 216–19
infant feeding 139–41
International Baby Food Action
   Network 140
introjection of fear 5–6
inverted quarantine 227–33
Iraq, invasion of 120

James, William 46
Jeffrey, Grant 30
jihadists 38
John of Salisbury 59
Johnes, Martin 241
Johnson, Lyndon B. 163
Jonas, Hans 164–7, 170, 245
Joyce, James 55–6
Judaism 51, 244
judgement, fear of 184–5, 231–2, 257–8
Julius Caesar (W. Shakespeare) 47

Kakutani, Michiko 238–9
Kant, Immanuel 253–4
Kateb, George 162
Kazin, Michael 162–3
Kerr, Margee 11
Kierkegaard, Søren 24, 54
Kingsley, Reverend Charles 121–3, 143
knowledge, fear and 85–90, 93, 96, 110

Laidi, Zaki 84
The Lancet 153
language of fear 2–5, 17–19, 29, 30, 142
language regulation see free speech
Lasch, Christopher 191–2, 216–17,
   228
Law, Bill 86
Lecourt, Dominique 88
Lee, Ellie 141
life expectancy 102–3

Little, E. F. 56–7
Little Ice Age 125
Locke, John 126
Loseke, Donileen 178
Lovelock, James 133–4
low-intensity fear 25
Lucretius 43–4
Lusignan, Bruce 12
Lyon, Jordon 180

Machiavelli, Niccolò 247–8
MacIntyre, Alasdair 179
Mack, Arien 161–2
Macvarish, Jan 78
Malleus Maleficarum (H. Kramer and J. Sprenger) 121–2
Manifesto Club 208
Marcus, George 99
martyrdom 38, 41
Marxism 166
masturbation 135–8
May, Theresa 116
Mclean, Ian 241
media division 20
media promotion of fear 10–19, 215–16, 218–19
medicalization of fear 35, 59–60, 61, 63, 64–5, 68, 195
Meier, Christian 242
Methodist Review 56–8
Metro 75
Mica, John 207
micro-aggression 217–18
Mill, John Stuart 221–2
millennial finances 103–4
millennial health 73, 102–3
Millennium Bug 30, 96
Mills, C. Wright 31
Mintz, Steven 250
modern slavery 115–18, 120
moral authority 110–12, 118–19, 151, 164, 179, 250–1

moral panic 107–9, 167–8
morality and fear 29–32, 35, 48, 49, 50–1, 52, 53–4, 112–41, 164
More, Henry 124
Moses 51
motivation and fear 151–2, 169–71
Mueller, John 21

Nash's Pall Mall Magazine 65
National Police Chiefs' Council, UK 219
National Union of Students 230
Nelson, Penelope 51
Nesbit, Jeff 116
neurosis 61
New Science 48–9
New York Times 3, 62, 201
Nicholson, J. H. 196
Nichomachean Ethics (Aristotle) 45–6
Nietzsche, Friedrich 221
9/11 terror attacks 12, 15, 83, 173, 249
Northwest Mining Journal 154

Obama, Michelle 73
Obeidallah, Dean 245
obesity 127–8, 133
O'Brien, Cardinal Keith 117
Observer 131
Occupy Movement 228–9
O'Grady, Captain Scott 10, 35
Old Testament 51
Oliver, Jamie 73
omens 47
'On Taking One's Life' (Seneca) 43
On the Nature of Things (Lucretius) 43
Onanism (S. Tissot) 135–7
Our Final Hour (M. J. Rees) 97

paedophilia 16–17, 174–5
Palin, Sarah 117
parenting *see* children, threats to
Parsons, Reverend Archibald 60

pedagogy, modern 195
  see also education/school system;
    student welfare
performance of fear 98–100, 149
personal identity and insecurity 216–19
personhood, meaning of modern
    178–9, 181–2, 201–2, 252–5
perspective of fear 141–3, 145–75, 258–9
phonics teaching method 114–15
Plamper, Jan 38–9
Plato 37–8, 48, 99, 166
police 179–81
politics of fear 141–2, 145–6, 161–72,
    173, 259
polluters, babies as 204–5
Pope, Alexander 104
Popular Science Monthly 55
possibilistic thinking 158
Precautionary Principle 160–1, 164–7,
    175, 235
Presidential Election (2016), US 2,
    207–8, 245
Prima Baby magazine 139–40
Prince, Dr William Rosecrance 58
Project Fear 2, 143, 168–9
prosperity and fear 14, 22–3
Prudence 256–7
psychic boundaries 228–9
psychology, early development of
    39–40, 57–8, 64–5, 66–7, 186–91
  see also Freud, Sigmund
'psychology of fear' idiom 61–3, 68
Psychoanalytic Review 60
The Public: A Journal of Democracy 93
public debate and opinion 245–8
Pucci, Linda 185

Quarterly Christian Spectator 108

race-against-time narratives 77–9, 85–6
  see also 'time bomb' metaphor
Reddy, William 98

Rees, Martin J. 97
Reformation 124
relationships, toxic 174, 202–3
religion 29, 30, 35, 38–9, 45–56, 81, 108,
    118–19, 124, 125, 134, 138, 150, 164, 244
the Renaissance 23, 95, 244, 247–8
The Republic (Plato) 37–8, 41, 166
Revenge of Gaia (J. Lovelock) 134
Revolution in Military Affairs
    (RMA) 41
Rhetoric (Aristotle) 25, 80–1
rhetorical idiom 4–5
Riesman, David 196
riscare 247
risk assessment and aversion 14–15,
    21–2, 179–81
risk, redefined 153–8
Robin, C. 52
Rochester, Andrew Gillies 57–8
Rollier, Auguste 130
Rolling Stone magazine 2
Romans 95, 241–2, 244
Roosevelt, Franklin D. 60, 67–8,
    95, 255–6
Rousseau, Jean-Jacques 136, 139
Rowell, Geoffrey 54
Rowlatt, Justin 132
Royal Commission on the Liquor
    Traffic in Canada 109
Royal Society 123
rules of fear 36–42, 64–5
Rumsfeld, Donald 90–1, 120
Russell, Bertrand 50, 53, 69, 71, 190
Russian military 38–9

safe spaces 227–33
safety 207–36, 259
Salvation Army 215
Sapere Aude 254
scepticism 132, 143–4
Schleicher, Andreas 86
Schneider, Stephen 99–100

science and scaremongering 127, 134–8,
   143–4, 164
   see also knowledge, fear and
Second Gulf War 9
Second World War 36, 42, 191
Selleck, R. J. W. 196
Seneca 43–4
Senko, Jen 11
sexual health 129, 134–8
Shaftesbury, Lord 49
Shakespeare, William 47
shaming 231–2
Shklar, Judith 170–1
Shorten, Bill 192
Sinclair, George 124
slavery, modern 115–18, 120
Small, Bishop John B. 55
small pox 73
social media 11, 130, 132, 215–16
social prosperity and fear 14, 22–3
Social Research 161–2
socialization of children 197–8,
   249–52, 258
Socrates 37–8
soldiers 10, 35–6, 37, 38–42, 180, 222, 225
solidarity and fear 171–3
Spee, Father Friedrich 126
Stearns, Peter 9, 40, 64, 186, 188, 209, 249
Stern, J. 160–1
Stiff Upper Lip, British 185–6
Stolberg, M. 137
Strauss, Steven 114
Strauss, William 198–9
Strossen, Nadine 230
student welfare 8, 181, 184–5, 198–9,
   211–13, 227, 229–31, 232–3, 235
Sue, Derald Wing 217
suicide bombers 38, 41
Summa Theologica (Thomas Aquinas) 52
Sumners, William Graham 150
Sun 114
sun exposure and health 129–32

superbugs 74
superstition 47, 81, 121–3, 143
surveillance, instruments of 234–5
survivalist mentality 191–2, 228, 239
Svendsen, Lars 22, 25, 26, 79
Szasz, Andrew 227

Tacitus 220
technology, fear of new 157–8
   see also future, fear of the; science
      and scaremongering
Temperance Movement 109
Temple Bar magazine 11–12
terrorism 12, 15, 21, 38, 41, 83, 96, 172,
   173, 249, 272
Tertullian 220
The Times 18, 62, 97, 240
Theophrastus 46
Thomas, Pat 140
Thucydides 21, 119
'time bomb' metaphor 75–8, 81, 93
Time magazine 6
Times Educational Supplement 195
'tipping point' 18
Tissot, Simon-Auguste 135–7
Toffler, Alvin 84–5
Top Santé magazine 130
Trump, Donald 2, 167, 207–8, 235, 245
Tweedy, Reverend Dr Henry 60

uncertainty and fear 25–6, 81–96, 111,
   143, 248–9, 257, 259
UNESCO 86
United Nations 120
universities and stress 229–30
   see also student welfare
the unknown 109, 111
'unknown unknowns' 90–3
Unseen campaign 116

Valéry, Paul 66
value, safety as a 219–25

the Vatican 138
'The Vice of Reading' (Anon.) 11–12
Vico, Giambattista 48–9, 50
Vietnam War 42
Viner, David 100
Voltaire 136
vulnerability, assumption of human
177–8, 181–2, 199–201, 228, 238,
239–41, 252–3, 255, 260

Walker, Kathy 79–80
Wall, General Peter 225
Walsh, David 250
Walters, Barry 204
War on Terror 234
Ware, Colin 127
warnings on toys 210–11
water, drinking 147–9
weather, extreme 14, 19, 72, 125–6

Weber, Max 41–2
Weekend Australian Magazine 17
Weekly Underwriter 101
Wiener, B. 160–1
Wildawsky, Aaron 222
Williams, Vogue 219
Wilson, Kelpie 205
witchcraft/witch-hunts 121–6,
143, 150
Wodak, Ruth 162
Wolfe, Alan 184–5
workplace bullying 192–4
World Health Organization 129
the 'worried well' 22

Yehuda, Rachel 160

Zavaliy, Andrei G. 183
zero harm society 224–7, 232

A NOTE ON THE AUTHOR

Professor Frank Furedi is Emeritus Professor of Sociology at the University of Kent. A public intellectual and commentator, he is the author of a number of acclaimed books including *Culture of Fear, Politics of Fear, Where Have All the Intellectuals Gone?* and *Paranoid Parenting.*

frankfuredi.com/@Furedibyte

A NOTE ON THE TYPE

The text of this book is set in Minion, a digital typeface designed by Robert Slimbach in 1990 for Adobe Systems. The name comes from the traditional naming system for type sizes, in which minion is between nonpareil and brevier. It is inspired by late Renaissance-era type.